The Household

The Household

Informal Order
around the Hearth

Robert C. Ellickson

Princeton University Press
Princeton and Oxford

Published by Princeton University Press, 41 William Street, Princeton, New Jersey 08540
In the United Kingdom: Princeton University Press, 6 Oxford Street, Woodstock, Oxfordshire OX20 1TW

Library of Congress Cataloging-in-Publication Data
Ellickson, Robert C.
The household : informal order around the hearth / Robert C. Ellickson.
    p. cm.
Includes bibliographical references and index.
ISBN 978-0-691-13442-0 (hardcover : alk. paper) 1. Households—Economic aspects. 2. Consumption (Economics) 3. Informal sector (Economics) I. Title.
HB820.E45 2008
339.4'7—dc22   2008003203

British Library Cataloging-in-Publication Data is available
This book has been composed in Adobe Caslon Pro
Printed on acid-free paper. ∞

press.princeton.edu

Printed in the United States of America

10 9 8 7 6 5 4 3 2 1

To the members of the household
who first instructed me in homeways:

Katherine Pollak Ellickson, my mother
John Chester Ellickson, my father
Margaret Ellickson Senturia, my sister
Barbara O'Leary Singleton (Nana)

Contents

Chapter 9

THE CHALLENGE OF UNPACKING
THE HOUSEHOLD 128

Preface

My aim in this volume is to help lay bare the organization of home life. Plato and Aristotle devoted attention to the household in ancient times, and since then analysts have examined it through a wide variety of lenses. My own is somewhat unconventional. I am a specialist in property law, a background that may confer some comparative advantage in analyzing the nature of personal entitlements around the hearth. On the other hand, I am, for a law professor, relatively skeptical about how much people look to law when shaping their ordinary affairs. Most of the rules that govern the hearth, I argue in this volume, are not derived from law but rather are household-specific norms that evolve from the repeated interactions of household participants. In this book, I address the factors that influence how individuals select their co-participants in home life (that is, how households are constituted) and how these clusters of individuals choose to govern themselves.

Households bring into play two of my principal scholarly interests. I have devoted much of my scholarly career to the empirical study of forms of land tenure and the role of informal norms in human affairs. The household is an institution that is land-based and, for the most part, informally governed. In retrospect, it seems inevitable that I eventually would be attracted to the topic. My experiences over several decades in teaching the subject of property to law students also deepened my resolve to investigate the reality of domestic life. The teaching materials conventionally used in property courses at American law schools touch on a number of potential conflicts among household participants. These include possible disputes among the co-occupants over the management of their shared space (a classic example of a "commons"), among the co-owners about how to manage their shared asset, and between landlords and tenants. I became increasingly frustrated that most property casebooks address many of these issues in an arid fashion that seems largely disconnected from the realities of domestic life.

In 2000, John Drobak, the Director of the Center for Interdisciplinary Studies at the Washington University School of Law, asked me to contribute a paper to the Center's inaugural conference, organized around the general topic of norms and the law. I decided to use this opportunity to think and write more systematically about the household. My short paper, "Norms of the Household," was eventually published in the conference volume, *Norms and the Law* (John N. Drobak, ed., Cambridge Univ. Press, 2006). With my appetite thus whetted, in fall 2005, I returned to the topic and devoted my sabbatical leave to the writing of a much more extended law review article on the subject. This I published in 2006 in the *Yale Law Journal* under the title, "Unpacking the Household: Informal Property Rights Around the Hearth" (116 Yale L.J. 226 [2006]). That article was pitched to a legal audience. This book, by contrast, although it draws heavily on "Unpacking the Household," has been reedited so as to be more accessible to the many historians, sociologists, economists, demographers, anthropologists, and political scientists interested in the organization of domestic life. I also address some new topics, expand some discussions, and provide fresh statistical compilations (much of it in the appendixes) on the nature of contemporary intentional communities and co-housing communities in the United States. Although the organization of this book reflects the structure of "Unpacking the Household," there are numerous changes in the text and footnotes. I thank Cambridge University Press and the *Yale Law Journal* for their permission to revise and expand those previous publications.

This project has been long in gestation and I have had much help along the way. I owe special thanks to Henry Hansmann and Robert Pollak for many enlightening conversations over numerous years. Margaret Brinig, Richard McAdams, and Henry Smith offered extended comments on early drafts that were particularly useful. I am grateful, in addition, for the contributions of Robert Ahdieh, Anne Alstott, Scott Altman, Jennifer Arlen, Stephen Bainbridge, Yochai Benkler, Hanoch Dagan, Eric Fleisig-Greene, Robert Gibbons, Oliver Hart, Jill Hasday, Joni Hersch, Robert Keohane, John Langbein, Amnon Lehavi, Avital Margalit, Daniel Markovits, Steven Nock, Serguei Oushakine, Eric Rasmusen, Roberta Romano, Martha Roth, Kim Scheppele, Scott Shapiro, Reva Siegel, Brian Simpson, Katherine Stone, Lynn Stout, Jay Weiser, James Whitman, Viviana Zelizer, and an anonymous reviewer. Thanks also to the participants in the Cornell University Social Science Seminar, the Harvard–MIT Organizational Economics Seminar, the Princeton Economics/Sociology Workshop, the Princeton Law and Public Affairs Seminar, and law and economics workshops at Harvard Law School, University of Southern California Law School, and Yale Law School.

Numerous Yale Law students made major contributions. William Baude and John Eisenberg helped with the early spadework; YiLing Chen-Josephson, Shyamkrishna Balganesh, and Jessica Bulman-Pozen, with polishing "Unpacking the Household"; and Katherine Lin and Dina Mishra, with preparing the book manuscript. YiLing and Kathy also aided in the assembly of statistics from primary sources. My deepest thanks to all. For institutional support, I am grateful to the Washington University School of Law, the American Center at Sciences-Po on Paris (where Pascal DeLisle generously accommodated me during my sabbatical in fall 2005), and, of course, the Yale Law School.

An author seeks a shepherd to guide a book through the perils of the creative process. The shepherd of *The Household* was Tim Sullivan, my splendid editor at Princeton University Press. I am indebted to Tim for his exemplary encouragements and wise counsel over many months. Thanks also to the highly professional members of the Press's production team—notably Jason Alejandro, Leslie Grundfest, Chuck Myers, and Karen Verde, a copyediting whiz. Kate Mertes, who prepared the index, is also featured in the text as the author of *The English Noble Household 1250 to 1600*, an invaluable study of mammoth households.

In order to shorten the length of the text, I have relegated much useful material to the endnotes. I have also provided a few dozen footnotes, primarily either to discuss substantive issues that are important but digressive, or to cite leading scholarly sources on issues especially pertinent to the structuring of life around the hearth.

Finally, I thank my wife Lynn, the sole co-occupant and co-owner of my house in New Haven, for her good sense, steadfast support, and cheering presence. Living with such a sterling housemate is an abiding blessing.

—*Robert C. Ellickson*
December 2007
New Haven

The Household

Chapter 1
How Households Differ from Families

An extraterrestrial visitor would immediately notice that most earthlings spend over half their time clustered together in small dwellings—working, eating, sleeping, and socializing. From on high, these household relationships plainly appear to be among the most basic of human arrangements. This book investigates, mostly from the bottom up rather than the top down, how people create and manage these domestic microcosms to which they can retreat from the hurly-burly of larger society.

Most homes have more than one resident and many have multiple owners. These household participants must devise methods of dealing with both the mundane and unexpected challenges of collective living. By devising better domestic practices—homeways, for short—a household's participants can greatly improve the quality of their lives. Designers of utopian communities deserve credit for recognizing this essential truth (but also reproach for failing to discern some economic realities that constrain household organization).

It is important at the outset to distinguish a household from both a marriage and a family, two closely related (and more extensively studied) social molecules with which it is commonly confused. A "household" is a set of institutional arrangements, formal or informal, that govern relations among the owners and occupants of a particular dwelling space where the occupants usually sleep and share meals.[1] By this definition, a studio apartment with a single owner-occupant is a household, and so is a kibbutz where hundreds of members dine communally. A study of a household thus is an investigation into the allocation of entitlements in a specific physical setting. The members of a household (that is, its owners and occupants) together manage a real estate enterprise that makes use of inputs of land, capital, and labor in order to provide shelter, meals, and other services. Members of an intimate household, through their repeated interactions, typically generate a set of norms to govern their behavior, including their duties to supply household inputs and their rights to share in household outputs.

Although often confused with "household," "marriage" denotes something else, namely a legal relationship between two people that is not specific to any one location. Over the course of a lifetime, an individual is likely to participate in dozens of different households, but in no more than one or two marriages. The state, which doesn't bother to regulate the formation and termination of household relationships, closely regulates entry into and exit from marriage. Of course, when marital partners cohabit a home they jointly own, their household ties are deeply intertwined with their marital ties. The domain of their marital relationship, however, differs significantly from the domain of their household relationship. Much of marital property law addresses entitlements to assets other than the marital home, such as children, financial accounts, and the spouses' aggregate human capital. In that sense, a marital relationship is broader and more multifaceted than a household relationship. Conversely, marital law does not apply to many significant household relationships. First, when marriage partners cohabit, other kinfolk and non-kinfolk commonly are present in their home. In the United States in 2004, for example, married couples were the sole occupants of less than 39 percent of multiperson households.[2] Second, a married couple need not cohabit. Indeed, in the United States, 7 percent of married persons do not live with their spouses.[3] These separated couples include, among others, spouses en route to divorce, spouses in commuting marriages, and spouses in marriages in which one member is institutionalized or on military duty. Third, marriage partners who cohabit are not necessarily also the co-owners of their dwelling unit; others may join them as co-owners, they may lease their dwelling from others, or their home may be owned by only one partner. To emphasize the institutional distinction between marriage and the household, the discussion to come commonly features relationships within nonmarital households.

In a liberal society, individuals voluntarily choose both their household and marital partners. "Family" ties, by contrast, are largely determined by biology. An individual, however, can also voluntarily add kinfolk by marrying or adopting, two highly legalized procedures. Nonetheless, families are far more stable than households. At death, the members of the decedent's family can be charted in a unique family tree. By genealogical convention, a family tree does not refer to a decedent's sequential household relationships, which typically were far more ephemeral and tangled (and also conceivably far more meaningful) than her family relationships. Family members, even more obviously than spouses, need neither cohabit nor co-own, and cohabitants and co-owners need not be kin. In the United States, the number of multiperson households in which none of the occupants had family ties increased almost sixfold between 1970 and 2004.[4] These nonfamily households, which contained 12.3 million people in 1998, appear in a wide variety of incarnations.[5] Examples include university students living as housemates, unmarried heterosexual couples, gay and lesbian partners, welfare recipients or recent immigrants clustering to economize on rent, and idealists teaming up in a commune.[6]

Most studies of the "family"—including those by leading scholars such as Gary Becker and the team of Shelly Lundberg and Robert Pollak—focus not on the structure of household institutions as such but on marriages, parent-child relationships, and nonmarital child custody.[7] An influential dissertation on the "family" by the editors of the *Harvard Law Review* addresses numerous issues that arise out of the legal regulation of households, but virtually never uses the word "household" and doesn't explicitly recognize that families and households are distinct institutions.[8] Even a scholarly work that includes the word "household" in its title commonly concentrates almost entirely on family, marital, and premarital associations.[9]

The household is eminently worthy of study as an institution distinct from marriage and the family. Even in industrialized nations, dwellings are still the sites of a large fraction of economic and social activity. According to a leading study by Robinson and Godbey, in 1985, American women, irrespective of their marital and employment status, were spending an average of 30.9 hours a week on housework, and men, 15.7 hours.[10] In the United States, recent estimates of the value of within-household production (most of it unpaid) have run from 24 percent to 60 percent of gross domestic product (GDP)—that is, to several trillions of dollars per year.[11]

The norms that govern household affairs, moreover, have had Promethean influence. Households have been ubiquitous throughout human history, and the rules that our ancestors developed to resolve problems arising around their hearths provided templates for achieving cooperative solutions in settings outside the home.[12] Even today it is typically within the household that children first learn how to recognize and deal with challenges posed by endeavors involving common property and collective enterprise. Much of the analysis to be offered here can be directly applied to the governance of other forms of real estate typically co-owned and co-occupied by intimates—for example, small farms and retail outlets. More grandly, study of the household promises to shed light on the organizational logic of larger and far more complex business entities that are based outside the home.

Given the importance and centrality of the household as a distinct institution, it is surprising that social scientists have tended to slight its study.[13] Consider the field of economics. Although the etymological root of "economics" is *oikos* (the ancient Greek word for household), prior to 1970 economists—with a few important exceptions such as Margaret Reid—paid no more than passing attention to home economics.[14] After 1970, Gary Becker, Robert Pollak, and other leading economists began to do foundational work on the domestic sector, but their works mostly stress the structuring and dynamics of marital and child custody relationships.[15] Legal scholars also tend to focus on issues of marital and family law, not on how people organize home production and consumption. This priority is understandable. Co-occupants who share a hearth usually dispense with written contracts and other legal formalities. When a domain generates little business for attorneys, legal scholars tend to turn their attention elsewhere.

While institutional economists and legal scholars have largely neglected the household as such, numerous demographers, sociologists, and social historians have examined the institution. In the first book of *The Politics*, Aristotle envisions the household (*oikos*) as the basic building block of more encompassing forms of political life—first the village, and, beyond that, the city (*polis*).[16] Plato, Thomas More, Charles Fourier, B. F. Skinner, and other utopian thinkers have imagined new institutional arrangements for providing housing and meals.[17] There have been incessant experiments with unconventional households, such as monasteries, kibbutzim, and, more recently, co-housing developments that enable nuclear households to engage in congregate dining several times a week.

Basic positive questions about the institution of the household abound. Why are the occupants (and also, for that matter, the owners) of a dwelling unit so often related by kinship? Why has the average number of occupants per household fallen, particularly during the twentieth century? More fundamentally (and to redirect questions Ronald Coase famously asked in another context), why don't all adults live alone? or, conversely, all in one huge household?[18] How do household members formulate their homeways— the rules that govern their relationships? And what sorts of rules are they likely to favor?

This book is an initial foray into developing answers to these sorts of questions. Its chief goals are to provide a structure for thinking about the household, to systematize and augment what is already known, and to stimulate scholars and students to devote more attention to the constitution and governance of the home. Much of the analysis in the ensuing chapters stresses how both background legal conditions and stubborn economic realities profoundly influence how people shape their home lives. One recurring thesis is that individuals, across cultures and historical eras, have tended to structure their households, even ones sustained by love and affection,[19] with a close eye to reducing the transaction costs of their domestic interactions. I assert that transaction-costs considerations, for example, typically prompt household participants to keep their numbers small (see chapter 4), tend to doom to an early demise a strongly communal intentional community with a secular orientation (see chapter 5), and help induce householders to become homeowners (see chapter 7). Because transaction costs exist in many forms, many of which are not directly measurable, the thesis that household participants are attentive to these costs is difficult to test quantitatively. In the end, the plausibility of the thesis therefore rests largely on the intuitive persuasiveness of the examples marshaled to support it.

My emphasis on factors that invariably affect how individuals set up households should not be interpreted, of course, as an assertion that cultural variables have no influence on the shape of domestic life. There is a massive literature on cultural differences in household institutions, including both classics such as E. Franklin Frazier's *The Negro Family in the United States* and many insightful contemporary works.[20] While unquestionably valuable, these particularized studies tend to downplay factors that affect household organization under all social conditions. A major aim of the present work is to complement these rich, but narrow, cultural studies by identifying forces with universal influence.

Chapter 2 sets the foundation. It begins by unpacking the three distinct relationships—co-occupancy, co-ownership, and landlord-tenant—that may exist within a household. It then introduces the notion of the "liberal household," that is, the sort of institution likely to emerge when background principles of law and norms generally support individual rights of self-determination. Chapter 3 offers reasons why individuals in a liberal society, when they form household relationships, are likely to choose to consort with intimates. This strategy, among its other virtues, enables household participants to coordinate informally and relatively cheaply. Chapter 4, the empirical heart of the book, marshals demographic evidence about household forms and demonstrates the wide popularity, in each of the three basic household relationships, of the strategy of consorting with intimates. Although much of the proffered evidence pertains to contemporary conditions in the United States, some attention is paid here and elsewhere in the book to households in other nations and other time periods. Chapter 5 raises the issue of the optimality of the process of household formation and reviews utopians' proposals for radical transformation of conventional household forms. Chapters 6 and 7 bring the theory of business enterprise to bear on the issue of household ownership and on the determinants of the number of participants in household relationships.[21] Like participants in a business firm, members of a household typically confer ownership on providers of at-risk capital, not on occupants who labor within a home. Particularly when some or all of the owners of a dwelling are absentees, this may give rise to the separation of ownership from control—a homespun version of a problem much analyzed in the business context.[22] Chapter 8 investigates alternative processes of internal household governance, including law, norms, and contracts. A central claim is that, in a liberal society, while law provides fundamental background rules that enable household formation, more specific small-bore private-law rules have little relevance to everyday domestic affairs. Instead of following legal niceties, intimate co-occupants and co-owners typically create household-specific homeways either by oral agreement, or even more commonly, through a pattern of informal gift exchange. Even non-intimates, such as a tenant and an absentee landlord, are likely to strive to avoid involvements with the legal system. Chapter 9 concludes with a brief synthesis and a discussion of opportunities for further exploration into the functioning of household institutions.

Chapter 2
Household Formation and Dissolution in a Liberal Society

Three Distinct Relationships that May Exist within a Household

When a recluse solely owns and occupies a dwelling unit, interpersonal conflicts over household arrangements cannot arise. Difficulties can surface, however, when two or more co-occupants face the challenge of sharing a domestic space. Indeed, the seeds of conflict in such circumstances are so fertile that writers of novels, dramas, and other works of fiction commonly favor story lines that feature cohabitants. In particular, many leading television series have been set in multi-occupant households. Many of these have featured married couples or families—for example, *I Love Lucy*, *The Cosby Show*, and *The Sopranos*. In others, such as *The Odd Couple*, *Three's Company*, and *Friends*, the principal housemates have not been related.

Besides the occupancy dimension, however, there is an ownership dimension to household organization. This can introduce two additional sources of relational complexity. First, there may be multiple owners of the occupied real estate and, second, some or all of them may not be occupants.* In short, the members of a household may need to

---

*Even the U.S. Census Bureau, an organization that has worked conscientiously to sort out the persons involved in households, has yet to

manage as many as three distinguishable relationships—
that among co-occupants, that among co-owners, and that
between owners and occupants (more familiarly, landlords
and tenants).[1] Figure 2.1 portrays these three spheres of
interaction. (As noted, overlapping marital and familial relationships commonly complicate the picture even further.)

A study of the household that fails to recognize these
distinctions risks muddying its portrayal of domestic life.
The U.S. Census Bureau, for example, treats a household's
occupants as its only members.[2] By contrast, Hanoch Dagan
and Michael Heller, in their influential article, "The Liberal
Commons," treat co-owners as the only relevant "commoners."[3] A household has both occupants and owners, however, and it is essential to consider the roles of each.*

To highlight the distinctions just offered, it is useful to
introduce a hypothetical household of greater than usual
complexity. Because the relationships within it are rich
enough to provide weekly comedy fare, I will refer to it as
the "Sitcom Household." This household has five occupants: Dad, a widower; Granny, Dad's widowed eighty-
year-old mother; Maureen, Dad's thirty-five-year-old di-
vorced daughter; Chip, Maureen's seven-year-old son; and
Nadia, a twenty-two-year-old from abroad whom Maureen
has hired to serve as a live-in nanny for Chip. They reside

---

propose a term to denote both the owners and occupants of a dwelling
unit. As the next sentence of text illustrates, in this book these participants occasionally are collectively referred to as *members*.

*Many outstanding scholarly works on families and intentional com-
munities similarly fail to distinguish between the differing roles of occupants and owners of domestic spaces. Examples include, in economics,
Gary Becker, *Treatise on the Family*; in history, Michael Grossberg, *Governing the Hearth*; and, in sociology, Benjamin Zablocki, *Alienation and
Charisma*, the leading study of intentional communities.

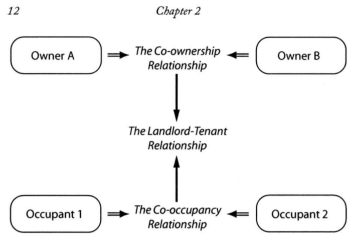

Figure 2.1. The Three Relationships Embedded
within a Complex Household

together in a large single-family dwelling, with Nadia in guest quarters situated over the house's attached garage. These five occupants provide virtually all household labor and consume virtually all household services. The ownership of the Sitcom House, however, complicates the structure of relations within it. Dad owns the house in equal shares with his sister, Aunt Audrey. After Dad's wife died a decade ago, Aunt Audrey and he acquired the house, each providing half of the down payment and taking title as tenants in common. Aunt Audrey resided in the Sitcom House for several years, but a few months ago she married, and she now lives elsewhere with her new husband.

The Sitcom Household illustrates the often distinct governance structures of marriages, families, and households. Aunt Audrey, the co-owner with Dad, is the only member of the dramatis personae with an ongoing marriage, but her marriage is not nested within the Sitcom Household because she doesn't reside there. Family relationships abound, but one resident (Nadia the nanny) isn't a family member.

Some family members (Granny, Maureen, and Chip), meanwhile, are occupants but not owners, and Aunt Audrey is an owner but not an occupant. This household illustrates the three distinct types of internal relationships, each with its own potential for cooperation or strife: the relationship among the five co-occupants, who must govern their commons; the relationship between the two co-owners, who must govern their joint investment; and the relationship between the co-owner group and co-occupant group, who must govern their landlord-tenant relationship. Note that only one of the members, Dad, is involved in all of these relationships and that he is involved on both ends of the landlord-tenant relationship.

Foundational Liberal Rights that Enable Individuals to Fashion Their Own Households

People can be thrust into household relationships that they would never voluntarily choose. A totalitarian state might dictate the combinations of participants in all household relationships and also closely regulate internal household practices. In *Utopia,* Thomas More envisioned a highly regimented system of this sort.[4] For many decades after it had abolished private property in land, the Soviet Union assigned families and individuals to specific dwelling units. In some situations, Soviet authorities compelled unacquainted persons or families to share an abode—the much-reviled *komunalka* system.[5] Slave-owners similarly were able to dictate where their slaves resided. In many societies, parents still arrange their children's marriages and thus, usually in practice, at least one of each child's housemates.

In a liberal state, by contrast, norms and laws support a

laissez-faire approach to household formation and dissolution. The core tenet of liberalism is that a competent adult presumptively can decide better than a state, master, parent, or other third party what arrangements best suit that individual. A liberal state therefore largely contents itself with establishing a set of background rules that grant individuals broad discretion to structure their own living arrangements.[6] Ordinary individuals, who lack the time and interest to obtain detailed legal information, commonly subscribe to the simplified conceptions of these basic liberal entitlements that are embedded in prevailing social norms. In this permissive environment, "liberal households" (to invoke a useful phrase coined by William James Booth) emerge.[7] These are the domestic arrangements that currently predominate in most developed nations.

The key entitlements necessary for a robust system of decentralized household formation are largely the same as those that underpin a market economy: private ownership of the basic inputs of household production (i.e., land, labor, and capital); freedom of exit from any sort of household relationship; and freedom of contract. Each of these three foundational entitlements warrants separate discussion.[8]

Private Property in Land, Capital, and Labor

Members of a liberal household voluntarily combine land, capital, and labor to generate a flow of domestic goods and services. A liberal system of household formation thus presupposes private property in these basic inputs. An unalloyed private property regime of course can have harsh distributive consequences. Those who lack land, capital, and valued labor skills need assistance from others to have meaningful choices among household arrangements. For example, on a given night in the United States, roughly one person out of two thousand is among the unsheltered homeless, that is, sleeps in a space not designed for residential use.[9] In the United States, as in other liberal societies, the administrators of a multitude of private and public transfer programs strive, with mixed success, to augment the choices of the destitute.[10]

A system of private property in land provides havens within which household members can fashion their own domestic arrangements. In a society such as the United States, the supply of private housing and building lots traditionally has been highly competitive. In most metropolitan markets, for example, the ownership of rental housing is not concentrated enough to confer monopoly power on a handful of suppliers.[11] Under these conditions, prospective household members can choose, subject to their budget constraints, among a wide range of locations, dwelling types, and forms of tenure. Conversely, in a society where a few government agencies or private firms control housing supply, or where land use regulations severely constrain housing arrangements, there is less freedom in household formation.

One of the fundamental entitlements of a private landowner is the right to exclude.[12] This liberal entitlement, which of course is subject to limitations, makes the owners of dwelling units the gatekeepers who control the identities of occupants and additional owners.[13] Maureen can neither arrange for her lover to move in without the approval of Dad and Aunt Audrey, nor can she compel them to allow her to become the third co-owner of the Sitcom House. Ambient norms, however, may constrain would-be excluders. In the memorable lines of Robert Frost's *The Death of*

the Hired Man, "Home is the place where, when you have to
go there,/ They have to take you in."

The right to accumulate private capital is another core
liberal property right. Without legal protection against con-
fiscation by either a government or a private taker, an individual would have little incentive to accumulate enduring
assets. In many settings, the protection of savings leads to
the establishment of intermediary financial institutions, some
of which then serve as specialized mortgage lenders. This
right to accumulate private capital enabled Dad and Aunt
Audrey to come up with the down payment and financing
they needed to purchase the Sitcom House. Partly because
holdings of private capital are protected, about 80 percent
of Americans, at some time in their lives, are able to become
homeowners.[14]

Ownership of one's own person and labor is the last of
the basic liberal property rights. Because self-ownership
entails the right to physically control the location and activities of one's own body, it is the entitlement most indispen-
sable to the liberal ideal of self-determination. A household
occupant commonly provides work around the home in exchange for receiving domestic services such as meals and
lodging, and, in some instances, wages. The Sitcom Household's au pair, Nadia, is voluntarily trading her labor for a
compensation package of this sort. In a nonliberal regime,
by contrast, a slave-owner or the state might own Nadia's
human capital and have the power to decide, among other
things, where she would live.[15] As a historical matter, most
slaves—whether chattel or debt—resided in or near their
masters' households. Indeed, Aristotle devotes much of his
pioneering discussion of the household in *The Politics* to
rationalizations for slavery.[16]

Well into the nineteenth century, upon marrying, a
woman typically ceded to her husband most of her powers

to contract and own property.[17] This compelled deprivation of a wife's ownership of her own labor was distinctly illiberal. The nineteenth-century scholar Henry Maine is renowned for his sweeping observation in *Ancient Law* that "progressive societies" had begun to move away from defining rights and duties as immutable outgrowths of family and marital status and toward entitling individuals to define these rights and duties by contract.[18] As Maine recognized, the key legal developments that gave rise to this trend were changes in property rights, namely legal conferrals of greater self-ownership rights on slaves, wives, and adult children who formerly had been under the thumbs of family and household heads.[19]

Freedom of Exit: Of Households "At-Will"

Because individuals may enter and exit, the membership rosters of both the co-owning and co-occupying groups in a particular household may change over time. As noted, a landowner's entitlement to exclude entails a plenary power to veto a proposed entry by either a new occupant or a new owner. But a household's owner typically has scant authority to keep an adult participant in place. A liberal legal regime, consistent with its overarching principle of self-determination, generally grants a legally competent person robust unilateral rights to exit from a household relationship.[20] This power of exit helps establish a threat point that influences the distribution of shares of household surplus.[21]

A co-occupant's right of exit consists of her privilege to physically remove both her person and her personal belongings from the previously shared abode. If Nadia wants to terminate her employment contract with Maureen, no one can force her to stay. Even if Nadia had previously promised Maureen that she would serve as a nanny for a certain period, in a liberal state Maureen could not obtain an injunction ordering Nadia to perform those personal services.[22] Laws against slavery and kidnapping also would bar Maureen from forcing Nadia to remain against her will.

The application of some basic law-and-economics concepts clarifies the nature of an occupant's exit entitlements in a liberal society. Because Nadia cannot waive by contract her right to physically exit, her entitlement to leave the household is, to use Ayres and Gertner's parlance, *immutable*.[23] On the other hand, if Nadia were to have promised Maureen to stay for a full year and then were to have broken that promise, a court might order her to pay damages to Maureen. The rule that an occupant can exit from a household without charge thus is not immutable but instead, in Ayres and Gertner's terms, is a *default*. To describe the legal situation another way, now in Calabresi and Melamed's influential terminology, those who want Nadia to remain a cohabitant cannot obtain *property-rule* protection of that desire, but they can contract with her to obtain *liability-rule* protection of it.[24]

A liberal state is also likely to grant a co-owner, as a default, unilateral power to exit from a co-ownership relationship. Unless Aunt Audrey had contracted otherwise, she would have two ways to force the end of her arrangement with Dad. First, she could sell her ownership interest to a third party.[25] Second, she could unilaterally bring a partition action, that is, petition a court to terminate the co-ownership of the Sitcom House and to divide up the asset according to her and Dad's shares of ownership.[26] In response to a plea for partition, a court may either split the formerly shared asset into separately owned pieces or, more likely in this particular case, order its sale and the subsequent division of the sale proceeds.[27]

This is not to say that exit by a co-owner is utterly unconstrained. A judge adjudicating a partition action may order, as part of the final accounting, a cross-payment to correct disproportions in the co-owners' prior sharing of benefits and burdens. In some instances, this cross-payment provides a dose of liability-rule protection to abandoned co-owners. American law also entitles co-owners to contract with one another to waive, for a limited time period, their entitlements to exit unilaterally by either sale or partition.[28] Thus, for reasons shortly to be presented, a co-owner's rights to terminate a relationship are less immutable than a co-occupant's rights. In addition, even in the absence of an express contract, norms typically constrain a person involved in an intimate co-ownership relationship from selling to another without the other owners' prior consent. Without Dad's consent, for example, Aunt Audrey would hesitate to sell her share of the Sitcom House to the leader of the local motorcycle gang. (Now there's the germ of a plot for a half-hour of comedy!)

Finally, participants in a landlord-tenant (owner-occupant) relationship commonly also can unilaterally end the relationship without much delay.[29] When a residential tenancy is month-to-month, the landlord and tenant each are free to terminate after providing a month or so of notice to the other. When a residential tenancy is at-will, either party can exit even more swiftly. At least as a legal matter, Granny can move out without prior notice, thus terminating her implicit tenancy-at-will with Dad and Aunt Audrey. Correspondingly, however, those owners can peremptorily order Granny to leave the house.

When a landlord and residential tenant have entered into a lease for a specific term, for example, one year, their respective exit rights are more complex.[30] Both parties are entitled unilaterally to end the relationship at the end of the term. In addition, in the event of a material breach of the terms of the lease, the party not in breach typically is entitled to terminate the relationship with dispatch at an earlier date. (The principle of freedom of contract, soon to be discussed, confers normative significance on negotiated lease provisions.) When the term of a residential lease has not yet ended and neither party is in breach, however, the tenant typically has more robust exit rights than the landlord. Just as a liberal society immutably entitles an occupant to run out on other occupants, it also immutably entitles a tenant to abandon a leasehold, although at the risk of liability for damages to the landlord. Maureen can't force Nadia, by dint of their labor contract, to work as an au pair, and Dad and Aunt Audrey, by dint of an express lease, can't force Nadia to dwell in the room over the garage. A residential landlord, by contrast, has no right to unilaterally rescind a term-of-years lease. If Nadia were to have negotiated for rights to occupy the guest quarters of the Sitcom House for a specific term and if she were not in material breach of that lease, her occupancy rights would be protected by a property rule, not simply a liability rule.

This asymmetry makes normative sense. A landlord's (and, for that matter, a co-owner's) duties are virtually never personal but instead delegable to others. If the law were to compel Dad and Aunt Audrey to lease the guest room to Nadia, it would not be forcing them to be personally present at the Sitcom House or at any other particular location. By contrast, if Nadia were personally required either to serve as a nanny for Chip or to inhabit the guest room, she would not be able to delegate those duties. Enforcement of those duties therefore would confine her movement. Even normally competent people occasionally enter into short-sighted or rash contracts. For paternalist reasons, a liberal society thus is unlikely to specifically enforce a promise by someone such as Nadia to be physically present in a particular household, just as it would not permit her to sell herself into slavery or indentured servitude. In the United States, however, the practical effects of this asymmetry between a tenant's and a landlord's exit rights are modest. Only in unusual contexts, such as in a cooperative apartment building or a state or city that controls rents or otherwise severely limits eviction rights, are residential tenants likely to have possessory rights that extend beyond a year or two.[31]

In sum, in a liberal society, the risk of exit by other participants typically looms over individuals enmeshed in all three types of household relationships. Of course, practical considerations such as social norms or the transaction costs of arranging a successor relationship commonly deter exit from a household relationship. As a legal matter, however, co-occupancy relationships among competent adults typically are at-will, and many co-ownership and landlord-tenant relationships are as well. Household ties thus tend to be far more fragile than either marital or family ties.[32] In contrast with divorce proceedings, which typically drag on for a year or more, and blood ties, which can never be sundered, many household relationships can dissolve in a twinkling.

Freedom of Contract

Liberal law also grants participants in a household relationship wide berth to tailor their internal arrangements according to their own tastes (at least when the interests of outsiders and helpless insiders such as children are not jeopardized).[33] Self-determination, the core liberal principle, is enhanced when people can both shape their own homeways and also rely on others' promises.[34] As chapter 8 explains, in practice household members commonly coordinate not by means of express contracts but instead by means of informal norms generated through a process of gift exchange. Individual endowments of the entitlements just canvassed—land, capital, and labor—provide starting points for both explicit bargaining and informal exchanges that create implicit norms.

In the United States today, people have notably more freedom to shape their household relationships than their marital relationships. The state forbids certain marital couplings and typically requires a waiting period before both entry into marriage and exit from it.[35] By contrast, especially when the welfare of children is not at stake, a liberal state generally enables an individual to enter into all three types of basic household relationships with whomever he chooses. A gay or lesbian couple unable to marry typically can cohabit, and co-own, without legal impediment. Want to organize a counterculture commune? The background rules of a capitalist state generally pose no obstacle. There are, of course, some constraints on the creation of household clusters. For example, ambient social norms may deter an unmarried heterosexual or homosexual couple from "living in sin," and zoning regulations may restrict the number and composition of a household's co-occupants. In a liberal society, however, those who want to create a highly exotic household arrangement usually can find a place to do it.[36]

Household Surplus and Its Distribution among Members

The participants in each of the three relationships in a complex household—co-occupancy, co-ownership, and landlord-tenant—can arrange for mutually beneficial exchanges of goods and services, including ones that take advantage of their affective ties. Gains that arise from this internal household trade can be termed "household surplus," an extension of the notion of "marital surplus," a concept fruitfully employed by legal scholars such as Amy Wax, and Elizabeth and Robert Scott.[37] In a liberal environment that honors freedom of contract, individuals can be expected to choose household forms and associates with an eye to maximizing shared gains of this sort.[38] As chapter 8 discusses, the magnitude of the surplus available within a household relationship depends in part on the participants' ability to develop and enforce—by norm, contract, or otherwise—substantive and procedural rules to deter opportunistic behavior. Although participants have an interest in maximizing their total shareable surplus, they inevitably fall short, often far short, of that ideal. One source of frustration is the transaction costs of coordinating—that is, search and information costs, bargaining and decision costs, and policing and enforcement costs.[39] Other impediments are inherent human incapacities, such as limited cognitive power and incomplete self-control.[40]

How do the participants in a household relationship divide surplus among themselves? According to Shelly Lundberg and Robert Pollak's succinct review of the relevant intellectual history, until a generation ago many economists modeled the family household as if all members had identical preferences.[41] Paul Samuelson explored the idea that household members were cohesive enough to resolve all issues by consensus. Gary Becker hypothesized the existence of an altruistic dictator who served as the household head and whose decisions would thwart opportunism by any household member.[42] (Startlingly similar is philosopher John Rawls's view that the persons deciding on arrangements from "the original position" should be thought of not as individuals but as "heads of families.")* These sorts of hierarchical conceptions of domestic life have fallen out of favor. As Lundberg and Pollak report, most economists who study the household now regard it to be more realistic and intellectually productive to apply game-theoretic models that treat household members as (potentially) independent agents.

I adopt this general analytic approach and apply it throughout the book. Some commentators, it should be noted, question the appropriateness of this rational-actor perspective on domestic relations. Milton Regan, for example, asserts that it is descriptively incomplete and may have negative expressive consequences.[43] Regan is certainly correct that love and altruism infuse many household relationships. The rational-actor perspective, however, can and should be enriched to take these sentiments into account. And, when the approach is enriched in this fashion, the risk that this mode of thinking will adversely affect the quality of home life largely evaporates.

The prevailing game-theoretic conception of household dynamics is easy to sketch. At the outset, it is worth emphasizing that the approach implicitly presupposes a backdrop of liberal entitlements, particularly an individual's self-ownership of labor and unilateral right to exit from an unsatisfactory household relationship. Under these conditions, each adult occupant of a household is seen as having the leverage to obtain a share of the domestic pie.[44] In game-theoretic terms, a household member's "threat point" is the utility level that member would obtain after carrying

---

* *A Theory of Justice*, 128–29. For a review of the debate between Rawls and his feminist critics over his unwillingness to apply his principles of justice to internal family affairs, see Susan Moller Okin, "Justice and Gender."

out the action most damaging to the other members.[45] To simplify, the following discussion assumes that a disgruntled participant's most potent threat is to exit from the household relationship. (In some instances the most potent threat actually might be another course of action within the relationship, such as violence, nagging, withdrawal from sexual relations, or, to invoke Theodore Bergstrom's memorable phrase, "burnt toast.")[46] Others in the relevant household relationship, to deter exit by a valued member, must allocate to that person enough surplus to make it more advantageous for that person to remain than to depart. If Dad wants Aunt Audrey to continue as a co-owner of the Sitcom House, he must ensure that she remains satisfied with that investment. If the other four co-occupants want Granny to remain an occupant, their rules governing use of the common spaces cannot be too harsh on her. Conversely, if Granny herself wants to remain in residence, she has to make her presence a net boon for Dad and Aunt Audrey, the (implicit) landlords who have the power to terminate her stay.

When a household member's opportunities to prosper on the outside improve, the risk that he or she will exit rises. Recognizing this reality, the other participants in the relevant relationship may prospectively allocate a larger share of the relationship's surplus to that person. In colonial Andover, Massachusetts, for example, as young men had increasingly good opportunities to the west, many fathers granted their youngest sons more land to dissuade them from migrating.[47] Even in present times, it is widely believed that a husband is likely to obtain a majority of the surplus from a marriage because he usually has greater opportunities to remarry after divorce, a prospect that commonly makes his threat of exit from a marital home more credible than his wife's.[48]

Changes in law and social norms outside the household can also alter threat points by influencing available opportunities and the transaction costs of exit. Enhancement of women's employment opportunities outside the home thus serves to boost their power within the home.[49] Modifications of divorce law that make it more likely for an ex-wife than an ex-husband to be awarded child custody and child support similarly enhance wives' bargaining power within ongoing marriages.[50] More generally, any legal reform that facilitates exit from a household relationship—whether by making it easier for a spouse to divorce, a co-owner to partition real estate, or a landlord to evict a tenant—strengthens the hands of the household participants best positioned to ally themselves with fresh partners.*

---

*If transaction costs were zero, the strongest version of the Coase Theorem would imply that easing legal barriers to divorce, for example, would not increase the incidence of divorce. According to that general proposition, first developed in R. H. Coase, "Problem of Social Cost," if it were efficient for a disgruntled wife to remain married, her husband would successfully bargain with her—regardless of her legal rights—to refrain from invoking her entitlement to divorce. Gary Becker and Elizabeth Peters have separately made this argument and offered data to support it. See *Treatise on the Family*, 331–34; "Marriage and Divorce." For a number of familiar reasons (arrayed in Ellickson, Rose, and Ackerman, *Perspectives on Property Law*, 200–32), however, the Coase Theorem's invariance proposition is unlikely to hold in domestic contexts. First, shifting an entitlement may have wealth effects. Second, because of bilateral monopolies and emotional complications in household settings, transaction costs may be high even though few are involved. Third, the asymmetry between an individual's willingness to pay and willingness to receive tends to make an entitlement stick where it is initially allocated. For these reasons and others, the most recent studies indicate that the advent of no-fault divorce did in fact raise divorce rates, at least temporarily. See Margaret Brinig, *Contract to Covenant*, 153–58; and Justin Wolfers, "Divorce Rates."

Chapter 3
The Predominant Strategy:
Consorting with Intimates

A person considering how to structure household relations in a liberal society faces a potentially intimidating number of choices. A graduate student who moves to a new university community, for instance, must decide whether to live alone or with others, what particular dwelling to inhabit, whether to buy or to rent that dwelling, and, if to buy, whether to bring in other co-owners. Of the three potential household relationships, co-occupancy is typically the strongest and most multi-stranded.* Many co-occupants spend as many as half of their waking hours at home and are apt not only to engage in conventional forms of household production but also to socialize a great deal with one another. Both co-ownership and landlord-tenant relationships, by contrast, tend to be less intense, but even they commonly involve both significant sums of money and interactions protracted over months or years.

Household relationships are rife with possibilities for opportunists. A bad occupant can abuse common spaces, pilfer personal property, neglect household duties, and evade

---

* "Most intuitive notions of the 'strength' of an interpersonal tie should be satisfied by the following definition: the strength of a tie is a (probably linear) combination of the amount of time, the emotional intensity, the intimacy (mutual confiding), and the reciprocal services which characterize the tie" (Mark Granovetter, "Strength of Weak Ties," 1361).

duties to landlords. A bad owner may shirk on management and maintenance duties and wrongly siphon off assets, to the detriment of both tenants and other owners. Yet in all phases of life, people tend to be more considerate of others' interests than cynics anticipate. Experimental studies suggest that the majority of people prefer to reciprocate favors even in one-shot interactions with perfect strangers.[1] Ex ante, an individual entering into a household relationship nevertheless would want to improve on those odds.

One strategy would be to rely, in the event of trouble, on the legal system to impose sanctions on a domestic malefactor. This strategy would favor the negotiation of written contracts, documents likely to be helpful in the event of litigation or threats thereof. At the other end of the spectrum is the option of structuring household relationships in a fashion likely to bring into play informal deterrents to domestic opportunism. Even in the absence of legal constraints, a participant in a household relationship may act in a cooperative manner to avoid, for example, pangs of guilt, retribution by others in the relationship, or the sting of negative gossip and ostracism diffusely administered by friends and neighbors.[2] As the data presented in the next chapter demonstrate, most people in contemporary liberal societies opt to rely mainly on these informal social controls.

As a result, the predominant household-formation strategy is, when feasible, *to consort with intimates*. Consorting with intimates, of course, is likely to be a source of great enjoyment in itself. But it can be expected also to have a great instrumental advantage: a colossal reduction of the transaction costs that need to be incurred to achieve intra-household cooperation.[3] From the start, intimates are more likely than those who are socially distant to behave cooperatively as opposed to opportunistically.[4] Intimacy thus facilitates the spontaneous trading of services, in many household situations a method of coordination far more efficient than formal bilateral contracting.[5] Intimates' early successes with this sort of gift exchange are likely to deepen mutual trust and to produce even greater levels of cooperation thereafter.[6] Individuals also are likely to care much more about how intimates, as opposed to relative strangers, regard them. This makes esteem sanctions among intimates especially potent.[7]

How does a person recognize a prospective intimate, especially when the candidate in question is not kin? Some key positive attributes, generally in order of decreasing importance, are: the prospect of continuing future interactions; the number of participants involved (the fewer the better); and homogeneity of tastes.[8]

Favoring Those with Whom One Will Have Continuing Relations

In any social context, the prospect of future interactions is well known to be conducive to trust and cooperation.[9] The expectation of continuing dealings also tends to make participants more willing to invest resources into strengthening their relationship. These are major reasons why, as the next chapter documents, a large majority of household relationships are based on kinship. Robert Pollak, a pioneering analyst of marriage and the family, identifies four features of family ties that tend to foster cooperative behavior.[10] First, evolutionary selection fosters altruism toward kin—especially toward persons who carry the same genes.* Kinship altruism motivates a person to act cooperatively without external prodding, thereby enabling kinfolk who co-occupy to arrange for productive activities that otherwise would be extremely difficult to monitor, for example, infant care or the cultivation of a delicate crop such as raspberries.[11] These self-executing first-party systems commonly are the most cheaply administered of all social controls.[12] Second, Pollak notes that expulsion from a kinship network is particularly costly, presumably because that network is irreplaceable. Because kinfolk tend to remain in contact with one another, they are particularly well positioned to informally punish opportunistic acts, a significant second-party deterrent. Third and relatedly, information about a relative's past actions and character tends to be unusually complete, a reality that reduces the transaction costs of informal interactions. Fourth, in most societies ambient social norms support loyalty to kin. An opportunistic act at the expense of kinfolk thus is particularly likely to provoke neighbors to inflict diffuse third-party sanctions, such as negative gossip. In sum, the ex ante strategy of consorting with kin exploits the relative durability of family relationships and brilliantly harnesses the capabilities of the many different informal systems of social control. It does not follow, of course, that this strategy guarantees cooperative outcomes.[13] As Tolstoy

---

*Kinship altruism tends to be strongest among those with the closest genetic ties (David Buss, *Evolutionary Psychology*, 220–46; Richard Dawkins, *The Selfish Gene*, 88–108). Household relationships thus are more likely to involve closely related kin (e.g., parents and children) than more distantly related ones (second cousins). On altruism within marriages and families, see Gary Becker, *Treatise on the Family*, 277–306; Margaret Brinig, *Contract to Covenant*, 85–86.

reminds us in the first sentence of *Anna Karenina*, not all families are happy.[14]

Should appropriate kinfolk not be available, the next best option may be to associate with persons who share either preexisting friendships or—commonly even better—the prospect of an enduring association multi-stranded enough to provide a wide variety of future sanctioning opportunities. Suppose an incoming second-year graduate student, Harrison, were seeking a housemate to share occupancy of a rental apartment during the upcoming academic year. All else equal, could Harrison place more trust in Talcott, a distant acquaintance from college who has no interest in eventually entering the same graduate discipline, or in Viviana, a graduate school classmate Harrison currently knows even less well? During their college years, Harrison may have learned something about Talcott's character (including the internalized norms that constrain Talcott)—a significant advantage as far as it goes.[15] To someone interested in finding a prospectively cooperative roommate, however, information about a candidate's past behavior may be less valuable than the prospect of having continuing social ties with that person. Suppose Harrison were to doubt whether Talcott and he would still be friends once their joint living arrangement had ended. If so, especially toward the end of their cohabitation, Talcott might become less trustworthy because he would be less concerned about how either Harrison or members of their circle of common acquaintances would treat him in the future. If Harrison were to conclude that Viviana and he actually had better prospects of being enmeshed in an enduring friendship and network of friends, the strategy of consorting with intimates might tilt Harrison toward living with Viviana.

Limiting the Number of Persons in the Relationship

For several reasons, as the number of persons in a household relationship increases, participants in that relationship are likely to become more opportunistic.[16] First, rising numbers commonly make it more costly to obtain the information needed to deter opportunism. A person who lives with just one co-occupant, upon discovering at breakfast that the refrigerator's container of orange juice is unexpectedly empty, immediately knows who the culprit is. A person with four other housemates, by contrast, would have to engage in more extensive detective work. Second, the larger the group, the greater the tendency to free-ride with respect to making contributions that would benefit the whole group. In the case of the empty orange juice container, if there were only two co-occupants, all of the benefits of informal punishment of the excessive imbiber would accrue to the enforcer. If there were a total of five housemates, by contrast, significant benefits would be externalized to others. Although, as chapter 7 explains, there also are advantages in associating with more co-occupants or co-owners, for most household participants "more" soon ceases to be merrier. Of the Americans living in nonfamily households, the number living in twosomes is over twenty times the number living in fivesomes.[17]

Favoring Homogeneity of Tastes and Stakes

Most people prefer to consort with those who share their attitudes and orientations.[18] When co-occupants have homogeneous tastes, they can more readily agree on what television shows to watch, what magazines to subscribe to, how to stock the refrigerator, and what friends to invite to dinner. When co-owners have similar discount rates and architectural tastes, they can more easily decide on what capital improvements to make. A landlord and tenant get along better when they share sensibilities about standards of housekeeping and levels of noise. As a result, to the extent that tastes vary according to attributes such as social class, age, gender, and ethnicity, participants in a household relationship can be expected to show a tendency to cluster accordingly.[19] This is especially true in the case of co-occupants, whose interactions are the most multi-stranded.

Whereas homogeneity in tastes is advantageous, homogeneity in skills is disadvantageous.[20] More potential gains from internal trade are available when the parties in a household relationship possess complementary talents. A great cook can benefit from living with a great electrician. A landlord who lacks home-repair skills may favor a tenant who has them.

Homogeneity—indeed, equality—of stakes and power in a household relationship also is likely to be advantageous.[21] Equality offers both consumption and transactional advantages. Equality is the most focal—that is, prominent—of available arrangements.[22] Human egalitarian traditions also have primal roots in hunter-gatherer life.[23] Perhaps partly for these reasons, many adults in a liberal society prefer to interact as equals.[24] Sociologists and economists also assert that equality among participants tends to foster cooperative behavior, partly because it reduces decision-making costs.[25] In part to avoid hassles about how to share rent and utility costs, graduate students who co-occupy are likely to prefer to rent a dwelling unit where bedrooms are roughly equal in quality. Residents of many intentional communities are ideologically committed to egalitarian distributions of both occupancy and ownership rights.[26] When co-owners' endowments of capital permit, they are likely to prefer to own in equal shares, and, in the absence of evidence to the contrary, judges will presume that they do.[27] Although the landlord-tenant relationship is inherently asymmetrical in many respects, lawmakers commonly attempt to establish certain symbolic equalities between the two parties. For example, state statutes typically set, for both landlords and tenants, the same minimum period for notice to terminate a month-to-month tenancy.[28]

Chapter 4

A Historical Overview of Household Forms

Most adults in a liberal society indeed prefer to consort with intimates when they enter into a co-occupancy, co-ownership, or landlord-tenant relationship. This chapter marshals statistics to support this basic proposition.

Occupants of Households: The Predominance of Small, Kin-Based Clusters

Veteran observers of households—that is, all of us—will not be startled by the fact that the occupants of most households in the United States can be counted on the fingers of one hand.[1] As table 4.1 indicates, 91 percent of the Americans living in housing units in 1999 were living in households with five or fewer occupants.[2]

As a nation becomes more prosperous, its households generally shrink in size. Not only are U.S. households small, they also have been becoming smaller.[3] The average number of occupants in an American home fell from 5.8 in 1790, to 4.8 in 1900, to 2.6 in 2004.[4] In 1790, 36 percent of American housing units contained seven or more persons; by 2004 this figure had fallen to 1 percent.[5]

Although households do tend to be somewhat larger in less developed countries, the American pattern is hardly exceptional. In 2005, average household size was 2.0 in Sweden, 2.5 in Japan, 3.3 in China, 3.5 in Brazil, 5.2 in India,

TABLE 4.1
Occupants of U.S. Housing Units, 1999*

Number of Occupants	Percent of Occupied Housing Units	Percent of Occupants of Housing Units
1 person	26.2%	10.2%
2 persons	32.9	25.8
3 persons	16.2	19.0
4 persons	14.8	23.2
5 persons	6.5	12.7
6 persons	2.2	5.2
7 persons or more	1.3	3.9
Total	100.0%	100.0%

*Calculated from data in U.S. Census Bureau, *American Housing Survey: 1999*, 62. Columns may not sum to 100 percent due to rounding.

and 10.0 in Senegal.[6] Peter Laslett, an eminent historian of the household, found that the average household size in England remained relatively constant from 1600 to 1900, at about 4.75.[7] By 1961, however, the number had dropped to 3.04.[8] Average household size fell in Japan by half after the nation industrialized, and in Sweden, by more than half during the twentieth century alone.[9]

Except in the largest households, such as intentional communities and group quarters, co-occupants typically are kinfolk. In 1998, 85 percent of the U.S. population resided in multiperson family households, that is, households in which there was a householder and at least one other occupant related to the householder by birth, adoption, or marriage.[10] In that same year, another 10 percent of the U.S. population—that is, two-thirds of those not residing in a family household—lived alone.[11] Chapter 1 made passing reference to the remaining 5 percent, that is, the 12.3 million people then residing in multi-occupant nonfamily households. Table 4.2 indicates the size distribution of these clusters of unrelated co-occupants. A comparison of

TABLE 4.2
U.S. Non-Family Households, 1998*

Number of Occupants	Percent of Nonfamily Households	Percent of Occupants of Nonfamily Households
1 person	83.19%	68.18%
2 persons	13.41	21.98
3 persons	2.18	5.37
4 persons	0.85	2.78
5 persons	0.24	0.98
6 persons	0.12	0.57
7 persons or more	0.02	0.15
Total	100.0%	100.0%

*Calculated from data reported in *Statistical Abstract: 1999*, 61. Columns may not total 100 percent due to rounding. The third column assumes (conservatively) that households of seven to nine occupants contain an average of eight occupants each. The percentages reported in table 4.2, like those in table 4.1, do not include in the denominator persons living in group quarters.

tables 4.1 and 4.2 reveals that housemates who lack kinship ties generally form smaller groupings than kinfolk do. In 1998, multi-occupant nonfamily households had 2.4 residents on average (and hence a median and a mode of 2 persons), while family households had 3.2.[12] As table 4.2 demonstrates, among the Americans living in nonfamily settings in 1998, three times more were in singles than in doubles, and four times more were in doubles than in triples. Only one nonfamily household in one thousand had six or more occupants.[13]

Again, the pattern in the United States is unexceptional. In Mesopotamia, from the beginning of recorded history, occupants of households typically have been related by marriage or blood.[14] This also has been true in Europe, in Asia and the Arab world, in Ghana, and indeed on all continents in all historical periods.[15]

Although small nuclear-family households now predominate, many other forms exist. For starters, a household whose occupants all are relatives need not be nuclear. In a poor African-American neighborhood, for example, it is not uncommon for a grandmother to raise her grandchildren.[16] Moreover, a household that is otherwise nuclear may include occupants who are not kinfolk of the householder. In the late nineteenth century, perhaps as many as one-fifth of U.S. households included at least one boarder or live-in servant unrelated to the household's head.[17] Today only about 5 percent of U.S. households do.[18]

Extended-family households are thought to have been predominant during the early historical periods of the ancient Near East, at least in rural areas.[19] The conventional image, fostered by Homer's *Odyssey*, is that of an enterprise of dozens of persons hierarchically governed by a *paterfamilias* who resides with several of his married adult children and their families.[20] Partly due to polygamy and (especially) slavery, households then might have included scores or hundreds of occupants. As cities and markets developed, however, there was a trend toward downsizing to the nuclear-family household.[21] The *oikos* of the Classical period in Greece, for instance, was a more compact institution than the Homeric household that had prevailed four centuries or so earlier.[22] Xenophon, a canonical source on Greek life during the fourth century B.C., portrays a Classical household that has a single husband-wife team at its core.[23]

David Herlihy, a leading historian of domestic life, stresses that households were highly diverse before the fall of the Roman Empire.[24] After that event, however, slavery went into decline and family farms managed by nuclear households came to the fore in northwestern Europe. In an influential challenge to the previously prevailing view that extended-family households had been the norm in Europe prior to the nineteenth century, Peter Laslett adduced evidence that the nuclear household in fact had predominated.[25] By medieval times, most English and French peasants were living in nuclear households whose number of occupants averaged on the order of six and seldom exceeded ten.[26] In far eastern Europe, however, larger and more complex households generally remained the norm.[27]

In sharp contrast to the conventional image of rural life in ancient times, only 1 percent of U.S. households now include two or more married couples.[28] Angel and Tienda attribute these exceptional arrangements mostly to the economic needs of the occupants, not to cultural traditions.[29]

A century ago, an American couple commonly took into their home an elderly parent who had become a widow or widower.[30] Extended-family households of this sort are now unusual. Three or more generations of the same family are present in only 3 percent of American households.[31] Chapter 2 introduced a hypothetical Sitcom Household containing *four* generations of occupants, an extremely rare arrangement. Although the cultural traditions of many nations, such as Japan and South Korea, have supported the formation of multigenerational households, these patterns are fast eroding under rising tides of prosperity.[32] In 1950, 80 percent of elderly Japanese were living with one of their children, but by 1990 the figure had declined to 50 percent.[33] In South Korea, the fraction of elderly women living with their children fell from 78 percent in 1984 to 47 percent in 1994.[34] In India, where a bride traditionally has moved into her husband's extended-family household,* the

---

*In some societies, custom may govern which kinship-based household, if any, newlyweds are expected to join. Most common is a patrilocal rule, like India's, that requires a young couple to live with members of the husband's family. See Baker and Jacobsen, "Postmarital Residence Rules." On Indian traditions generally, see Gail Minault, ed., *Extended Family*.

average household size is 5.2; in the United States, the average size of an Indian-American household is 3.1.[35]

As mentioned, nonfamily households tend to be smaller than family households. Large numbers of nonkin, however, sometimes do co-occupy a residential complex that delivers common meals and other collective domestic services. At present, over 50,000 people in the United States reside in housing units where seven to nine unrelated individuals sleep and eat their meals.[36]

An additional 3.7 million persons voluntarily live in complexes that the Census Bureau calls "group quarters."[37] A resident of a group quarters may have a separate sleeping space but typically eats meals in a congregate dining facility. The voluntary group quarters category includes institutions such as dormitories, fraternities and sororities, military quarters, elder-care facilities, residential complexes of religious orders, and intentional communities. (The category excludes, however, the 4.1 million "institutionalized" persons living under supervised care or custody in facilities such as orphanages, nursing homes, and penitentiaries.)[38] Nonkin who cluster in large numbers may be able to take advantage of efficiencies of scale in the production of shelter, meals, social interactions, and other valued services, but at the sacrifice of individual autonomy and privacy.[39] Not surprisingly, these arrangements disproportionately attract those who are single, childless, and relatively impecunious; while 5.4 percent of Americans aged eighteen to twenty-nine years live in a voluntary group quarters, the percentage falls to 0.6 percent for those aged thirty to forty-nine years.[40]

"Intentional communities," although fewer in number, warrant special attention in part due to their central role in utopian thought. An intentional community can be defined as a self-governed association of ten or more adult residents, most of them unrelated, who as a matter of ideology not only share living spaces but also dine together for some or all of their meals.[41] In 2007, the number of communities in the United States that met this definition can be very roughly estimated at 1,000.[42] Appendix A in this book provides data on the characteristics of 490 of them. In most intentional communities, including notably the settlements of Benedictine monks and the Hutterian Brethren, members are unified by a common religious belief. A significant minority of intentional communities, however, are secular. This group includes most co-housing communities, most back-to-nature communes, and most Israeli kibbutzim. The median U.S. intentional community has two to three dozen adult residents. Few communities—well less than 5 percent—provide housing for one hundred or more adults.[43]

An intentional community can be described as "strongly communal" if its members dine together for a majority of meals. As appendix A indicates, a religiously based community is far more likely than a secular one to satisfy this criterion (and also, for that matter, to require its members to pool their outside earnings).[44] If members share some meals but less than a majority of them, as in most co-housing communities, the community can be characterized as "weakly communal." In 2007, the total adult population of strongly communal intentional communities in the United States appears to have been less than 30 thousand.[45] By comparison, in that same year, 30 million adult Americans, perhaps to the dismay of Robert Putnam, were living alone.[46]

Owners of Dwelling Units

The owners of a dwelling unit conventionally are defined as the persons so identified in pertinent deeds and court decrees.[47] There have been no comprehensive surveys of the ownership of all forms of residential structures in the United States. However, particularized surveys of the ownership of real estate in general, and of private rental housing in particular, have revealed a now-familiar pattern: about 90 percent of private dwelling units of all types are owned either by one or two individuals. Because 40.9 percent of households have three or more residents (see table 4.1), co-owner groups on average thus have even fewer members than co-occupant groups. Moreover, when a twosome does co-own, the individuals involved usually are intimates—most commonly marriage partners, self-identified unmarried partners, or other kinfolk such as the two siblings who hypothetically own the Sitcom House.[48]

Studies of the grantees of all forms of land transfers, a somewhat overly broad category for present purposes, support these assertions. Shammas, Salmon, and Dahlin sampled deeds recorded in Bucks County, Pennsylvania, between 1890 and 1980. In 1890, almost all real estate was in the name of a single individual (typically the husband in the case of a married couple). By 1980, almost 70 percent of Bucks County deeds named a husband and wife as co-grantees (typically as joint tenants with right of survivorship).[49] William Hines, in a study of deeds recorded in Iowa between 1954 and 1964, found that about 40 percent of the deeds named single grantees and another 56 percent named a husband and wife.[50]

A more recent and far more comprehensive source is the Property Owners and Managers Survey (POMS) that the U.S. Census Bureau conducted in the mid-1990s to determine the identities of owners of private residential rental buildings.[51] Because co-owners of rental housing don't have to live together, one might expect that they would tend to be somewhat less intimate than owner-occupants. The Census Bureau nevertheless found that the co-ownership of rental housing, even of mid-sized apartment buildings, is mostly a mom-and-pop enterprise.

Rental housing comes in many forms. About one-third of all rental units are single-family properties. At the time of the POMS, the landlords of 47 percent of these were single individuals, and the landlords of another 41 percent were pairs of individuals.[52] What about multifamily buildings? The buyers of such buildings commonly have to aggregate more substantial amounts of capital and are likely to be more concerned about spreading investment risks. It is therefore predictable that the purchase of a multifamily building would involve somewhat larger numbers of owner-investors, possibly ones formally organized in some form of business association. Nonetheless, the POMS found that single individuals and pairs of individuals owned 59 percent of the units in the nation's private multifamily rental structures.[53] They owned 88 percent of the units in 3–4-unit multifamily buildings, 67 percent in 10–19-unit buildings, and 25 percent in 50-plus-unit buildings.[54] Even the owners of rental complexes with 50 or more units are more likely to be organized as a limited or general partnership (41 percent) than as a for-profit corporation or real estate investment trust (24 percent).[55] Co-owners, like co-occupants, plainly see advantages in limiting the number of people with whom they have to coordinate.*

---

*Compare, with the POMS data, George Sternlieb's findings in his classic studies of slum tenements. In 1964, when Sternlieb first studied Newark, just over 50 percent of the tenements were owned either by individuals or by husband-wife pairs, and under 20 percent by corporations (*Tenement Landlord*, 122, 253). (Sternlieb also found that approximately 40 percent of the tenements were owned by a landlord who owned no other rental property; ibid., 122.) By 1972, of the slum properties not

Residential Landlord-Tenant Relationships

Because the landlord-tenant relationship may be highly fractious, an occupant can benefit greatly from having an intimate landlord. Most Americans, perhaps surprisingly, succeed in this quest. The principal ploy is to engage in what experts in industrial organization call "vertical integration,"[56] that is, to live in a self-owned dwelling (or in one that is owned by other co-occupants). In 2003, 68 percent of occupied U.S. dwelling units had at least one owner-occupant, up from slightly less than half during the period 1900 to 1940.[57] And, of the dwellings that have at least one owner-occupant, in a remarkable 96 percent, *all* of the owners reside there.[58] In this respect, the Sitcom House, which is partly owned by an absentee, Aunt Audrey, is a distinct outlier.

The desire for this arrangement—homeownership—runs deep. When asked by pollsters in 1999 which items on a list of two dozen constituted part of "the good life," Americans included "a home you own" more often (88 percent) than any other item, including "a happy marriage" (76 percent) and "a lot of money" (57 percent).[59] The pattern in the United States is not exceptional. In most Western European nations, the majority of dwellings are owner-occupied.[60] The earliest historical records indicate that owner-occupancy of a house was common in ancient times as well.[61] There have been exceptions, of course, notably the various Communist collectivizations that shifted formal ownership of all land to the state, but these have mostly proved to be ephemeral.[62]

---

owned by the City of Newark, almost two-thirds were owned by individuals or husband-wife pairs (Sternlieb and Burchell, *Tenement Landlord Revisited*, 56).

A group of co-occupants unwilling or unable to acquire a dwelling unit, but nonetheless desirous of a trustworthy relationship, can seek to rent from a landlord with whom the group has close ties. According to one of the most intensive studies of landlord-tenant relations—an early 1970s Rand survey of residential rentals in and around Green Bay, Wisconsin—"[t]wenty percent of the single-family residences and an appreciable number of units in multiple dwellings were occupied by relatives of the landlord."[63] Tenants can also seek to rent an apartment in a small building owned by individuals who currently reside in another unit of that same building. In the United States, a building containing two to four dwelling units is indeed more likely than not to be owner-occupied.[64] In part because repeat face-to-face interactions tend to foster cooperation, many tenants have reason to prefer living only steps away from their landlords.[65] Not all tenants, of course, succeed in cozying up to their landlords in any one of these fashions: about one-quarter of co-occupant groups in the United States face the unlovely prospect of dealing with landlord at arm's length.*

---

*Given that 68 percent of homes are owner-occupied (see text accompanying note 57) and that a significant minority of tenants rent from either family members or friends, this is the approximate fraction that remains. On why a co-occupant group might choose to rent, see chapter 7, text accompanying notes 46–48.

Chapter 5

Are the Household Forms that
Endure Necessarily Best?

Many utopian thinkers, from Plato on, have placed reform of the household at or near the top of their agendas. Critics have two basic grounds for questioning the worthiness of a liberal society's conventional household institutions.[1] The first is that the actual process of household formation in a given liberal society may be too beset with imperfections to produce sound outcomes.[2] More radically, some critics challenge the normative soundness of liberalism itself. The lackluster histories, in a wide variety of cultures, of experiments with collectivized living, however, suggest that conventional household institutions do have significant intrinsic merits.

Utopian Designs of Unconventional Households

For millennia, drastic reform of the conventional household has been a central theme of the utopian canon.[3] The reasons for the enduring appeal of this literature are obscure. Human psychology evolved during an era when people lived communally as hunter-gatherers.[4] Perhaps humans as a result may be evolutionarily inclined to favor depictions of relatively complex domestic arrangements. In hunter-gatherer bands, however, kinship ties typically are strong,[5] yet utopians rarely envision kinship as the glue of an intentional community.

Visionaries instead have imagined settlements where dozens or even hundreds of unrelated adults dine together and reside in collectively governed housing. In *The Republic*, Plato proposes that the governing class of Guardians share dwellings, storehouses, wives, and a modest food allotment.[6] Thomas More's *Utopia* depicts a fictional island where each city row-house is occupied by ten to sixteen adults—assigned to it by central authorities—who take their meals in yet larger groups in common dining halls.[7] In the nineteenth century, Friedrich Engels, Charles Fourier, Robert Owen, and other utopian socialists sharply criticized conventional households, partly on the ground that they were venues for the oppression of women.[8]

The United States has been particularly fertile ground for the imagining of alternative household forms.[9] Two peaks of intellectual ferment were the Utopian Socialist era of 1824–1848 and the Woodstock era of 1965–1978. Edward Bellamy's *Looking Backward*, one of the best sellers of the late nineteenth century, envisions a future of nuclear-family households whose occupants rent their dwellings from the state, eat meals cooked in public kitchens, and obtain household cleaning and nursing services from assigned members of a national industrial force.[10] In *Walden Two*, B. F. Skinner depicts a community of nearly one thousand persons who share a common eating facility and reside in personal rooms located within a complex of buildings governed by a six-person Board of Planners.[11]

Possible Imperfections, from a Liberal Perspective, in the Process of Household Formation

Utopian visionaries rarely articulate their reasons for doubting the soundness of conventional household forms. Even within the liberal paradigm there may be some facially plausible reasons for questioning the merits of ordinary domestic arrangements. In brief, a given society may fail to establish sufficiently liberal background conditions for household formation, may not adequately deal with issues of externalities and personal incompetence, and may adopt regulatory and fiscal policies that distort individuals' decisions about how to organize their homes.

When a given society's law and norms insufficiently protect the core entitlements of private property, freedom of exit, and freedom of contract, a committed liberal has reason to doubt the optimality of its conventional household institutions. Two vignettes from Russian history illustrate the perversities of household formation under illiberal conditions. As noted, the Soviet Union at times assigned several previously unacquainted families to share an urban housing unit.[12] These *komunalkas* persisted not because they were popular with occupants (quite the contrary!), but rather because occupants lacked exit options due to the state's monopolization of housing supply and control over residency permits. Conditions in Russia prior to the October 1917 Revolution were more subtly illiberal. Residents of rural repartitional villages (*miri*) then commonly were mired in a rigid sociopolitical system that afforded them few choices and scant exit opportunities.[13]

In addition, even a state whose basic aspirations do comport with liberal ideals inevitably falls short in practice. A liberal state must control intra-household violence, for example, to ensure that domestic participants truly are free to exercise their powers of exit. No legal system, however, can detect and prevent all forms of private coercion. Acts and threats of domestic violence in fact are depressingly common and in most jurisdictions consume a large fraction of police time.[14] An occupant who otherwise would leave a suboptimal household may decide to remain solely out of fear that a decision to depart would provoke a violent response by an abandoned housemate. Moreover, exit is not completely costless even when there is no risk of violence. An occupant who leaves a household, for example, must incur moving expenses, the transaction costs of winding up intra-household claims, and the sacrifice of any household-specific human capital.[15] And a risk-averse occupant may remain in a household solely because of fear that a seemingly better prospect would not pan out.[16] Liberal critics of conventional practices thus have some normative basis for questioning prevailing household forms.

Liberal critics also may be skeptical of how well a generally liberal state has dealt with the two principal potential imperfections in a laissez-faire system of household formation: externalities and lack of personal competence.[17] In the absence of appropriate policies addressing these considerations, a liberal observer may lack confidence in the merits of a society's evolved domestic institutions.

Many areas of liberal law address the complications posed by pervasive externalities. At a back-to-nature commune with scores of occupied dwellings, both members and neighbors may receive governmental help in controlling occupants whose activities threaten the spread of disease.[18] Similarly, when increased risks of fire and disease would result from substandard housing conditions, housing codes may force a landlord and tenant to agree on a higher level of quality than those two parties otherwise would choose. When co-owners are numerous and when unilateral exit by one of them would be highly disruptive, the state may limit a co-owner's right of partition.[19] More controversially, liberal lawmakers may seek to forbid consensual household arrangements that offend public morals—for example, occupants who live in a polygamous fashion.[20]

In addition, a liberal state properly adopts various paternalist policies to protect incompetent persons from entering into inadvisable household relationships. Members of a
significant fraction of the population—notably children and
the mentally disabled—are barred from exercising powers of
ownership and choosing their residences. Unable to protect
themselves by exit, these individuals are potentially vulnerable to abuse by those who govern their living spaces. Liberal legal systems respond by attempting to prevent other
household occupants from neglecting or abusing children,
incompetent adults, or, for that matter, pets.[21] One conception is that the state tries to assure that the rules of a household that contains helpless members are identical to the
rules that would exist if those members were not lacking in
capacity.[22] Even legally competent individuals, however,
are susceptible at times to errant and compulsive decision-
making.[23] A liberal state responds, for example, by paternalistically making some entitlements immutable, including an
occupant's entitlement to decamp from a household.[24]

Finally, a liberal critic of conventional household institutions might contend that the state has not only mishandled
these externality and paternalism issues, but also that it has
pursued other small-bore public-law policies that have distorted individuals' choices of household forms.[25] ("Small-
bore," hardly a precise term, denotes a legal rule whose scope
and impact is insufficient to qualify it as one of the "foundational" rules of a liberal society that were discussed in
chapter 2).[26] Government regulations, for example, may unjustifiably limit household options. Draconian zoning ordinances can overly restrict owners' choices about what to
build and occupants' choices about where and how to live.
The law of intestate succession can confer co-ownership of
a house on several surviving heirs who never would have

chosen that arrangement on their own.[27] A stiff rent-control program deprives landlords and tenants of freedom of contract, limits their ability to exit from their relationship, and crimps housing production and maintenance.[28]

Government taxation and spending programs similarly can distort the shape of household institutions. For instance, the rules that govern eligibility for welfare benefits or liability for income taxes may capriciously influence an individual's choice of co-occupants.[29] Many observers contend that the Internal Revenue Code excessively subsidizes homeownership.[30] Massive government support for subsidized housing projects can crowd out the private production of housing. By concentrating the supply of low- and moderate-income housing in a few institutional providers, this policy can diminish less affluent tenants' choices of landlords, locations, and building types. This has been one source of frustration for immigrants living in the suburbs of Paris, for example.

Is Liberalism Overly Destructive of Solidarity?

The foregoing qualms about the optimality of existing household forms all were articulated from within the paradigm of liberal thought. But if liberalism itself were unsound, the household forms that evolve under liberal background conditions plainly would not be worthy of deference.* Some

---

*Some feminist scholars contend that liberalism fails to recognize that individuals are not autonomous decision-makers but instead are socially interdependent. See, for example, Linda McClain, "'Atomistic Man' Revisited." See also sources cited in Maxine Eichner, "Dependency," 1288 n.12, 1289 n.13. And compare Milton Regan, *Pursuit of*

critics of liberalism, such as Duncan Kennedy and William Simon, appear to regard robust rights of exit—a core principle of liberalism—as particularly corrosive.[31] Similarly, a social conservative who values stability in domestic arrangements may support covenant marriage, a bond designed to be resistant to divorce. As Albert Hirschman famously observed, ease of exit from an association may reduce willingness to participate actively in its affairs, or, in his terms, to exercise voice and to commit oneself to loyalty.[32] It thus is possible that untrammeled liberal rights to terminate household relationships impede the achievement of the deepest forms of domestic solidarity.[33]

A liberal, however, has a number of responses. First, American law recognizes and responds to the concerns embedded in this critique. A competent occupant or owner who hungers for a particularly close-knit relationship is entitled to waive certain exit rights—for example, to agree to be liable to those abandoned in the event of departure.[34] Second, the dynamics of household formation are better analyzed from an ex ante than an ex post perspective. People are far more likely to be willing to enter into a relationship when they know they can readily exit from it later. On balance, robust exit rights thus actually may help bring

---

Intimacy, which expresses concern about the effects of individualistic ethics on family institutions.

A sensible liberal commentator should acknowledge, however, that individuals are constrained, often for the benefit of others, by internalized norms, altruistic feelings arising out of love and family ties, gift-exchange obligations, diffuse social pressures, legal rules, and other influences. See generally chapter 8. Liberal principles favor individual self-determination, not in a social vacuum but within the bounds of these constraints (Michael Walzer, "Communitarian Critique of Liberalism," 20–21).

people together. Third, a participant's power of exit can improve the quality of an ongoing household relationship in various ways. Some liberals claim that maintaining a relationship when ready exit from it is possible is the deepest expression of solidarity and commitment.[35] In addition, a participant's threat of exit helps deter other participants from denying that participant a satisfactory share of household surplus.[36] A person who is unable to exit is vulnerable to exploitation, and exploited persons are likely to become malcontents whose presence poisons household interactions. Difficulties in exiting, for example, accounted for some of the misery of co-occupants' lives in *komunalkas* and contribute to the bitterness of landlord-tenant relationships in rent-control jurisdictions.[37]

The Unpromising History of Experiments with Unconventional Household Forms

For the reasons just canvassed, it is foolhardy to deem extant household institutions to be even close to perfectly optimal. Utopians have imagined, however, that many individuals would prefer to be involved in household relationships that involve far more people than conventional households do. Each year in the United States, there are dozens of new attempts to create intentional communities.[38] The founders of intentional communities sometimes encounter zoning problems and other hurdles, but their legal advisors seldom regard these as insurmountable barriers.[39] The historical record indicates, however, that, at the end of the day, few individuals want to entangle themselves in highly complex household relationships.[40]

A strongly communal settlement whose residents live in

social isolation and share a common ideology is apt to endure longer than one that lacks these features.[41] The nature of the ideology also matters. Because regular participation in common religious rituals appears to help sustain solidarity and cooperation, an intentional community united by religious belief tends to fare better than a secular community.[42] The Hutterian Brethren (an Anabaptist offshoot dating from 1528), and the Order of Saint Benedict (established in 530), are prominent examples of long-lived religious sects that have devised a replicable form of long-lasting intentional community. Seeking to comply with the biblical precept of living with "all things common,"[43] both sects require the residents of each of their communities to dine together for virtually all meals. According to the Brethren's own figures, in 2007 there were 124 separate Hutterite colonies in the United States, most of them in the northern Great Plains.[44] These settlements have an average population of about ninety, a majority of whom are children.[45] In the same year the Benedictines claimed a total of about 150 monasteries, convents, and other residential institutions in the United States.[46] They report that these communities lodge an average of forty members, all of whom are adults.[47]

Secular experiments with strongly communal forms of intentional community tend to be far more ephemeral than these Hutterite and Benedictine settlements. Within a handful of years, many nonreligious groups either disband completely or succumb to creeping capitalism, that is, to reforms that lessen sharing among members. This was true during the Utopian Socialist era of 1824–1849, when Fourierism, Owenism, and the like inspired the creation of, among others, Brook Farm in Massachusetts, New Harmony in Indiana, and the Icarian Colony at Nauvoo, Illinois.[48] It also was true during the Woodstock era of 1965–78, a period that gave rise to a large burst of experiments in collective living. Benjamin Zablocki, a preeminent authority on the subject, reports that a newly established Woodstock-era commune had roughly a 30 percent chance of enduring for four years or more.[49]

Israeli kibbutzim have had a far longer life expectancy, but also hardly have been free of travail. Founded decades before the establishment of the State of Israel in 1948, the first kibbutzim were both secular and strongly communal. By 2003, a total of 270 kibbutzim, 16 of them religiously oriented, were dotted about the country.[50] These communities are large, with 400 residents on average.[51] Since the mid-1980s, traditional kibbutzim have been in crisis. The communities had long benefited from loans from kibbutz federations and special government-supported banks. The declining electoral fortunes of the Labor Party led to reductions in this outside support and plunged many communities into severe financial difficulty.[52] In addition, the younger members of many kibbutzim began to cool on the collectivist ideal.[53] In response to these adversities, many settlements, particularly those with a secular orientation, have privatized some previously collectivized functions. Originally committed to congregate dining at no charge, most kibbutzim have begun to charge fees for meals and to permit members to have separate kitchens.[54] Between 1991 and 1998, the percentage of communities that had discontinued the practice of regularly serving a communal evening meal rose from 9.2 percent to 57.8 percent.[55] As a result, a majority of kibbutzim can no longer even be characterized as "strongly communal."[56]

In addition, most kibbutzim subsequently began to shift individual housing units to a more privatized form of ownership. The earliest kibbutz cooperative associations leased their lands from the Jewish National Fund, a charitable organization. The State of Israel, after its establishment in

1948, largely assumed the Fund's role as lessor. In 2004, the Israeli Cabinet approved a new form, the "renewing kibbutz," that over half of kibbutzim had adopted by early 2006. In a renewing kibbutz, the state is empowered to transfer a specific housing unit by long-term lease to an individual member, with the kibbutz holding a right of first refusal in the event of a proposed further transfer.[57] This privatizing reform, along with the others, returned many kibbutzim to viability.[58]

In recent decades, co-housing has become a relatively active sector in the otherwise stagnant movement to create secular intentional communities. Pioneered in Denmark in the 1970s, the co-housing template offers a potentially durable form of weakly communal life.[59] A typical co-housing settlement consists of a few dozen dwelling units, each designed for separate ownership and for occupation by either a single individual or members of a conventional household. (In a Hutterite community or traditional kibbutz, by contrast, a married couple typically was granted the exclusive right to occupy a sleeping quarters, but not the right to sell or rent those premises to others.) As in a condominium development, the owners of the co-housing units also share ownership of the community's common areas. In co-housing, the most important shared asset is the "common house," a facility designed to permit the preparation and serving of collective meals, the defining feature of the movement.[60] About three-quarters of co-housing communities offer collective dining opportunities at least twice a week.[61] Only a few communities, however, provide group meals on a daily basis, a service that would qualify them as "strongly communal."[62]

Moreover, even advocates of the co-housing model insist that each dwelling unit must come equipped with a separate kitchen, even though those facilities readily enable unit occupants to opt out of the collective meal. The FAQ section of the website of the Cohousing Association of the United States once included the following:

If I live in cohousing, will I have my own kitchen?

You may well wonder why we have put this seemingly insignificant question [second to] the top of our list. Frankly, because it is the single question most frequently asked of cohousing enthusiasts. Yes, every cohousing community does have a common kitchen, but community meals are usually prepared and served in the common house only two or three times each week. Can you imagine 25 or more households each trying to separately prepare 18 or 19 meals a week in one kitchen? That would be well nigh impossible. So yes, each residence has a fully equipped—and usually spanking new—private kitchen. Really.[63]

Despite the enthusiasm of its promoters, the co-housing concept does not seem to have tapped into a large, previously unserved market. The first newly constructed cohousing development in the United States opened in 1991.[64] By 2005, there were slightly more than eighty occupied cohousing complexes in the United States, with a combined total of over two thousand housing units. From 1991 to 2005 in the United States, co-housing represented less than one housing start in 10,000.[65] Toward the end of that period, the number of newly opened projects had plateaued at about a half-dozen per year.*

The near universality of private kitchens in both kibbutzim and co-housing communities indicates that communi-

---

*See appendix B, table B.1. According to self-reports by the groups, the number of adult residents in Benedictine and Hutterite settlements in the United States, taken together, greatly exceeds the total number in co-housing developments. See appendix A, table A.1.

tarian practice has veered sharply away from the visions that Plato, Fourier, Skinner, and others contributed to the utopian canon. Contemporary critics of conventional living patterns generally have become less interested in reforming institutions *within* conventional households and more interested in improving social relations *among* neighboring households. Those who hunger for deeper social interactions, it is now thought, can satisfy their hunger beyond the walls of their dwellings. New Urbanists, a highly influential school of urban planners, feature conventional dwelling units in their communities, but seek to enhance contact among neighbors by, for example, including front porches and placing housing units close together.[66]

Even skeptics of liberalism seem to be mainly interested in enhancing inter-household, as opposed to intra-household, solidarity. Kennedy and Simon, for example, tout the potential of the limited-equity housing cooperative.[67] Owner-occupants who buy units in one of these ventures must agree to sell back, on departure, their proprietary interest to the remaining co-owners at a below-market price. This heavy tax on exit can be expected to reduce owner-occupant turnover, thereby possibly enhancing solidarity among the cooperative's households. Demand for these communities in fact has proved to be tepid. Many former limited-equity housing cooperative associations, including all four in the 4,500-unit Co-op Village complex on Manhattan's Lower East Side, have voted to eliminate their resale-price ceilings.[68] It is notable, nevertheless, that Kennedy and Simon join with the New Urbanists and co-housing advocates in accepting the conventional household as their basic social building block. Similarly, feminist critics such as Martha Fineman and Vicki Schultz, who aspire to radically transform conventional husband-wife relations, seem not to be troubled by the prospect of a future in which small, intimate households continue to predominate.*

The central fact is that conventional households—small, typically family-based, and commonly owner-occupied—have predominated in the face of competition in widely diverse eras and sociolegal environments. Although small-bore public-law policies, path dependence, and nonliberal ideologies undoubtedly can affect the shape of prevailing household institutions, particularly the incidence of home-ownership, their influence on the size and composition of occupant groups tends to be either minor or ephemeral. The conventional kinship-based household persists not because individuals lack imagination or spurn interfamily solidarity, but rather because this traditional form has inherent advantages. Even a weakly communal blueprint for dwelling and dining, such as co-housing, tends to founder on that most mundane of shoals: transaction costs. As the next three chapters demonstrate, transaction costs powerfully influence all features of household institutions, in particular the structuring of ownership, the numbers of participants, and participants' systems of internal governance.

---

*Fineman urges the abolition of marriage as a legal category but proposes the conferral of special legal protections on participants in certain caregiver relationships, such as mother-child pairs, whose members in practice are highly likely to co-reside in a small household (*The Neutered Mother*, 8–9, 228–36). Schultz favors converting much currently unpaid household work performed by insiders to paid work performed by outsiders ("Life's Work," 1900–1902). Her discussions of ideal domestic relationships, however, typically assume the continued prevalence of small households headed by intimate partners. See, for example, "Life's Work," 1957 n.305. But compare on page 1939 of same, the suggestion, in passing, of the desirability of creating more households that are not centered on a nuclear family.

Chapter 6

Choosing Which of a Household's Participants
Should Serve as Its Owners

The legal owners of a house typically are the grantees named in the most recent deed conveying the premises.[1] This group of owners almost always includes all the individuals who provided equity capital—that is, the funds used to defray the portion of the purchase price not financed by means of a mortgage. After initially acquiring title, these owners typically provide any additional infusions of equity, perhaps to cover deficits incurred in ownership operations or to finance improvements to the premises.[2] What are the powers of a household's owners? Why, among all the various parties involved in household operations, are contributors of equity capital (as opposed to, say, providers of household labor) typically designated as owners? Transaction-cost considerations lie at the heart of the story.

Basic Concepts in the Theory of the Ownership of Enterprise

According to the theory of the firm, the owners of an enterprise have two key entitlements: the power to make *residual control decisions* and the right to receive *residual financial flows*.[3] Participants in a household, like participants in a nondomestic enterprise, tend to bundle these entitlements together and confer them on a single set of designated proprietors, such as Dad and Aunt Audrey, the owners of the Sitcom House.

When Dad and Aunt Audrey acquired the dwelling, they assumed broad powers to decide the use of the premises, the people who could enter it, and the circumstances under which it might be transferred to another.[4] These are examples of control decisions. The owners of a household, however, commonly choose to trade or give away some of the sticks in the bundle of entitlements they originally acquired. Although Nadia is not one of the owners of the Sitcom House, her agreement with Dad might explicitly entitle her both to dwell in the guest room over the garage and to paint its interior in a color of her choice. Granny, through a process of gift exchange with Dad and Aunt Audrey, might have acquired implicit rights to live rent-free in the Sitcom House. Young Chip might even charm Dad into ceding him control over whom to invite to an adult dinner party.

Owners' *residual* control powers are the ones that they originally acquired but have not yet traded or given away. If, as is almost certain, Dad and Aunt Audrey's express and implicit obligations to the various occupants are partial, they retain the power to decide many issues. Has the time arrived to charge Maureen rent or to ask her to find another home for Chip and herself? Can Nadia invite her lover to move in with her? Should a swimming pool be built in the back yard? If Aunt Audrey wants to withdraw her capital and Dad is willing to move to a smaller nest, has the time come to put the Sitcom House up for sale?

The owners of a household (in their roles as owners, as distinguished from other possible roles such as occupants or family members) are primarily interested in controlling household behavior that affects the value of their residual financial claims. For example, because Dad and Aunt Audrey incur opportunity costs when they cede space to an occupant, they are likely to want to assure themselves an adequate reciprocal flow of compensating benefits from that occupant. If they concluded that Granny, given her level of contributions to them as owners, already controlled *enough* space within the house, they would resist her attempts to take over the dining room table as a site for her jigsaw puzzles. Granny's choice of home reading material, by contrast, would not normally affect the value of the space that Dad and Aunt Audrey controlled. Their implicit lease with Granny thus would limit her use of the dining table, but not her choice of books.

Or, suppose Maureen wants to bring a dog into the Sitcom House as a personal pet. Because the presence of the dog might negatively affect the residual value of the shared environment, Maureen certainly would have to obtain Dad's (and possibly Aunt Audrey's) approval. In this instance Dad and Maureen are enmeshed in three conceptually distinct relationships: father–daughter; co-occupant–co-occupant; and (implicit) landlord–tenant. The last of these relationships significantly boosts Dad's power to influence Maureen's dog decision. If Maureen herself were the sole owner of the Sitcom House, Dad's control over her choice of pets would plummet.[5]

Housemates also have to determine who is entitled to receive the residual financial flows of domestic operations. Figure 6.1 portrays the flows of resources to and from the main participants in a household's economy. Entitlements to some of these flows may be governed by express contracts. For instance, a labor contract may establish the compensation owners are to pay a domestic worker; a lease, an occupant's rental obligation to owners; and a mortgage, the

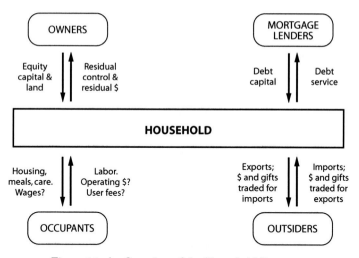

Figure 6.1. An Overview of the Household Economy

owners' financial obligations to a secured lender. In most households, entitlements to many internal flows are protected by household-specific norms that the members generate through repeated informal interactions.[6]

As in a business firm, the *residual* financial flows in a household enterprise are the ones that remain unallocated after all existing commitments that govern inflows and outflows have been honored. The value of the owners' equity in the household is the discounted present value of these residual flows.[7]

As noted, the owners of a household, like the owners of any type of enterprise, typically have both the power to make residual control decisions and the right to receive residual financial flows. Scholars of business enterprise argue that the patrons of a firm benefit from the bundling of these two types of residual rights because this increases owners' incentives for prudent management.[8]

To illustrate, suppose that the roof of the Sitcom House

has begun to leak, an eventuality not governed by contract among the members, nor by norm, nor by housing code. If the owners of the household (Dad and Aunt Audrey) have residual control powers, they have the exclusive authority to decide whether and how to repair the roof, but also the burden of bearing the attendant costs. Reshingling the roof would be in the owners' financial interest only if the cost of the project would be exceeded by the increase in the discounted future occupancy value of the household premises. Generally, one who bears the financial consequences of a decision is likely to deliberate more carefully than one who does not bear those consequences. Bestowing on the owner of a household both residual control powers and residual financial claims thus tends to improve the quality of household decisions. This proposition, however, does not pinpoint *which* of the various providers of inputs into household operations should serve as owners.

Why Suppliers of a Household's At-Risk Capital Tend to End Up Owning It

Like any enterprise, a household is associated with a variety of "patrons" (to borrow a useful term from Henry Hansmann).[9] Figure 6.1 identifies the four chief patrons involved in a typical household's economy. The arrows in the figure indicate possible inflows and outflows from each patron. Two of the patrons—owners and occupants (together, the "members")—have been featured in the previous discussion. Owners contribute equity, either in cash (for instance, a down payment on a house) or in kind (for instance, a gift of previously acquired land). Occupants supply most household labor. A household's internal rules also may require occupants to help defray operating expenses and to pay user fees. Maureen, for example, might be obligated to contribute to the cost of groceries and to pay for her long-distance telephone calls. Figure 6.1 indicates two other patrons who may have stakes in a household's decision-making: mortgage lenders and outsiders. Lenders provide debt capital. Outsiders contract with owners or occupants to provide some goods and services—such as groceries and lawn-mowing—that are consumed within the household.

The patrons of a household combine their various inputs of labor, capital, land, and personal property to generate flows of goods and services that include, by definition, shelter and meals for occupants.[10] In a family household, the range of services is likely to be especially broad and may include, among others, emotional and medical care, child training, and entertainment. Household members typically distribute most of these outputs to occupants, either as obligations owed under the household's contracts, norms, and other rules, or as gifts. Love-infused households are sites of staggering amounts of altruistic gift-giving, especially between spouses, from parents to minor children, and from adult children to elderly parents.*

As figure 6.1 indicates, occupants also may deliver some

---

*See, for example, Gary Becker, "Altruism in the Family." Many long-term cohabiting couples also end up making gifts that pool their financial assets. See Marjorie Kornhauser, "Love, Money, and the IRS," 84–91, a review of pertinent empirical studies. Because an outside observer cannot easily distinguish between an altruistic gift and a gift made with the expectation of reciprocation, empirical analysis of domestic property rights is inherently difficult.

household outputs to outsiders. For example, they may invite casual guests to share accommodations or home-cooked meals. In addition, they may export goods and services produced within the home. Prior to the Industrial Revolution and the emergence of the conception that the home and workplace are "separate spheres," most products in fact were manufactured within households.[11] Contemporary zoning ordinances, by contrast, commonly attempt to limit the operation of home businesses.[12] Nonetheless, partly due to advances in telecommunications, about 5 percent of the paid U.S. workforce still works exclusively at home for outside customers or outside employers.[13]

Those jointly involved in an enterprise have an interest in allocating ownership rights to the category of patrons that values ownership most highly. Conferring rights in this fashion reduces patrons' total costs of obtaining needed factors of production. In addition, patrons benefit from allocating ownership in a manner that reduces the transaction costs of governing the enterprise. The suppliers of some factors, if not granted the protection of ownership rights, might insist on being protected with contractual guarantees that household participants would find costly both to draft and to administer. The selection of a governance system for a household (or any other enterprise) thus is a positive-sum game. All patrons, including non-owners, can maximize household surplus by minimizing the sum of (1) deadweight losses arising from suboptimal governance decisions, and (2) the transaction costs of governance. In Hansmann's terms, this is the "lowest-cost assignment of ownership."[14]

Of the various patrons that figure 6.1 identifies, outsiders who trade with the household are the least plausible candidates to serve as owners. Because they rarely are knowledgeable about household conditions, they tend to be poorly qualified to make residual control decisions. In addition, unlike providers of at-risk capital, outsiders typically have simple means of protecting themselves from opportunistic acts by other patrons. For instance, a disgruntled outsider who provides an ephemeral service can withhold future services, and a provider of a durable good or permanent physical improvement can insist on being either protected by lien or paid in advance.

Nor is an outside mortgage lender a plausible candidate for ownership of a household. Besides being relatively poorly informed about domestic issues, an outsider who lends capital typically can, like the bondholder of a business corporation, use both covenants and security interests to protect itself against household practices that would jeopardize repayment of the mortgage loan. It also can reduce its risks by limiting the amount of its loan. Like a bondholder, a mortgage lender desires to ensure that a borrower has an equity stake in the mortgaged property that is sufficiently large to deter the borrower from taking excessive risks with the property. The residual claimants of a home that is fully leveraged may be tempted, especially if they would not be personally liable for losses, to engage in overly risky projects, such as installing an exotic sauna or bringing in a potentially destructive pet. If a project of this sort were to pan out, the borrowing owner would reap all the gains, but if it were to fail, the owner might bear none of the losses.[15] The loan-to-value ratio of a first mortgage thus rarely exceeds 80 percent (absent government or private mortgage insurance).[16]

Occupants, on the other hand, are facially plausible candidates to serve as the owners of a household insofar as they typically do have detailed knowledge of the enterprise. If occupants were to own a household, they conceivably could raise all the capital they needed by means of either loans (perhaps secured by junior mortgages) or retained earnings.*

To anticipate the possible merits and demerits of occupant ownership, consider a hypothetical household that twelve communards might wish to establish on a farm in Tennessee. Three of the twelve (the "trust-fund kids") between them have enough capital to establish the enterprise. The other nine are impecunious. Because founders of contemporary intentional communities typically are strongly egalitarian, members of the group might balk at letting the three trust-fund kids put up the entire down payment and assume exclusive ownership of the farm. Instead, the twelve might prefer that the deed transfer the land to all of them as owners in tenancy-in-common. Under that arrangement, to amass the needed down payment, the twelve would borrow funds from the three, perhaps securing that loan with a junior mortgage on the property. The twelve might anticipate that this arrangement would enable them to labor together on the farm, consume some of its produce, sell surplus produce to outsiders, and have enough net income to service all mortgage debt, including that owed to the three trust-fund kids among them. If the communards later were to need additional capital, they might imagine that they could obtain it either out of retained earnings or further loans from the trust-fund kids. Would an occupant-ownership arrangement of this sort be a viable alternative to a more conven-

---

* Scholars of business organization have analyzed the analogous possibility of a worker-owned business firm that borrows all needed capital. See, for example, Henry Hansmann, *Ownership of Enterprise*, 75–77. And there indeed are some enduring instances of worker ownership of a firm. See Gulati, Isaac, and Klein, "Kerala Dinesh Beedi."

tional form of household ownership? I return to this concrete example after discussing the issue in more abstract fashion.

In practice, the patrons of households typically confer ownership (that is, rights to make residual control decisions and receive residual financial flows) on their suppliers of equity capital. Even the patrons of the most idealistic intentional communities usually adhere to this custom.[17] The literature on the ownership of enterprise suggests four basic reasons for this result, which I will discuss in order of increasing complexity and weightiness.

Equity investors in households tend to be few in number and stable in identity. The providers of a household's equity capital are likely to be less numerous than its occupants. The Sitcom Household (to invoke another hypothetical case) has four adult occupants, but only two suppliers of equity. Two people can make decisions more easily than can four. Although these particular numbers are no more than artifacts of a fictional example, ownership clusters in fact tend to be smaller than occupant clusters. As mentioned, about 90 percent of the private housing units in the United States are entirely owned either by one or two individuals (in the latter case, typically by a married couple).[18] By empowering a smaller number of equity contributors to govern, a multi-occupant household can reduce its decision-making costs without forgoing economies of scale in household production and consumption.

In addition, equity investors in a household tend to turn over less frequently than household occupants do.[19] Even in an owner-occupied nuclear-family household, peripheral occupants such as Nadia the au pair are likely to come and go, and so might some individual family members such as Granny. The list of occupants of a large, nonfamily household is likely to be even more unstable. To avoid the complexities of absentee ownership by former occupants, a departing occupant might be required either to transfer his ownership interest to a successor occupant or to sell it back to the remaining occupants.[20] The negotiation of those transfers, however, would significantly increase the transaction costs of beginning or ending a period of occupancy in a particular dwelling. Unless scrupulously recorded in public records, a revolving door of occupant-owners also would confuse vendees, contractors, mortgage lenders, tax collectors, and other outsiders in need of assurance about the current state of title to a household premises. By adding to transaction costs, occupant ownership thus is likely to disadvantage all of a household's patrons.

Suppliers of capital tend to bear risks better than suppliers of labor do. A risk-averse person is helped by the diversification of her combined holdings of human capital and financial capital. An occupant who has specialized and nontransferable skills in housework already is somewhat invested in the dwelling she occupies. Particularly if she has little financial capital, for reasons of diversification she may prefer not to have a share of the ownership of the residual financial claim in the same dwelling. Other less risk-averse patrons of the same household also likely would not want her to serve as an owner. For example, if Granny and Nadia were co-owners of the Sitcom House and neither had much in the way of savings, they might be overly cautious about taking on more household debt to finance the replacement of the leaking roof. If Aunt Audrey, another co-owner, had a larger and more diversified financial portfolio, she would be less wary of the downside risk of the roof project and therefore annoyed by their excessive caution.[21] This narrow point leads to a more general one.

The interests of suppliers of capital tend to be more homogeneous than the interests of occupants. Hansmann stresses the transaction-cost advantages of conferring ownership on persons whose interests are homogeneous.[22] The interests of suppliers of equity capital to a household typically are more homogeneous than are the interests of the household's occupants (whether in their capacities as consumers of domestic services, suppliers of domestic labor, or both). For example, Dad and Aunt Audrey, in their capacities as equity investors, have similar financial stakes in any roof repair project that might be undertaken.[23] This would reduce their decision-making costs.

A roof repair project, by contrast, would affect occupants in different ways. The construction activity might inconvenience some occupants more than others. Moreover, the occupants of the bedrooms that previously had been particularly vulnerable to roof leaks would obtain special benefits from the repair. If occupants, and not capital providers, controlled the decision over whether to replace the roof, these differences might cause fractiousness.

In addition, homogeneity of ownership interests facilitates the calculation of shares of ownership. Capital contributions are especially easy to value. Although some account may have to be made of the date at which a contributor provided capital, figuring out the shares of a household's equity capital is likely to require no more than simple mathematical calculations. This is not the case for labor inputs, for which difficult valuation problems loom. If labor were the residual claimant in the Sitcom Household, for example, the occupants might wrangle over the fractional interests that, say, Maureen and Granny should be accorded. Granting each adult occupant an equal share of ownership would greatly reduce these transaction costs, but that approach also would misalign incentives by failing to correlate ownership shares with work contributed.

Because suppliers of at-risk capital are those most vulnerable to opportunism, they value rights of control more than others do. Suppliers of at-risk capital to a household are especially vulnerable to opportunism by other patrons. In a liberal society, a household worker who feels exploited can exit immediately with most of her human capital in tow.[24] A supplier of debt capital can insist on the protection provided by a senior security interest, and outside suppliers of goods and services can insist on simultaneous bilateral exchange. A supplier of at-risk capital, by contrast, turns over a long-lived asset that opportunistic household managers could either expropriate or expose to unduly high risks, say, by skimping on maintenance or taking in pets with destructive tendencies. Oliver Williamson argues that transaction costs prevent non-owner providers of at-risk capital to business firms from negotiating contracts that adequately protect them from these sorts of risks.[25] Similarly, the various patrons of a household enterprise are likely to recognize that the approach that would best minimize their overall costs would entail bestowing ownership on those among them who are equity investors. The common-law rules of co-ownership anticipate this preference. When co-owned real estate is partitioned, there is a default presumption that it is owned in shares proportionate to capital contributions.[26]

The various considerations just canvassed show why occupant-ownership of the hypothetical Tennessee commune would be unwise. Twelve cannot decide nearly as quickly as three. In some contexts, the impecunious will be overly cautious about new projects. When three of the owners are lenders and nine are not, there will be a potentially divisive heterogeneity of interests on some issues. Finally and most seriously, as time passes, the three trust-fund kids are likely to find themselves victims of opportunism by the majority. With little or no equity at stake, the nine might be lax about avoiding risky projects, maintaining the commune's buildings, keeping out troublemakers, paying property taxes, and so on. The three trust-fund kids thus eventually might condition their additional infusions of capital on their obtaining more rights of control.

The historical record supports this analysis. The founders of intentional communities, although not conventionally associated with capitalistic practices, typically have implicitly recognized the advantages of conferring ownership on providers of capital. Even during the height of the idealistic Woodstock era, the modal form of land ownership in a rural commune in the United States was ownership by one or a few members, with corporate ownership the next most common form.* Contemporary advocates of co-housing urge that the new communities be organized, at least initially, as limited liability corporations, with shares allocated in proportion to investments made.[27] Indeed, it is difficult to find a single instance of worker ownership of an intentional community. Ownership by a trust, however, is a form that might serve occupants' interests, provided that the trustees

---

*Benjamin Zablocki, *Alienation and Charisma*, 64, table 2–3. Zablocki does not indicate, however, whether the shares in corporate communes were owned solely by equity investors or by others as well. A legal advisor to creators of contemporary intentional communities urges them to take title to land in the name of a nonprofit corporation, partnership, or limited liability corporation (Rob Sandelin, "Legal Issues for Communities"). See also Carl Guarneri, *Utopian Alternative*, 59–61, stating that many Fourierist phalanxes were organized as joint-stock companies; and Karl Peter, *Hutterite Society*, 178, reporting that land in Hutterite communities is usually held in corporate form.

were so instructed.[28] Real estate indeed has been held in
trust form at some rural U.S. communes, including, apparently, Brook Farm during its early years.[29] Governance by
trustees, however, may be in tension with the participatory
democracy that communards tend to favor. In addition, as
Williamson would predict, the trustees of an intentional
community are likely to have a devilish time raising capital.
For example, the organizers of Brook Farm, one of the most
famous utopian experiments, were perennially short of working capital.[30] Nathaniel Hawthorne, one of the original
providers of seed money to Brook Farm, eventually resorted
to a lawsuit when seeking the return of his investment.[31]

The foregoing discussion of the optimal allocation of
household ownership has neglected a potentially complicating consideration. Household-specific human capital,
such as knowledge about how to deal with a particularly
cranky oven or neighbor, is valuable on site but has no value
in an alternative location. As a result, a domestic worker
may underinvest in acquiring home-specific knowledge and
skills.[32] Household participants therefore may want to devise a method of eliminating this disincentive.[33] In some
situations, the award of an ownership share in the dwelling
in question might be an appropriate means of accomplishing
that end.[34] This may be one reason, in addition to altruism,
why a breadwinning spouse who provides all the capital to
purchase a house commonly is willing to add the name of the
homemaking spouse to the deed as a co-owner.[35]

This method of encouraging a home worker to invest in
household-specific human capital, however, introduces new
problems. A lumpy award, such as an ownership share in a
dwelling, inevitably is a crude quid pro quo for fine-grained
efforts to amass another asset—in this instance, human
capital devoted to the management of the same dwelling.

And, if co-ownership were to be awarded at the outset of the household co-participation, the capital providers would bear the risk that the worker might never make the effort to acquire the relevant skills.[36] Moreover, splitting ownership rights among two or more classes of patrons inevitably creates complications. If the suppliers of both financial capital and household-specific human capital were to share ownership of a household, transaction costs would escalate because both the number and the heterogeneity of the decision-makers would increase.[37] In sum, a household's members are wise to search for another method, such as a measured return flow of informal gifts, to reward those among them who have disproportionately invested in home-specific skills.[38]

As a general matter, investor ownership of a dwelling offers decisive transaction-cost advantages in all cultural contexts. Several millennia ago, the creators of conventional households began to refine this system of conferring ownership on equity providers, and it soon became predominant in the domestic sector.[39] In subsequent historical periods, the promoters of nascent commercial enterprises were readily able to adapt this time-tested model when structuring their business associations.

Chapter 7
The Mixed Blessings of Joining with Others

Although most adults strive to avoid unwieldy households, most also choose not to live and own alone. This chapter addresses the factors that influence how many people join together in the various household relationships. Economists have produced a deep literature on the scale and scope of internal household enterprise.[1] This work focuses primarily on the questions of whether and when co-occupants can gain by adding to their numbers or taking on more activities. Less attention has been paid to the analogous issues that arise in the other two household relationships—that is, to the advantages and disadvantages of bringing in more co-owners, and to the merits and demerits of owning what one occupies.

Adding Co-Occupants

Those who cluster around a hearth must decide the scale and scope of their joint domestic endeavors. In analyzing the considerations that may influence co-occupants' decisions on these fronts, it is useful to start from a static perspective and then move to a dynamic analysis that considers the possible effects of changing background conditions.

Neoclassical economists have long assumed that the patrons involved in an enterprise have an incentive to operate at an optimal scale. Boosting the number of household occupants, for example, may reduce per capita costs of supplying some goods and services. Security from an alarm system and heat from a central heating system are pure public goods or nearly so. For these, it may be literally true that "two can live as cheaply as one." In addition, there are efficiencies of scale in the production and consumption of many household goods and services that are rivalrously consumed. Per capita food costs, for example, fall as the number of occupants rises.[2] An increase in numbers may make it easier for housemates to assemble an efficient production team (for example, to grow a crop or move a sofa), and also to specialize in their work both within and beyond the home. For example, researchers have found that, all else equal, marriage (a relationship highly correlated with cohabitation) increases a husband's outside wages by 10 to 30 percent.[3] Historically, multi-occupant households have served, along with families, as key providers of informal social insurance; the larger a household, the more easily its occupants can spread risks of calamities such as injury and illness.[4]

But there are also countervailing inefficiencies of scale.[5] For starters, the transaction costs of managing a shared household space tend to rise precipitously with the number of occupants.[6] In addition, an occupant's ability to control the attributes of a shared domestic environment declines as the number of housemates rises. A person who lives alone has broad control over the music played, the food served, and the guests invited. Those who live with others, by contrast, must make compromises.* The sharing of household

---

*See Karsten Mause, "The Tragedy of the Commune"; and Melinda Ligos, "Wanted: Roommate," a newspaper article presenting a litany of complaints by owner-occupants who had taken in boarders. But compare Penelope Green, "Getting To Know You," a journalistic description of

spaces diminishes privacy as well as autonomy. The more housemates one has, the less secure the information about one's sexual partners, medical problems, and eccentric tastes.[7] Having many housemates also enhances the risk of contracting a communicable disease. As a result of these sorts of countervailing considerations, over 90 percent of adult Americans residing in nonfamily households forgo the advantages of size and live either alone or with only one other adult.[8]

Taking the size of a co-occupant group as given, what factors might influence the scope of the members' joint domestic endeavors? In his classic work on the theory of the firm, Ronald Coase hypothesized that a firm's managers, when considering how to obtain a needed good or service, would compare the relative costs of internal production and external trade and then choose the cheaper option. Foreshadowing his later work, Coase asserted that these decisionmakers would include in their calculations what have come to be known as transaction costs.[9]

As Margaret Reid presciently noted in 1934, household occupants, whatever their number, repeatedly confront make-or-buy decisions analogous to those faced by a firm's managers.[10] Instead of cooking their own meal on a given evening, for example, occupants can go out to a restaurant or arrange for an outside vendor to deliver a meal to their home.[11] Putting the transaction-cost implications of the alternative choices to one side, housemates incur deadweight losses when they choose the more costly production alternative. Typically, this consideration weighs in favor of buy-

---

how five single adults ages 23 to 36, most of them newcomers to the New York City area, had located each other on www.craigslist.org, an online classified advertising site, and then co-occupied an apartment in midtown Manhattan mostly for social reasons.

ing from outsiders because labor and capital are unlikely to be as specialized within a home as they are within the economy at large. Considerations of transaction costs, on the other hand, usually favor home production; dealing with outsiders tends to be more complex than dealing with insiders, and home production commonly enables savings in transportation costs, such as the hassle of group travel to a restaurant. Coase's theory implies that, when choosing whether to make or buy, decision-makers strive to minimize the sum of the deadweight losses and transaction costs that they incur. Because transaction costs tend to be lower among intimates, Coasean theory thus anticipates that five co-occupying adults with strong social ties would share home-cooked meals more frequently than another fivesome without those ties. Intimates would dine together at home not only because they are apt to especially enjoy each other's company but also because they can more expeditiously co-ordinate home production.

In general, both the scale and scope of the typical household economy has been shrinking. Particularly during the past century or two, the median number of household occupants has fallen sharply.[12] In addition, even controlling for size, household occupants have been shifting away from internal production and toward acquiring goods and services through trade with outsiders. A few centuries ago, a household's occupants were likely to grow much of their own food, make much of their own clothing, and erect their own dwellings. In 1840, de Tocqueville provided a vivid portrait of the members of an American nuclear-family household living on the frontier. The stalwarts in his fictional vignette had cleared their own land, built their own log house, and hewn their own furniture.[13] A twenty-first century household in a developed nation, by contrast, is far less self-sufficient ("autarkic" is the fancy synonym).[14]

What dynamic factors account for these trends? Demographers and social historians have mostly attributed them to technological and demographic changes. But shifts in background laws and norms have also played a significant role.

For a number of reasons, technological progress tends to shrink both the size of households and the scope of occupants' activities.[15] New forms of transportation and communication, such as the motor vehicle and the telephone, tip housemates away from internal production because they reduce the transaction costs of trading with outsiders more than they reduce the transaction costs of internal coordination. Technological innovations also foster greater specialization of labor. This disfavors home production because highly specialized skills typically are more valuable when sold in the external labor market than when applied around the house.[16] In both industrial and post-industrial societies, many adult housemates thus are likely to work for outside employers and to devote a large portion of their take-home pay to the acquisition of household goods and services from outside vendors.

Technological innovations also make people wealthier, and wealthy people, all else equal, seem to prefer to live with a smaller number of co-occupants (at least, other than servants).[17] Household life is a bundled good. When choosing a home, an individual chooses—to name two of many attributes—a heating system and a domestic social environment that offers a certain level of autonomy and privacy. An increase in prosperity affects demand for these two particular attributes quite differently. In a poor society where wood is the primary fuel for heat, the laboriousness of keeping a wood fire ignited gives rise to significant economies of scale and thus tilts individuals toward living with more housemates. An invention such as the gas-fired furnace, however, greatly reduces the laboriousness of home heating and with it the value of living with others. Home heating, moreover, is an example of what economists call a "normal good"—that is, the sort of commodity that draws down an ever lesser fraction of a household's budget as the household grows richer. For both these reasons, as a society prospers, the scale economies of keeping a wood fire going become less salient.

Conversely, privacy and autonomy within a home are both "superior goods"—that is, attributes of domestic environments that most people, as they become wealthier, are apt to spend a greater fraction of their disposable income to attain.[18] As a nation's wealth increases, this increasing itch for privacy helps to induce adult children to depart from their parental homes at a younger age.[19] In the United States, for example, the proportion of single adults aged twenty to twenty-nine that were living with their parents fell from about 70 percent in 1940 to about 40 percent in 2000.[20]

Trends in privacy-seeking by the elderly have run in the same direction and are even more dramatic.[21] The percentage of widows over age sixty-five living alone increased from 12 percent in 1910 to nearly 70 percent in 1990.[22] Dora Costa's careful study of the living arrangements of elderly American males over the course of the twentieth century provides some of the most convincing evidence that privacy is a superior good. Costa reports that, in 1900, 72 percent of retired men over age sixty-five were living, irrespective of the residence of their wives, with either one of their children or another relative. By 1990, the fraction had plummeted to 19.8 percent.[23] Costa investigated whether this change was driven more by increased demand (i.e., senior men's preferences for greater privacy and autonomy) or by reduced supply (i.e., children's diminished generosity toward elderly fathers). She concludes that seniors' quest for privacy has been the main driving force.[24] Once one of the poorest groups in

American society, the elderly have prospered as a result of retirement programs, old-age assistance, and the general increase in national wealth. Able to afford a wider range of housing choices, about two-thirds of unmarried elderly Americans of both sexes now live by themselves.[25]

A variety of demographic changes, such as greater urbanization, a higher incidence of divorce, and increased age at first marriage, also have reduced the average size of co-occupant groupings.[26] The two most influential of the demographic changes have been the increase in life expectancies and the drop in childbearing. Thanks largely to innovations in health care and birth control, the life expectancy of an American at birth rose from forty-seven years in 1900 to seventy-seven years in 2000, and, simultaneously, birthrates fell by half.[27] The upshot, of course, is that there now are relatively fewer children and far more elderly. During their lifetimes most people currently living in a developed nation will have devoted far fewer years to raising their own minor children than to serving as the parent of an adult child. Parents are far more likely to want to live with their own minor children than with either their adult children or their own parents. Now that there are fewer minor children to go around, this asymmetry contributes to the continuing drop in average household size.

The effects of legal conditions on the size and scope of household economies have been less recognized. It is useful to distinguish, as always, between the potential effects of basic background norms and laws, as opposed to small-bore rules such as zoning practices and taxation policies.[28] Although small-bore rules certainly affect how individuals shape their household institutions, basic legal conditions arguably matter far more.

First, households tend to be smaller in societies where norms and law provide effective support for the core liberal entitlements identified in chapter 2—private property, freedom of exit, and freedom of contract. Households are likely to be relatively large, for example, in an illiberal society that tolerates slavery. This is a natural upshot of empowering the master of a household to bring in and keep occupants against their will. Conversely, the emancipation, both legal and informal, of wives and adult children from the clutches of a *paterfamilias* helps to open households' exit doors.[29]

Second, the establishment of the rule of law, or at least of informal order, makes it easier for occupants of households to negotiate and enforce contracts with outside vendors.[30] By making "buy" options more attractive relative to "make" options, the advent of the rule of law thus tends to reduce both the number of household occupants and the scope of household production. For example, in a society where strangers can be trusted to honor contracts, insurance companies and mutual-aid societies can emerge and relieve households and families of some of their traditional burdens of spreading the risks of individual disability. And as contracting with outsiders spreads, social capital and trust tend to deepen, further facilitating external trade.[31]

Events in ancient Greece, medieval England, and modern Israel can serve to illustrate the point. Although slavery remained well ensconced during Greece's Classical period, the *polis* matured into a more effective governing institution. Many of the early Greek city-states succeeded in improving the local trading environment, for example, by bringing law and order to the surrounding territory and by providing a public marketplace (the much-celebrated *agora*). By Aristotle's time, Athenians were active shoppers and their households had fewer occupants and were less autarkic than the households of the Homeric era.[32]

English noble households became gargantuan during the late Middle Ages. The average number of occupants in an earl's household rose from around 35 in 1250 to about 200 by the late 1400s, with some households then having as many as 500 residents.[33] The occupants typically included the noble's immediate family, friends and retainers who assisted in entertaining, and a multitude of hired servants. The resident staff produced many of the goods and services consumed on the premises, including communal meals, defense against marauders, religious ceremonies, arbitration of disputes, and education.[34] According to Kate Mertes, noble households expanded in size during a period when England was politically unstable and lacked centralized control.[35] After 1485, the King, Parliament, and royal courts gradually became better at providing defense, adjudication, and other public goods. As England stabilized, noble householders were able to trade more easily with outsiders. Over the course of the next centuries, the scale and scope of earls' household economies shrank steadily.[36]

The story in Israel is broadly similar. Jews' insecurity in rural Palestine, especially prior to 1948, heightened the attraction of the kibbutz—a potentially huge household heavily engaged in production for internal consumption. Practices such as collective dining promised to enhance solidarity among kibbutzniks, a major asset in an environment where mutual defense efforts against organized enemies might be necessary. However, as internal conditions within much of Israel stabilized, defense considerations became less salient and trade between households much easier to conduct. By the end of the twentieth century, in many parts of the country the traditional kibbutz form had come to be seen as obsolete.[37]

Adding Co-Owners

Issues relating to the optimal scale of a dwelling's ownership associations are distinct from the analogous issues for
occupancy associations. An owner—that is, a provider of
at-risk capital—can foresee both advantages and disadvantages to joining with other investors. Co-ownership facilitates the diversification of risk and the pooling of capital, perhaps enabling, for example, two young single professionals to
purchase a dwelling unit in an expensive housing market.[38]
The primary downside of bringing in more co-owners, of
course, is the escalation of transaction costs. The owners of
a dwelling unit regularly confront decisions about potentially complex matters such as a repair or improvement,
dealing with tenants (paying and nonpaying), and payment
of insurance and property tax bills. It is highly advantageous
to be able to resolve these issues expeditiously.[39]

For prospective owners, reducing the transaction costs
associated with the ownership relationship typically domi-
nates other concerns. Although a homebuyer theoretically
could bring in an outside investor as a co-owner to raise
funds for a down payment, in the United States, only 4 percent of owner-occupied dwellings are partly owned by a
non-occupant.[40] Even the largest of apartment complexes
are more likely to be owned in partnership than in corporate form.[41] In short, most owners, like most occupants,
tend to balk at bringing in more co-participants.*

---

*The popularity of timeshare projects, which can have myriad nom-
inal owners (each with a separate time slot), is puzzling. A well-marketed
timeshare development taps into a buyer's anticipated pleasure in feeling
that he owns, or at least will be able to brag that he owns, a share of a
dwelling unit in a prestigious location, even though the buyer can't con-

Ambient norms and small-bore legal rules may shape individuals' decisions about how many nominal co-owners to have. During the twentieth century, for example, the social norm governing how a married couple should take title to their marital home seems to have shifted away from the husband taking title solely in his name and toward both spouses taking title as co-owners.[42] A married couple that is legally sophisticated may elect to take title solely in the name of the person less likely to be pursued by creditors or, conversely, in both names in order to avoid the complications of probate proceedings and (in community property states) to reduce income tax liabilities.[43] The influence of small-bore law on ownership forms appears to be limited, however, because many home-buying couples apparently receive little to no legal advice about how to take title.[44]

Choosing between Owning and Renting a Home

Economists have amassed a large body of work on residential tenure choice.[45] This literature identifies some advantages of renting. To begin with, occupants unable to raise funds for a down payment to purchase a dwelling simply have no other option. In one survey, for example, 51 percent

---

trol the furnishing of that unit and will have a difficult time selling his interest in it. The administrative clumsiness of the timeshare form has provoked some website-based commentators to question its quality as an investment. See, for example, J. Robert Taylor, "Timeshare Ownership Equals Disaster," and Stephen Nelson, "Timesharing 101." Nelson asserts, "As a rough guide, resale prices more closely reflect the cost of the unit absent the sales and marketing program, or roughly 50 percent of the new sales price." Curtis Berger's law-review article, "Timesharing in the United States," provides an overview of the rise of this institutional form.

of renters stated that they were tenants primarily because they could not afford to buy.[46] Occupants who do have sufficient savings nevertheless may still prefer to rent in order not to tie up a large chunk of their capital in an illiquid and undiversified investment.[47] Also, because renting involves smaller stakes, occupants usually can both commence and terminate a home rental far more rapidly and cheaply than a home purchase.[48] For those who put a high value on ease of residential mobility, this is a significant plus.

On the other hand, although housing historically has not been a source of abnormally high investment returns, buying a home certainly can be financially advantageous on balance.[49] The Internal Revenue Code confers on homeowners a variety of significant income tax benefits.[50] The main inherent advantage of homeownership, however, is that it greatly eases coordination of domestic life. An owner of land has plenary (although not unlimited) power to control, into the indefinite future, both the use of the property and who is present on it. A landlord, when entering into a lease with a residential tenant, retains a reversion that becomes possessory when the lease ends. As a result, absent rent controls, a tenant lacks security of tenure beyond the term of the lease. In addition, even during the rental period, the provisions of the lease are likely to limit a tenant's control over both the physical condition of the premises and the identities of additional occupants. People who place a high value on long-term security of possession and on autonomy of control thus have good reason to own, not rent. This is a primary reason why two-thirds of U.S. housing units are owner-occupied.[51]

Transaction costs underlie this key advantage of owning a home. If transaction costs were zero, an occupant, regardless of whether he started out as an owner or renter, would end up exercising an identical set of possessory entitlements. An occupant who started out with only a short-term lease, for example, would be able to continually renegotiate with the landlord to extend the term of possession as long as that occupant continued to be the person who valued possession of the premises most highly. When he ceased being the most highly valuing possessor, he would terminate the arrangement. This termination date would be identical to the date on which he would have sold the premises were he to have owned them from the outset. In a zero-transaction-cost world, in short, purchasing a home would not increase security of tenure.

The economic literature on tenure choice recognizes, if indirectly, that a key advantage of homeownership is its capacity to reduce the transaction costs of coordinating domestic life.* When a home is owner-occupied, there still is an implicit landlord-tenant relationship between the owners and the occupants, but that relationship typically involves intimates. An arm's-length landlord-tenant relationship, by contrast, is apt to be far less trusting during the course of the relationship (midgame) and is especially rife with possibilities for opportunism during the terminal period of the relationship (endgame)—a stage that many intimates anticipate never even reaching. In the real world,

---

*See Henderson and Ioannides, "Model of Housing Tenure Choice," 99–102, where the authors stress the "fundamental rental externality" that is rooted in a landlord's difficulties in monitoring a tenant's use and maintenance decisions. Joseph Williams, "Agency and Ownership of Housing," 84, 90, pursues this theme and finds, as numerous other investigators have, that owner-occupied houses are better maintained than rented houses. See also Mark Wolfson, "Generalized Lease-or-Buy Problem," 163–65.

where the transaction costs of achieving mutually beneficial outcomes are positive, a tenancy between relative strangers is inherently messier than homeownership.[52]

An example helps clinch the point. Suppose that a sitting tenant wished both to extend the term of his lease and also to persuade the landlord to install new kitchen cabinets. The landlord and tenant would be situated as bilateral monopolists who could deal only with one another.[53] If opportunistic, the landlord, aware that the tenant had put down roots and faced positive moving costs, might insist on extortionate terms. The two parties then might engage in protracted wrangling or fail to exploit their potential mutual gains from trade. These unlovely scenarios would be far less likely to play out in a relationship among intimates.

The transaction-cost advantages of eliminating the arm's-length landlord-tenant relationship have enhanced the popularity of condominium housing. Beginning in 1961, state legislatures explicitly validated the condominium form, thereby reassuring mortgage lenders and title insurers, two sets of actors highly attentive to obscure provisions of small-bore private law. Congress also provided a boost by extending to condominium owners the standard tax advantages of homeownership. Condominium projects then blossomed.[54] Henry Hansmann, one of the most perceptive analysts of institutional forms, persuasively argues that a large association controlled by occupants typically is less adroit than a landlord with hierarchical power at governing the common elements of a multifamily building.[55] Association members are more numerous, and they also have heterogeneous interests when the alteration of a specific common area would particularly affect adjacent units. Hansmann therefore concludes that the condominium form is inefficient for a large apartment building. In his view, developers choose this means of governance partly out of fear of rent control but mainly to enable their purchasers to enjoy tax subsidies.[56]

This analysis, however, undervalues the transaction-cost savings that the condominium form makes possible, namely, the elimination of the arm's-length landlord-tenant relationship with regard to the *interiors* of individual condominium units. To return to the prior example, an owner-occupant of a condominium unit can arrange for the installation of custom-designed kitchen cabinets far more easily than can a residential tenant. In some contexts, these savings in internal governance costs could more than offset the transaction-cost disadvantages that Hansmann associates with the collective governance of a building's common areas.

Transaction-cost considerations also help explain why housing cooperatives have trouble competing with condominium projects.[57] A cooperative housing association, unlike a condominium association, typically takes out a loan secured by a blanket mortgage encumbering the interiors of members' dwelling units. As a result, the governing board of a housing cooperative is apt to closely scrutinize both buyers' financial qualifications and also members' proposed changes in unit interiors—policies that increase the transaction costs of building governance. These additional complications partly explain why condominium units tend to command significantly higher sales prices than co-op units do.[58]

A change in a small-bore legal policy may influence the size of households, but the effect typically is small.[59] The history of the condominium form illustrates, by contrast, that particularized legal reforms can greatly influence residential tenure choices. A nation's tax and spending policies and systems of mortgage finance are especially likely to affect householders' choices between owning and renting.[60]

Homeownership rates vary widely in Western Europe, for example, from 40 percent in Sweden to 80 percent in Ireland.[61] Sweden's low figure is partly due to its policy choices. Between 1965 and 1974, Sweden, a land of roughly 4 million households, supervised the construction of 1 million housing units (the "Million Programme"), a majority of which were subsidized rental apartments.[62]

Legislative debates over bills that would affect residential tenure choices tend to be politically charged because, after becoming a homeowner, a person's politics tend to become somewhat more conservative.[63] Homeowners tend to pay closer attention to property tax burdens, for instance, and are more likely to oppose rent controls.[64] Great Britain has been a notable battleground for fights over small-bore housing policy. By 1979, Britain had built enough subsidized rental projects ("council housing") to accommodate one-third of its population. To reverse this long tradition of government-encouraged renting, during the 1980s Margaret Thatcher and the Tories sold over 1 million of these individual units to their occupants.[65]

Chapter 8
Order without Law in an Ongoing Household

Participants in each of the three basic household relationships have an interest in coordinating their efforts to augment the surplus that is available for them to share. Co-occupants, for example, can benefit from improving their system of dividing up household chores; co-owners, their system for keeping the books; and landlords and tenants, their system for dealing with a leaky faucet. Even in the informal setting of the home, participants have rules—commonly unwritten and even unarticulated—that govern the assignment of responsibilities for handling these sorts of tasks. In addition, participants can benefit from rules that restrain affirmative misconduct, such as carving one's initials into the kitchen counter. Together, these homeways, which may arise from a wide variety of sources, provide the backbone of everyday domestic life.

As Lisa Bernstein has demonstrated in another context, participants during the midgame of their relationship may look to different rules than they would in endgame.[1] In midgame, all participants in a household relationship by definition are currently satisfied with their shares of the surplus and anticipate that their relationship will continue. During this stage, they are likely to rely mostly on rules of their own making, such as household-specific customs and contracts, rather than on external legal rules. Endgame commences when participants first anticipate that some or all of them soon will terminate the relationship. In endgame, the rules of the legal system are more likely to become influential.

This chapter analyzes how participants in household relationships create or borrow the homeways that govern their midgame affairs. The focus is on midgame rules because legal scholars have devoted far more attention to endgame rules, and also because domestic life, especially among intimates, is mostly played out in midgame. Although the legal rules that govern partition, eviction, and other household endgame matters plainly are worthy of study, the significance of these laws tends to be exaggerated. Intimates involved in a household relationship are highly unlikely to structure their affairs "in the shadow of" these endgame laws.[2] Many household intimates anticipate that they will remain friendly forever, even after their home ties cease, and thus that their relationship will never reach the endgame stage. And even those who are less optimistic about the future are likely to envisage that the stakes at issue when a household relationship goes bad will be too puny to be worth taking to a lawyer.

The formal rules of family law, by contrast, may well affect the interactions of spouses and unmarried couples during midgame.[3] Family law aspires to govern, after divorce, the distribution of marital assets and the support and custody of children. These issues tend to involve stakes far higher than the stakes involved in most co-occupant, co-owner, and landlord-tenant conflicts. In addition, the state typically insists that a marriage end only with a formal divorce proceeding, primarily because a marital split can greatly affect the future prospects of both minor children and the spouse who didn't precipitate the divorce. As a result, intimate partners can anticipate that the endgame of a marriage or co-parenting arrangement will be highly legalistic. In light of these expectations, they may be at least somewhat attentive to the rules of family law even while their relationship is healthy.

The Tendency toward Welfare-Maximizing Substantive and Procedural Rules

To enhance their shareable surplus, the participants in a household relationship can be expected to gravitate toward low-level rules that serve to minimize the sum of (1) dead-weight losses caused by failures to exploit potential gains from associating with each other, and (2) transaction costs.[4] To apply a cost-benefit approach of this sort, the participants must regard all varieties of costs and benefits to be commensurable and capable of being discounted to present value.[5] Benefits from association, of course, include the pleasures of social interactions as well as receipt of more conventional goods and services.[6]

Stated in the language of economics, the norms of a group of household intimates are predicted to require a participant to assent to a low-level rule that is Kaldor-Hicks efficient for the group.[7] Suppose some participants anticipate that they would suffer net losses if a particular rule were adopted. If these participants simultaneously anticipated that the new rule would confer net benefits on others in the domestic relationship that in the aggregate would exceed their own losses, the losers nevertheless are predicted to accede to it. The enduring and multi-stranded nature of an intimate household relationship makes these partial sacrifices individually palatable. In most situations, the participants can easily compensate those who lose out in one aspect of the relationship by making offsetting adjustments in other strands. For example, if the duty of vacuuming the Sitcom House's floors is regarded as burdensome, an informal rule that assigned that task to Dad could be counterbalanced by the assignment of other onerous chores to other occupants, such as window washing to Maureen. The power of each individual to exit unilaterally from a household relationship encourages participants to embrace this give-and-take approach.[8] This method of interaction commonly enables them to achieve long-run results that in the aggregate improve the situation of each one of them—that is, overall outcomes that are not only Kaldor-Hicks efficient, but Pareto superior.*

An implicit utilitarian pact of this sort promises to enhance shareable surplus. By embracing the Kaldor-Hicks calculus, participants will not only incline toward adopting rules that minimize deadweight losses, but also succeed in simplifying their decision-making process. The Kaldor-Hicks approach has the advantage of ignoring complicating considerations such as distributive consequences, and can be applied to a low-level problem of any sort. For household participants attuned to transaction costs, the relative simplicity of the approach is a great advantage. By adopting it, members can anticipate not only steadily increasing the size of their shareable pie, but also not losing too many crumbs in the process.

Like legal rules, some low-level household rules are sub-

---

*Even interacting parties who are not intimates commonly show a strong tendency to choose outcomes that maximize their joint profits. See Hoffman and Spitzer, "Experimental Law and Economics," 1009–12, a review of the authors' experimental findings. See also Stephen Garcia et al., "Profit Maximization versus Disadvantageous Inequality," reporting that members who self-identify with a group are inclined to give, at least in the short-term, more weight to total group profit than to equal outcomes among group members. See also Norbert Kerr, "Group Decision Making," 90–92. On the ethics of applying this Kaldor-Hicks approach in contexts where the members' actual future outcomes are uncertain, see Adler and Sanchirico, "Inequality and Uncertainty," a source that includes a thorough review of the pertinent literature.

stantive, and others procedural.[9] When choosing among rules of either type, members of a household can be predicted to take into account the same sorts of considerations that scholars address when evaluating the efficiency of a legal rule.

Substantive rules. The basic substantive aim of cooperative household participants, in their low-level interactions, is to internalize externalities arising from behavior within their relationship. This is achieved when a participant's own product from his actions or inactions is made to equal the product for all participants. Thus, co-occupants and co-owners should take account of the effects of their actions and inactions on their co-participants. Co-occupants' customs, for example, are likely to call for the imposition of negative sanctions on an occupant who tracks dirt into the house or hogs the only television set, and for the conferral of informal rewards on an occupant who prepares an unusually splendid dessert. Similarly, a tenant should treat the premises as he would treat them if he owned the landlord's interest (and vice versa).[10]

The substantive rules applicable to a household relationship also are likely to impose special duties on participants who have private information. Household rules generally should allocate losses from household accidents, for example, to the participant who has the best information about potential accident costs and accident prevention costs as well as the best ability to act on that information.[11] For example, the risk of a roof leak that arises without any tenant involvement usually is best assigned to a landlord.[12] When a participant is considering taking a significant action that would alter the status quo, household rules can be expected to require that participant to provide advance notice to the others in the relationship. Co-occupants' norms thus are likely to require an occupant who intends to host a party to clear that undertaking with the other housemates. Co-owners' norms similarly are likely to require that one of them provide advance notice to the others before making a capital improvement to the premises. Likewise, a tenant who plans to paint the interior walls typically must notify the landlord before proceeding.

In addition, household participants often can augment their shareable surplus by obligating those who possess a comparative advantage in performing a task to take on that task.[13] For example, household rules—implicit or explicit—may require the occupant who is the best cook to do most of the cooking and the owner who is most skilled with heating systems to work on maintaining the furnace. Although these sorts of special duties impose special burdens, again, those burdens can be offset by adjustments of rights and duties in other strands of the same relationship. In practice, of course, ambient norms governing gender roles are likely to influence how male and female co-occupants divide up responsibilities.[14]

Procedural rules: on the advantages of seeking consensus. Procedural rules govern how participants in a household relationship make collective decisions—for example, how they go about creating new rules, adjudicating the application of a rule to a given situation, or administering internal sanctions. Like substantive rules, procedural rules entail varying combinations of net benefits and transaction costs. It may be worthwhile for household members to go through a thorough but costly procedure, for example, when that approach would cool tempers and thus likely be, to borrow Bernstein's useful phrase, "relationship-preserving."[15] One of the great advantages of a small and intimate relationship is that it enables participants to economize on transaction costs by using informal procedures. Debate around a dinner table need not proceed according to Robert's Rules of Order. Unlike the dozens of owners of a co-housing community, three intimates who co-own residential real estate need not schedule regular weekly meetings, prepare formal agendas, or keep written minutes.[16] Even in an absentee landlord-tenant relationship—typically the most distant of all domestic relationships—investigators have found that the participants are likely to achieve a comfortable mode of interaction.[17]

When a group has three or more members, the decision rule that participants apply to determine when they have resolved a contentious issue is of great importance. Suppose ten graduate students co-occupying a house were considering whether or not to host a party at their abode. Possible decision rules include: (1) majority vote; (2) consensus—that is, debating the issue until no member objects to a particular proposed outcome; and (3) unanimous vote. Superficially, consensus and unanimity appear to be identical decision rules, but they are not. In a consensus-oriented group, the discussion leader typically does not ever call for a formal vote on an issue (or even conduct a straw poll), but instead declares, after open debate, that consensus on the issue appears to have been achieved.[18] If one or more members then publicly objects, debate continues. In a group governed by consensus, the members of a frustrated majority are free to informally sanction, with negative gossip and the like, dissenters who have refused to go along with the decision for the greater good of the collective. A unanimity rule, by contrast, requires the taking of a formal vote and implies that a stance of uncompromising dissent is within the rules of the game; indeed, balloting may be secret and, when it is, a lone dissenter need not fear the sting of social ostracism.

In their valuable article on the "Liberal Commons," Dagan and Heller urge lawmakers to declare that majority rule is the default decision rule for a group of "commoners."[19] When members number in the hundreds, as they do in most kibbutzim, majority rule indeed is a common approach.[20] But a group of ten graduate students is highly unlikely to proceed in this fashion. When household participants are intimates and number no more than several dozen, a mountain of evidence indicates that they typically favor making decisions by consensus—a procedure, to repeat, that is distinct from seeking unanimity.[21] The great majority of secular intentional communities in the United States employ consensus as their *only* decision rule.* Eighty-two percent of co-housing communities, for example, report that they proceed exclusively in this fashion, and another 14 percent report that they mostly do.[22] And there is some evidence that smaller groups of conventional co-owners also prefer to wait until former dissenters are willing to accede to a proposed course of action.[23]

A quest for consensus can result in long and tedious meetings, the delay of valuable projects, and even stalemate. Nonetheless, even self-interested participants in an intimate household relationship have good reasons for trying to proceed in this fashion. The process of striving for consensus assures, better than majority rule (especially in its less participatory forms), that debate over a proposal will

---

*See appendix A, table A.2. Benjamin Zablocki's survey in the 1970s of 120 intentional communities similarly found that occupants, numbering twenty-five on average, tended to be hostile to voting and to favor consensus-seeking (*Alienation and Charisma*, 200–201, 250–56).

fully inform proponents about opponents' concerns.[24] To accomplish this end, experts advise the owner-occupants of a co-housing project not only to seek consensus at their meetings but also to make use of cards color-coded to indicate intensity of support or opposition to a measure.[25] Because the participants are engaged in repeat play and know each other well, each should discern the long-term personal disadvantages of exaggerating the strength of their sentiments on a particular issue. When a process of decision-making succeeds in accounting for genuine intensities of preference, it is more likely to result in outcomes that enhance members' overall welfare.[26] In addition, when participants are intimate, their efforts at consensus-seeking are less likely to result in a costly impasse than if they were to seek unanimity. Those disadvantaged by a proposed measure can be predicted to go along with it, partly on account of social pressure, once they perceive that others strongly favor it.[27] And, as always when there are multi-stranded social relationships, a participant who relents for the overall good of the group can later be informally compensated when other decisions come before the house. Finally, unlike both unanimity-rule and majority-rule systems, a process of consensus-seeking signals that participants are intimate and trustworthy. Those who engage in consensus-seeking thus are likely to derive more pleasure from their decision-making process as such.[28]

As participants become more numerous or heterogeneous, governance by consensus becomes increasingly difficult. Some co-housing communities therefore have adopted a two-stage procedure. In the first stage of decision-making, members seek to reach consensus. Whenever that effort fails, they proceed to a second stage in which they apply a supermajoritarian decision rule.[29]

Sources of Household Rules: In General

Participants in a household relationship can generate their own homeways in a variety of fashions and also can extract them from a variety of external sources. This section offers a brief and generally abstract survey of these various sources of social control and sets the foundation for the three flesh-and-blood sections that follow. Those three sections delve into the social-control techniques used by participants in each of the basic household relationships: co-occupancy, co-ownership, and landlord-tenant.

The overall system of social control is an amalgam of rules involving first-, second-, and third-party controllers. First-party rules include internalized norms and personal ethics that an individual enforces upon himself.[30] Second-party rules are those that participants in the governed relationship generate. These rules include relationship-specific norms that evolve from participants' practices over time, contracts among participants, and rules promulgated by formal organizations that participants may establish.[31] Third-party rules are produced by outsiders; these include ambient social norms generated by diffuse social forces and laws decreed by governments.[32]

Commonly, the controller that makes a rule also is the agent that enforces it. For example, state bureaucracies may enforce law and an individual may self-enforce his own personal ethics. But hybrid systems of social control also are common. Participants in a household relationship, for instance, could use an express contract to create a rule and then rely entirely on external controlling agents—perhaps neighborhood gossips or courts—to enforce that contract.[33]

Two major themes are developed in the remainder of this

chapter. The first theme is that, the more intimate the participants in a household relationship are, the more likely they are to make use of second-party as opposed to third-party rules.[34] The second theme is that increasing intimacy among participants brings a particular type of second-party rule to the fore, namely the household-specific norms that arise out of patterns of gift exchange.

Internal sources of rules: the relative merits of contracts and relationship-specific norms. When creating their own homeways, participants in a household relationship are likely to make some use of both contracts and relationship-specific norms. The latter require a few sentences of introduction. Relationship-specific norms are informal expectations about how each participant *should* behave in the future. They emerge from participants' spontaneous (i.e., unnegotiated) successes in coordinating with one another.[35] The standard label for these sorts of reciprocal acts of cooperation is "gift exchange," a much-studied process of low-level coordination.* (Gift exchange must be distinguished from purely altruistic gift-giving, which also is extremely common within households.)[36] The particularized "customs of the household" that emerge from its history of cooperative practices

---

*For a concise overview of alternative theories of gift exchange, see Thomas and Worrall, "Gift-Giving," 315–17. Valuable entryways into the vast literature on the subject include, in anthropology, Maurice Godelier, *Enigma of the Gift*, and Marcel Mauss, *The Gift*; in sociology, Peter Blau, *Exchange and Power*, David Cheal, *Gift Economy*, and George Homans, *Social Behavior*; in economics, George Akerlof, "Labor Contracts as Partial Gift Exchange," Fehr and Gächter, "Economics of Reciprocity," and Janet Landa, *Trust, Ethnicity, and Identity*; and in law, Yochai Benkler, "Sharing Nicely," Melvin Eisenberg, "World of Gift," Melanie Leslie, "Enforcing Family Promises," and Eric Posner, "Gifts and Gratuitous Promises."

are somewhat analogous to the varying "customs of the manor" that evolved in medieval English villages.[37]

For a process of gift exchange to be mutually beneficial, each participant must keep a rough mental account of who has contributed what and who has received what.[38] The account should be no more than rough because an excessively close mental reckoning of a balance of informal trade manifests distrust (and indeed, among married couples, is associated with a greater likelihood of divorce).[39] Because domestic gift-giving can be fitful, temporary imbalances of trade are likely to arise. A participant who becomes convinced that she will obtain an insufficient flow of net benefits from the process can be expected to respond with escalating self-help measures. As her grievances deepen, her informal remedies might progress from gentle reminders, to more caustic comments, to conspicuous refusals to perform customary duties, to threats of exit, and perhaps even to actual exit from the household relationship.[40]

In selected contexts, contracts between household participants are better than household-specific norms at inducing cooperative behavior. Contracts are particularly useful when participants face a discrete challenge that they haven't confronted before, when they anticipate that they may disagree on the values of certain outcomes, and when they are untrusting (as, for example, a tenant and absentee landlord may be).[41] When participants in a household relationship do contract with one another, they commonly will regard an oral agreement to be sufficient. Reducing an agreement to writing, however, can help parties prove the substance of their agreement both to one another during midgame, and also to a third party in the event of an endgame dispute.[42]

In many household contexts, however, especially when

the participants are intimates, gift exchange is superior to bargained-for exchange. Consider, for example, the choices available to an unmarried but romantically involved young couple who are about to cohabit for the first time. With a view to enhancing the overall quality of their co-occupancy experience, the couple might contemplate, among others, the following four options:

1. the negotiation of a complete written contract specifying the two parties' respective rights and duties in every aspect of their forthcoming co-occupancy relationship;
2. the negotiation of a bare-bones written agreement requiring one participant to provide "housekeeping services" (or some other vaguely defined bundle of duties), and requiring the other periodically to pay that provider a specified amount of money;
3. the negotiation of a bare-bones oral agreement requiring one participant to provide certain categories of services, say "shopping and cooking," and the second to provide other categories of services, say "cleaning, laundry, and yard work"; and
4. muddling through, that is, relying primarily on gift exchange, whereby each participant would unilaterally perform most tasks without prior negotiation, in the hope of eventually receiving an adequate flow of return gifts.

Among trusting intimates, the gift-exchange process, the last of these four alternatives, has as many as three potential advantages over the various forms of express contracting.[43] The first advantage of gift exchange is—no surprise here— lower transaction costs.[44] Participants who are confident that their spontaneous reciprocal exchanges will be mutually advantageous can avoid the hassle of negotiating, interpreting, and enforcing explicit terms of trade. The negotiation of a written contract covering all household contingencies would be impossibly expensive to draft. While a bare-bones contract (oral or written) could be negotiated in minutes, it is likely to be rife with ambiguity and to invite haggling over interpretation.[45] Do "housekeeping services" include paying the bills? Are "cooking" obligations to be relaxed when the designated cook falls sick? How often should the person with "cleaning" responsibilities sweep out the garage? And so on. For the relationship to prosper, the two parties would have to be able to engage in an informal give-and-take to resolve these sorts of ambiguities. But if they could succeed at such a give-and-take, they likely also could succeed by muddling through without an overarching contract. Informal gift exchange of course entails transaction costs of its own, in part because co-occupants must keep rough mental accounts of how they stand with one another. But, among trusting intimates, these costs tend to be lower than the transaction costs of negotiating and enforcing an express contract, whatever its degree of complexity.

A second advantage of gift exchange is that it can be kept money-free (in contrast to the hypothetical couple's second option, the exchange of housekeeping services for a periodic wage). Because money is fungible, most outsiders that provide household services, such as commercial housecleaning firms, prefer cash transactions to barter transactions. Intimates, by contrast, typically have a strong aversion to engaging in monetized transactions with one another.* Just as

---

*See Margaret Radin, "Market-Inalienability," and Ellickson, *Order Without Law*, 61–62, 78, 234–36 (describing the preference of neighbors in rural Shasta County, California, to use in-kind gifts, not money, to

a well-socialized dinner guest arrives bearing the gift of a
bottle of wine and not a twenty-dollar bill, intimate housemates don't pay wages to one another. Monetary compensation tends to be counterproductive among housemates
because it displaces intrinsic motivations to perform the
same task and fails to enhance the social status of the recipient in the eyes of outsiders.[46] Moreover, by serially ex-
changing in-kind gifts, participants in a household relationship can signal their mutual feelings of intimacy and
trust.[47] This mode of exchange thus enhances prospects for
cooperative interactions in the future.[48]

   Third, recent research indicates that a process of reciprocal gift-giving, apart from other instrumental advantages,
may intrinsically generate utility for its participants.[49] There
is neurological evidence, for example, that reciprocated acts
of cooperation generate pleasure.[50] And one team of exper-
imenters found that individuals regarded the outcomes of
informally reciprocated exchanges as fairer than the outcomes of negotiated exchanges, even when the material results were identical.[51] In sum, intimates have many reasons
for preferring to create their homeways by means of spontaneous gift exchanges as opposed to express contracts.*

   Internally organized hierarchical relationships. As participants become more numerous, the administrative costs of

---

compensate one another). See also Viviana Zelizer, *Purchase of Intimacy*
(analyzing the use of money in intimate relationships of all sorts); Ertman and Williams, *Rethinking Commodification*; and note 61 in this
chapter and accompanying text. But compare Vicki Schultz, "Life's
Work," 1901–06, an assertion that workers especially value paid work.

   *But compare Martha Ertman, "Commercializing Marriage," 55–59,
urging a marrying couple to execute a written agreement; Marjorie
Shultz, "Contractual Ordering of Marriage," 328–34, advising married
couples to make greater use of written contracts and also urging courts
to enforce such contracts even when the marriage is ongoing.

both contracting and gift exchange rise precipitously. Members of a twosome have a single one-on-one relationship to keep in healthy balance. In a threesome, there are three of these one-on-one relationships. In an eightsome, there are twenty-eight. In a group of 50, there are 1,225.[52] The relative efficiency of establishing a centralized hierarchy to coordinate actions thus grows markedly with group size. In addition, increased size tends to erode intimacy and trust, and with them the attractiveness of more decentralized systems of coordination.

A co-occupant or co-owner group that includes dozens of participants therefore commonly creates a formal organization responsible for handling many of its coordination issues.[53] A hierarchy, of course, is a mixed blessing. The formalization of governance gives rise to administrative costs and rigidities and opens up the possibility that unfaithful agents will seize the reins. For members of a small group, the creation of a governing body is, on balance, highly unlikely to be worth the bother. But for a large group, the existence of a permanent administrative structure supervised by specialized managers can give rise to significant efficiencies. A hierarchical solution is essential in, for example, a timeshare development, where owner-occupants rotate in possession as often as weekly and have virtually no face-to-face contact. Some legislatures indeed require the developer of a timeshare project to designate a management entity prior to marketing shares in the project.[54]

External source of rules: the relative merits of ambient social norms and laws. Instead of developing their own rules or hierarchies, participants in a household relationship can follow an externally validated system. The two main choices are ambient social norms, that is, informal rules of appropriate behavior, and laws, the formal rules promulgated by governments.

Ambient norms generally are enforced in diffuse fashion by neighbors and members of other external social networks. These norms commonly have great influence on the nature of midgame domestic arrangements, in part because participants in a household relationship may have previously internalized many of them.

In a liberal society devoted to freedom of contract, neighbors and other potential informal enforcers are likely to grant participants in a household relationship broad leeway to tailor their own homeways, even idiosyncratic ones.[55] Like liberal lawmakers, liberal neighbors are most likely to enforce ambient norms applicable to the internal practices of a household when violation of those norms would harm either outsiders like themselves or helpless insiders.[56] For example, if a group of co-occupants were to neglect maintenance of a house's front-yard landscaping or were to abuse children inside the house, neighbors might respond with negative gossip or more severe sanctions.

In a liberal society, the legal system performs a crucial role in helping to ensure basic individual entitlements such as private property, freedom of exit, and freedom of contract. These backdrop entitlements underpin all interactions among household members.[57] Public-law rules that govern relations between citizen and state, such as tax and welfare policies, also may significantly influence the housing stock, co-occupants' rent-or-buy decisions, and perhaps the composition of co-occupant and co-owner groups.[58] By contrast, the small-bore *private-law* rules that either legislatures or courts promulgate are not likely to have much influence on midgame household relations among intimates. A central finding of empirical legal scholars is that low-stakes disputes among individuals in a continuing relationship tend to be resolved beyond the shadow of the law, that is, without regard to nominally applicable legal rules.[59]

Although in some contexts this peripheral role of private-law rules may be partly attributable to the participants' lack of confidence in the legal system, in all situations a major factor is the participants' desire to avoid the transaction costs involved in learning applicable law and pursuing legal remedies. Indeed, if an intimate were to seek to resolve a midgame domestic dispute by filing a lawsuit, the other participants typically would deem that legalizing step a grievous violation of the customs of the household.[60]

Rules for Co-Occupants

Drawing on the various sources just surveyed, co-occupants develop rules to resolve mundane issues such as how to assign the duty of vacuuming the floors and the power to control the television remote. As noted, intimate housemates are likely to rely mainly on an ongoing process of gift exchange to generate "customs of the household" that implicitly resolve many of their coordination issues.* To supplement

---

*Critics of the gift-exchange process among housemates assert that it systematically advantages the powerful, men in particular, to the disadvantage of women. See, for example, Vicki Schultz, "Life's Work," 1899–1902, applauding the trend toward greater contracting out of household work on the ground that outside employees can more readily engage in collective action to protect themselves from adverse working conditions. See also Mary Becker, "Patriarchy and Inequality," characterizing the existing social structure as overly patriarchal and critiquing liberal models of social interactions. These critics do not accept, at least in the context of intergender relations, the premise that background legal and social conditions in the United States are liberal—that is, that occupants can use either voice or exit to avoid exploitation within the home.

The results of empirical studies designed to shed light on the subject are mixed. Wives in good marriages tend to be happier, and wives in bad marriages tend to be unhappier, than unmarried women. See sources

these household-specific norms, they may enter into explicit contracts with one another, create an internal governing hierarchy, and import rules from outside norm-makers
or lawmakers.

Oral contracts. New housemates commonly converse about
how rooms are to be allocated, chores performed, and bills
paid. Intimates are apt to structure these agreements, however, in a fashion that signals that they indeed are intimates.
For example, a domestic oral contract is far more likely to
call for, or presume, in-kind compensation as opposed to
monetary compensation.[61] As noted, in most contexts a
transfer of money signals social distance. Feminist scholars
who favor monetary compensation for household labor implicitly recognize this point and stop short of advocating
spouse-to-spouse payments for the performance of discrete
domestic tasks.* Parents sometimes do pay their children

---

cited in Brinig and Nock, "Marry Me, Bill," 432–33; see also Lee, Seccombe, and Shehan, "Marital Status and Personal Happiness." A large
majority of wives report that they regard the division of labor within
their homes to be fair. See Lennon and Rosenfield, "Division of Housework," 507, and sources cited in Stephen Nock, "Time and Gender in
Marriage," 1977. But compare Jessie Bernard, *Future of Marriage*, 27–28,
tables 10 and 14–16, offering evidence that marriage tends to be detri-
mental to a woman's health.

*See, for example, Martha Fineman, *Autonomy Myth*, 31–54, 284–91;
and Nancy Folbre, Invisible Heart, 49–51, 109–13, two commentaries
that urge *governments* to compensate caregivers within households. See
also Susan Okin, *Justice, Gender, and the Family*, 180–81 (opposing cash
compensation for particular household tasks, but advocating that each
spouse receive half of any paycheck earned for work performed outside
the household); Joan Williams, *Unbending Gender*, 129–31 (urging
adoption of legal rules that would divide equally, after divorce, former
spouses' assets and future incomes). See generally Catharine MacKinnon, *Feminist Theory of the State*, 63–80 (reviewing, mostly from a Marx-
ian perspective, arguments for and against the payment of wages for
housework).

for performing extra chores around the house (in part to prepare them for employment relations outside the household), but tend to feel ambivalent about making these payments.[62]

Because insistence on a written document signals distrust, intimates are likely to prefer an oral deal to a written one.[63] Even when participants regard their oral promises to be informally binding, they are likely to avoid saying anything to imply that these obligations would be legally enforceable; in an intimate relationship, the keeping of a promise is likely to do more to enhance the relationship when participants perceive that performance was in no way legally coerced.[64]

Written contracts. In endgame, courts are more likely to enforce an obligation that has been reduced to writing.[65] A number of commercial firms sell sample contractual forms designed to help housemates structure their relationships. These forms tend to be aimed at helping an unmarried couple resolve, in midgame, the sharing of operating expenses owed to outsiders and, in endgame, the disentangling of personal property and financial accounts (and, if relevant, post-separation obligations of partner and child support).[66] The forms in *Living Together: A Legal Guide for Unmarried Couples*, now in its twelfth edition, focus almost entirely on those issues, as opposed to the allocation of physical spaces, the assignment of household chores, and the articulation of rules of deportment. As the authors put it:

> The contracts included in this chapter [on "living together agreements"] pertain only to property and finances. They do not cover the day-to-day details of your relationship, such as who will do the dishes, who will walk the dog, how many overnight guests you'll allow, and whose art goes in the living room. A court won't—and shouldn't be asked to—enforce these kinds

of personal agreements. If your agreement includes personal as well as financial clauses, a court might declare the entire contract illegal or frivolous and refuse to enforce any of it—including the more important financial clauses. Obviously, you need to be clear with your partner on things such as house-cleaning and cooking. Just don't mix up these day-to-day issues with the bigger legal issues of living together.[67]

One of *Living Together*'s co-authors, Frederick Hertz, an Oakland attorney who has long urged unmarried cohabiting couples, both straight and gay, to negotiate written agreements, has admitted that only a "miniscule fraction" of them in fact choose to do so.[68]

A few commentators even advise co-occupants who are not romantically involved, and whose prospective relationships thus are far simpler, to negotiate written contracts.[69] These "roommate agreements" may be sensible when housemates are particularly untrusting, for example, after a Manhattan real estate agency has brought together utter strangers who share only an interest in splitting rental costs.[70] Co-occupants also might benefit from a written agreement when their stakes are unusually high, perhaps because their lease has a term of several years or because they live in a rent-control jurisdiction.[71]

Some colleges and universities encourage students who are roommates to negotiate detailed written contracts to govern behavior within their shared space.[72] These contracts make the most sense, if they ever do, when roommates are total strangers, such as entering freshmen.[73] Many students, who likely have a better sense than university administrators about the optimal amount of formalization of living arrangements, resist drafting roommate agreements and instead prefer to talk a few things through and otherwise rely on unstructured give-and-take.

Formal organizations of co-occupants. An intentional community that includes at least several dozen residents usually has some sort of formal central authority, both to handle internal matters and also to enter into contracts with outsiders.[74] These institutions vary widely in form. When the owners of an intentional community also all reside there, the governance of both co-owner and co-occupant affairs may be consolidated in a single central authority. As a matter of ideology, members of most secular communes are likely to prefer a highly participatory form of governance involving frequent group-wide meetings.[75] As the number of residents grows, however, this arrangement becomes less practicable. Thus, while a small co-housing community may make its decisions in group-wide sessions, a larger one is likely to rely significantly on representative democracy, such as governance by an elected board of directors.[76] Large intentional communities typically become more hierarchical as time passes.[77] For example, kibbutzim, most of which have hundreds of residents, have been shifting governance responsibilities away from their general assemblies and toward boards of directors, elected councils, and designated officers.[78] Perhaps to avoid this level of bureaucratization, the residents of most newly founded intentional communities, as appendix A shows, now tend to keep the number of adult occupants down to two or three dozen.[79]

Some intentional communities opt for a more autocratic form of governance that places authority over co-occupant affairs in the hands of a leader or small leadership group that the occupants cannot unseat. In these instances, the implicit or explicit leases between the household's owner and the occupants require occupants to obey this designated executive (who usually is either the owner or the owner's agent). Roughly 90 percent of religion-based intentional communities are organized in this fashion.[80] For example, Hutterite communities historically have been governed by six designated male elders.[81] A single elder heads a community of Bruderhof, whose members, like the Hutterites and Benedictines, pool most of their property for biblical reasons.[82] Members of the Oneida community conferred absolute power on their theocratic leader, John Noyes.[83]

Historically, many large family-based households have been headed by hierarchs, who typically obtained sole ownership through inheritance, usually according to rules that favored senior males.[84] Surveying practices in the Classical period in ancient Greece, Aristotle asserted in *The Politics* that "every household is monarchically governed by the eldest of the kin."[85] In a gargantuan medieval English noble household, the earl or other owner issued "ordinances" to govern the conduct of the co-occupants and hired stewards to supervise internal affairs.[86]

These hierarchically organized households were descendants of the ancient *paterfamilias* form, exemplified by the Homeric extended-family household.[87] The *paterfamilias* model has been particularly prominent in societies that deny the basic liberal rights of self-ownership and free exit to slaves—and often to wives and some adult children as well. Despite these unsavory aspects, the *paterfamilias* form enabled significant reductions in the transaction costs of organizing family and household affairs, an advantage that has undoubtedly contributed to its prevalence in nonliberal societies. Although the selection of a single household owner according to mechanical inheritance rules may devolve leadership into the hands of an incompetent, this system at least reduces the amount of energy younger family members waste in currying favor with their elders.[88] More important, by vesting controlling powers in a single person, the *paterfamilias* form enables some centralized structuring of the affairs of dozens or even hundreds of co-occupants. By identifying a single authoritative household leader, it also expedites dealings with outsiders, such as neighboring households. Even in the nonliberal settings where the *paterfamilias* form flowered, ambient norms commonly evolved to temper abuses by the household head. Social norms, for example, directed the law-giver (*kurios*) in a Homeric household to promote a shared sense of affectionate belonging (*philia*).[89] In addition, a *paterfamilias* or feudal lord commonly was unable to sell the household premises and pocket the proceeds. Instead, he was under some obligation to give other family members access to it and, upon his death, to pass it on according to the same mechanical rules of succession by which he had obtained it.

Although the *paterfamilias* form can enable transaction-cost savings, the form conflicts with central liberal values. It is no surprise then that with the spread of liberalism and the rise in wealth in recent centuries, the *paterfamilias* form of governing co-occupant affairs—while showing some staying power in China, India, the Arab world, and elsewhere—generally has been in decline.[90]

Ambient social norms. As the history of the *paterfamilias* form illustrates, widely honored customs can greatly influence the composition of co-occupant groups and also their homeways. In many societies, adult children are under social pressure to live with or near their aging parents. Ambient norms concerning gender roles, particularly if they have been internalized, are likely to strongly influence the allocation of co-occupants' tasks.[91] By looking to customary gender roles for guidance about what gifts of labor to make, co-occupants can reduce their transaction costs of coordination.[92] Adherence to traditional gender roles was routine even at Woodstock-era communes nominally committed to gender equality.[93] If widely embraced, however, ambient norms that pressure women into disproportionately performing certain domestic tasks may impair women's shares of household surplus.[94]

Legal rules. Foundational legal rules, such as protection of an individual's right of exit, also shape the basic structure of the co-occupant interactions. Except when the welfare of outsiders or helpless insiders is at stake, however, lawmakers usually are reluctant to enact small-bore measures to govern the niceties of housemates' internal affairs.[95] Indeed, the U.S. Supreme Court has struck down, as a violation of the constitutional right to due process of law, a number of state attempts to regulate home behavior and the composition of co-occupant groups. For example, in *Lawrence v. Texas*, the Court invalidated a statute criminalizing the consensual act of sodomy within the privacy of a home.[96] And in *Moore v. City of East Cleveland*, it struck down an ordinance that had prohibited a grandmother from living with two grandsons who were not brothers.[97]

Judges similarly are unlikely to be willing to hear a common-law claim between current housemates. Suppose a graduate student were to file in small claims court an action for damages against a *current* housemate whom she accuses of having failed to carry out agreed-to household chores. A judge almost certainly would dismiss the complaint, and for good reason.[98] If a party enmeshed in a multi-stranded relationship were ordered by a court to render compensation for inappropriate behavior in a single strand, he might respond by making offsetting countermoves in other strands—

for example, by being surlier at the dinner table. A court that recognized the likely necessity of continuing judicial oversight of a complex web of intimate relations understandably would refuse to get involved in midgame affairs in the first place. (By analogy, most courts decline to reach the merits of a civil complaint filed by one spouse against the other prior to endgame, that is, before the two have either initiated a divorce proceeding or begun to live apart.)[99] This does not, however, leave the victim without recourse. The cohabitation relationship would likely provide her with numerous opportunities to employ self-help to discipline the offender, and she also could exit from the relationship (and, after exit, conceivably initiate an endgame legal action).

Even if judges were willing to apply small-bore private-law rules to resolve midgame disputes between housemates, most competent adults would ignore those rules and legal opportunities and instead rely on cheaper nonlegal means of controlling one another. In a well-known study, Vilhelm Aubert found that no lawsuits had been brought under the Norwegian Housemaid Law of 1948 during its first two years because, to curb employer abuse, housemaids continued to rely entirely on their ability to exit from the household.[100] Partly because resort to law is so expensive and partly because judges resist getting involved, any sort of midgame lawsuit between the co-occupants of a household is highly exceptional, absent the prospect of collecting from a liability insurance company or other third party.[101]

To further illuminate the variety of homeways, it is useful to highlight two of the many substantive challenges that co-occupants may face.

The extent of privatization of household spaces. Besides developing rules to govern behavior in their common spaces,

co-occupants have another major option: the privatization
of selected parts of their joint domain.[102] The public spaces
of a household are a form of commons, vulnerable to classic abuses such as overuse and inadequate maintenance.[103]
One of the standard antidotes to a potentially tragic commons is the conversion of particular spaces and objects from
common to individual ownership. By awarding a particular
housemate virtually complete control over a particular bedroom, for example, a group of co-occupants can internalize
to that person most of the costs and benefits of the use
and maintenance decisions involving that room.[104] Virginia
Woolf, in *A Room of One's Own*, famously contended that "a
woman must have money and a room of her own if she is
to write fiction."[105] (In the same work, however, Woolf also
admitted that Jane Austen had written her novels in her
house's common sitting room.)[106] The fine-grained rules of
a household may not only allocate rooms but also grant a
particular occupant special rights to use a certain chair, television set, or parking space (although perhaps only at special times).[107] Privatization measures of this sort can not
only reduce the transaction costs of coordination, but can
also create individual zones of autonomy and privacy within
the larger domain.

Privatization also has disadvantages, of course. The chief
one is the elimination of the other housemates' privileges to
use the privatized space. Moreover, privatizing efforts may
entail the sacrifice of other benefits of sharing, such as risk-
spreading, exploitation of scale economies in production
and consumption, and the social pleasures of communal
interactions.[108]

Co-occupants' decisions to privatize need not be explicit.
A particular housemate's repeated and exclusive use of a space
may give rise to an informal entitlement. However, privati-

zation of a valuable space, such as an entire bedroom, has major domestic repercussions; even intimate co-occupants thus may resort to oral contracts, perhaps prior to moving in, when assigning these spaces. In less intimate environments such as co-housing communities, owner-occupants routinely enter into written contracts that precisely identify their shared and unshared spaces.

Privatization practices vary widely in intentional communities. Leaders of many religion-based settlements such as those of the Benedictines and the Hutterites are ideologically committed to sharing and thus try to resist the inevitable pressures toward greater privatization of space. Even in Hutterite settlements, however, families have separate bedrooms and at least semi-private sitting rooms.[109] Many secular intentional communities are significantly privatized; as noted, in kibbutzim and co-housing developments, private dwelling units with full kitchens have become virtually universal.[110]

When co-occupants anticipate periods of grossly unbalanced labor contributions. Co-occupants contribute labor—an input typically provided in a more fine-grained fashion than owners' capital—to their household's economy. In many households, the fine granularity of labor readily enables housemates to keep their rough interpersonal accounts in balance. In some situations, however, one housemate may ask another to render for many years, and without prompt recompense, a valuable flow of domestic services and speak of eventually correcting the imbalance by bestowing major rewards in the distant future. Two classic scenarios are these: A co-occupying adult cares for an aging relative, expects to be appropriately awarded in the relative's will, but is not.[111] An unmarried homemaker provides a valuable flow of domestic services to a cohabiting breadwinner who does little in return except to vaguely promise major future rewards; after the couple separates, the breadwinner fails to deliver.[112]

How might vulnerable gift-givers protect themselves in such situations? One option is to insist, early in the housemate relationship, on a written contract that specifically spells out the gift-giver's entitlements to future compensation. If the co-occupants were intimates at the time, however, insistence on a written contract would send a strong and potentially damaging signal of distrust.[113] The vulnerable party's better option therefore may be to make clear that she will reduce her levels of gifts and perhaps even consider exiting from the household unless the recipient starts providing, now rather than later, a more adequate flow of return gifts.

These gripping scenarios frequently give rise to litigation in endgame. Lawmakers in most states have not been sympathetic to a plaintiff who is unable to ground his claim for compensation on a written contract. This stance may be attributable to the difficulties a court typically has in determining both the oral promises that were made and also the gifts that actually were exchanged while the relationship was ongoing. More fundamentally, a judge might decide to reject a claim of this sort on the ground that the claimant had helped cause the problem by failing to insist on either a written contract or more prompt recompense.

Rules for Co-Owners

The co-ownership of residential property typically commences when a transferor executes a deed that vests title in two or more concurrent owners.[114] Surveys indicate that intimate couples, typically spouses, are the exclusive co-owners of a large majority of the co-owned housing units in the United States.[115] Although a co-ownership relationship, as such, is unlikely to be as multi-stranded as a co-occupant relationship, co-owners inevitably have numerous issues to resolve among themselves. Serious conflicts among co-owners may arise over whether an occupying co-owner owes rent to a nonoccupying co-owner, under what circumstances a co-owner who has unilaterally borne the cost of an improvement is entitled to compel other co-owners to share that expense, possible limitations on the rights of a single co-owner to initiate a partition action, and other such issues. In the event of litigation among co-owners, a liberal legal system stands ready to apply a complex set of small-bore private-law rules to resolve these sorts of disputes.[116] Because tiffs among co-owners potentially involve significant stakes, individuals about to jointly acquire residential property might be expected to hire attorneys to learn about the default legal rules and to tailor a written agreement that modifies some of them.[117]

There appear to have been no surveys of how frequently co-owners, prior to endgame, seek the advice of attorneys or enter into written contracts with one another. Various scraps of evidence, however, strongly suggest that most intimate co-owners strive to manage their midgame affairs without the counsel of lawyers and also without fleshing out their mutual obligations in writing. One team of investigators found that 58 percent of surveyed home co-purchasers had received no advice from any broker, attorney, or other intermediary even about the basic issue of whether to take title as joint tenants with a right of survivorship or in some other form.[118] Evelyn Lewis, author of one of the most searching studies of co-ownership, asserts that written agreements among co-owners are unusual.[119]

Two leading legal publishers each offer no more than a few
legal forms to govern co-owner relations, in sharp contrast,
for example, to the hundreds of pages of forms they each
offer to govern landlord-tenant relations.[120]

Individuals who co-own residential real estate by the
twos, threes, and fours are extremely unlikely to engage in
midgame litigation. Like intimate co-occupants, most intimates who co-own correctly anticipate that they will be
able to use gift exchange and discrete oral contracts to resolve any issues that they may confront while their relationship remains healthy. A co-owner typically is entitled to
petition for a judicial accounting during midgame and
also in endgame.[121] To obtain evidence of the stage at which
a co-owner is more likely to seek this legal remedy, an examination was made of the most recently reported state
court decisions involving accounting actions initiated by a
tenant-in-common.[122] Between 1914 and April 20, 2006,
the date of the search, state courts published a total of fifty-
eight decisions in cases that involved a proceeding of this
sort. In fifty-three of the fifty-eight (91 percent), the court's
opinion revealed that the plaintiff had initiated the accounting action in endgame—for example, after the co-
owners had become embroiled in a partition, divorce, or
probate action.[123] One has to search back to 1956 to find a
decision in an accounting action that implies that the liti-
gants intended to continue to own together after the lawsuit at hand had been resolved.[124]

Although litigation among intimate co-owners is far more
common in endgame than during midgame, even in endgame it is highly exceptional (unless the breakup coincides
with a marital divorce, a highly legalized proceeding). Most
unmarried co-owners can anticipate that they will not have
to turn to lawyers when they terminate their relationship.

While there are many contemporary legal treatises exclusively devoted to landlord-tenant law, treatises on the traditional forms of concurrent ownership are few and mostly dated.[125] This is indirect evidence that co-owners rarely turn to attorneys in endgame. Most intimate co-ownership relationships, particularly during midgame, thus are structured not in the shadow of the small-bore private law of co-ownership, but beyond that shadow. Like the rules of intimate co-occupants, most of the rules of intimate co-owners arise not from the law books but from informal processes of gift exchange and oral contracting.

The formal legal rules of co-ownership of course are likely to have more bite when the members of a group of co-owners are either numerous or untrusting, or the value of the co-owned real estate is exceptionally high. In situations such as these, co-owners at the outset of their relationship may hire an attorney to draft a written document formalizing portions of their relationship. For example, multiple absentee owners of a large residential complex commonly are formally organized as a corporation, partnership, or trust.[126] Even in these contexts, however, co-owners are likely to anticipate that, by becoming social chums, they could reduce their legal expenses in both midgame and endgame.

Rules to Govern the Landlord-Tenant Relationship

Roughly three-quarters of residential co-occupant groups in the United States deal with an intimate owner, most commonly someone who is an owner-occupant.[127] In these intimate circumstances, the owners and occupants are unlikely to conceive of themselves as antagonists, but rather as

the voluntary co-members of an in-group. This shared per-
ception is conducive to trust and trustworthiness, and relations are likely to be sunny.[128] The remaining one-quarter
of landlord-tenant relationships, however, involve parties
at arm's length. Of all household relationships, these non-
intimate leaseholds pose the greatest risks of estrangement
and are the ones most likely to give rise to both written contracts and litigation in endgame. This section addresses, in
turn, these two different kinds of relationships.

In many owner-occupied households there also are non-
owning occupants—commonly children or other relatives
of one or more of the owners. An owner is not likely to
charge a co-occupying relative rent, and is even less likely to
insist on the execution of a written lease. Parents exasperated with the sloth of a stay-at-home adult child, however,
ultimately may decide to charge him rent and formally assign him domestic duties. A wake-up call of this sort
teaches the child that, among competent adults, a flow of
gifts cannot go entirely unreciprocated. Elderly live-in relatives, by contrast, are likely to understand the implicit duty
to return gifts and therefore, when able, are apt to contribute money and services to support ongoing household
operations.[129] Intimates, however, would be unlikely to
refer to a senior's contributions as "rent," an alienating term
that connotes social distance.[130]

An owner-occupied household also may include some occupants—such as boarders and live-in domestic workers—
who are not relatives of the owners. According to Census
data, roughly three-quarters of unrelated adults of this sort
do not pay rent to the owners with whom they live.[131] Instead, they may help maintain their welcome by providing
money for selected household operations or by rendering
valuable domestic services, such as childcare or yard work.

An unrelated lodger is somewhat more likely to contribute money to support household operations in situations where the household residents are black or Hispanic, or don't include a married couple.[132] An owner and a socially distant lodger conceivably may enter into a written contract—for example, when an au pair is brought in from abroad. Because contracts are inevitably incomplete, however, even under those circumstances a formal arrangement may not be worth the hassle.[133]

Arm's-length residential tenancies tend to be frostier. They can give rise to a host of substantive and procedural disputes that are complex enough and litigated frequently enough to have inspired the authorship of numerous legal treatises.[134] Especially in rural areas and small cities, however, landlords' and tenants' interests in maintaining good local reputations can give rise to a surprisingly high level of trust among non-intimates. And, in all settings, landlords are likely to prefer to rent to tenants who can provide positive references from former landlords, a practice that helps deter tenant opportunism.

In the less expensive segments of the rental housing market, a lease between a tenant and an absentee landlord traditionally was oral.[135] Many absentee landlords, however, have come to prefer a more formalized relationship that includes, for example, a security deposit. Purveyors of legal forms offer numerous versions of written residential leases, and their use is spreading.[136] In poor neighborhoods, the increasing formality of residential leases likely is partly attributable to the maturation of legal service programs and the advent of the Section 8 housing voucher program, which requires a participating landlord to employ a one-year written lease.[137] A landlord and tenant are especially likely to execute a written document when the stakes are high (for example, the term is long or the dwelling unit is expensive) and when the parties anticipate remaining socially distant (for example, the landlord is a corporation or other institution).

Once a tenant and absentee landlord reach endgame, they are unlikely to have any compunction against turning to attorneys and courts to help resolve their disputes. At every stage, however, an absentee landlord and a tenant are likely to recognize the advantages of resolving their differences in more informal fashion. During midgame, for example, if they can settle their disagreements by applying lease provisions and ambient norms, they save the expense of learning and applying small-bore landlord-tenant law.[138]

Rent controls and project-based housing subsidy programs spawn some of the most legalized of midgame relationships between landlords and tenants. Even if they have come to hate one another, a landlord and tenant governed by one of these programs have difficulty severing their relationship. Special legal provisions sharply limit a landlord's power to end a tenant's stay, and a disgruntled tenant may not want to leave if her departure would entail losing an attractively priced abode. Anticipating the risk of especially frosty midgame relations in these contexts, a landlord is likely to insist in advance on a detailed lease. When exasperated by an unresponsive landlord, a tenant is likely to prefer to hire an attorney (or, if eligible, to seek free help from a legal services office) rather than to exit and give up the subsidy.

For instance, in New York City, where rent controls have a long history and subsidized housing projects are especially prevalent, residential landlords and tenants are uncommonly likely to turn to lawyers and courts to resolve spats arising out of ongoing leases.[139] The State of New York has created a special court exclusively devoted to residential landlord-tenant litigation in the city. This court has 50 judges, over 1,000 nonjudicial employees, and handles over 350,000 cases per year, making it, by its own report, "one of the busiest courts in the world."[140]

Chapter 9
The Challenge of Unpacking the Household

Households—institutions that lie literally at our doorsteps—warrant greater attention. Many of the most valued human interactions occur within dwellings. Social scientists plainly can gain much from a better understanding of how people structure their home lives. I conclude with some thoughts about how scholars of domestic arrangements might orient their endeavors.

Even the most eminent commentators too often muddle their depictions of home life by failing to distinguish among three closely associated, but conceptually distinct, domestic institutions: the household, the family, and the marriage relationship. A household is an enterprise that one or more adults consensually establish in a particular dwelling unit in order to produce and consume shelter, meals, and other domestic services. Although a household commonly is family- or marriage-based, it need not be. To enable individuals to create households of their own design, a state must protect freedom of contract, freedom of exit, and private property rights in land, labor, and capital. When these liberal conditions prevail, competent adults tailor their own household institutions through voluntary contracts, commonly ones that are oral or implicit. A liberal society makes little effort to regulate an adult's entry into, or departure from, a co-occupancy, co-ownership, or landlord-tenant relationship (at least in the absence of rent control). Relatively unconstrained market forces, in short, largely determine the shape of household institutions.

Family and marital relationships differ significantly from household relationships. A family tie based on kinship is not consensual but rather arises involuntarily out of the fact of common ancestry. To be sure, an adult does volitionally add a family member when she marries or adopts a child. But the process of voluntarily adding to or subtracting from the membership of a family is far more legalized than the process of altering the members involved in a household relationship. This is one reason why, especially in liberal societies, involvements in household relationships tend to be more ephemeral than in family or marital relationships. An elderly adult who has married only once may have been a long-term co-occupant of dozens of different dwellings and a co-owner of more than a few.

Why are governments and civil societies more concerned about the structure of marital and family relationships than the structure of household relationships? The citizens of a polity have a vital interest in fostering the creation of small and enduring social units to which they can delegate continuing responsibility for the care of minor children (and also, perhaps, infirm adults). A family, most of whose members are glued together by immutable genetic ties, generally is a far superior unit for these purposes than is a household, whose members need not be linked in this fashion. Societies rightly recognize that a minor child benefits far more from having a continuing relationship with a caring adult than a continuing residency in a particular dwelling. Laws and social norms thus both insist that responsibility for caring for a minor child "runs" with a parent or other guardian, wherever the parent and child might be, and not, for example, with ownership of the dwelling where the child was born. To build on the relatively reliable genetic foundation of this system of parental obligation for children, societies develop informal norms that require individuals to show special loyalty to blood relatives, spouses, and children (natural or adopted).[1] States also signal the importance of family institutions by enacting laws that formalize entry into, or exit from, a marriage or child custodianship.[2] Governments thus solemnize marriages and adoptions, register these official events in public records, and resist individuals' attempts to marry or adopt informally.[3] By conferring special significance on family relationships, these norms and laws reinforce the relative permanence of family ties.

The state's laissez-faire approach to household formation, by contrast, lowers the stakes involved in a household relationship and thereby contributes to its relative informality and impermanence. A young unmarried parent need not obtain advance state approval before sending a child to live with a grandparent. The state does not insist that married people live together and, as noted previously, 7 percent of married Americans do live apart.[4] When co-occupants, co-owners, or a landlord and tenant reach endgame, they are not required to go to court to file for a "divorce." When a legalized marriage or child-custody relationship breaks down, by contrast, both lawyers and judges tend eventually to become involved. Given this asymmetry, it is understandable that commentators on domestic life, especially legal scholars, have mostly focused on marital and family relations— the domestic ties in which spouses and children typically have the greatest stakes. This scholarly engrossment with family law, however, has left open many untapped opportunities for the study of household institutions as such.

Unlike legal scholars, many social historians, sociologists, and anthropologists in the Geertzian tradition have recognized the significance of homeways. These investigators, however, have tended to shun overarching theories and instead to stress the influence of particular cultural traditions on household structure and governance. While much of this work is valuable, culturally oriented scholars should also be alert to variables that universally shape household institutions. The influences of changes in background demographic and technological conditions have long been recognized. In this book, I have stressed the role of some less-recognized variables, particularly background legal principles and transaction costs.

People form their domestic institutions under a backdrop of foundational legal rules. When a traditionally illiberal society first embraces the basic liberal principles of private property, freedom of exit, and freedom of contract, it enables the emergence of a dynamic market in household forms. Similarly, when a society succeeds in bringing the rule of law to a broad territory, it enables its residents to trade more easily with outsiders, a development that reduces the scope of internal household production.

My most persistent theme has been the importance to household members of economizing on the transaction costs of home governance. There are great advantages, in all societies at all times, of limiting the participants in a household relationship to a small number of intimates. This strategic approach to household formation promises to greatly reduce decision-making and monitoring costs. In addition, because intimates tend to be relatively trustworthy, the strategy of consorting with intimates enables co-participants to coordinate mainly by means of gift exchange, a transactional method typically both cheaper and more satisfying than formal contracting.

Transaction-cost considerations underlie the overwhelming tendency of household members to confer ownership of their dwelling on those among them who have contributed the at-risk capital needed to acquire it. Contributors of capital are the domestic participants typically most vulnerable to exploitation. Bestowing ownership on capital providers tends to be the cheapest way for all participants to deal with this risk and thus tends to benefit them all. While the most visible domestic relationship within a home is that among the household's co-occupants, the conferral of ownership on capital providers creates two important additional household relationships, namely, that between the co-owners and that between the group of co-owners and the group of occupants. The demographers, social historians, sociologists, and others who examine the structure of domestic life should not overlook these additional participants and their interworkings.

Even some of the best empirical studies of households are far too undertheorized. Consider, for example, Sterling Delano's painstaking and generally praiseworthy history of Brook Farm, the intentional community created in West Roxbury, Massachusetts, in 1841.[5] Charles Fourier, the early-nineteenth-century French social critic, urged the creation of large planned communities—Phalanxes—whose members would apply "industrial principles" to domestic life.[6] In 1844, George Ripley and the other leaders of Brook Farm embraced Fourierism and set about constructing a Phalanstery building containing nearly one hundred small dwelling rooms and a dining hall capable of seating over three hundred persons. A fire totally destroyed Brook Farm's Phalanstery prior to the building's completion and no effort ever was made to reconstruct it.[7] The entire Brook Farm endeavor had fizzled out by 1847. The other two dozen efforts in the 1840s and 1850s to create Fourierist communities in the United States fared no better. Delano nevertheless puzzlingly attributes Brook Farm's failure to the personal shortcomings of the community's leaders and financial backers.[8] Brook Farm's basic problem in fact was a built-in and utterly mundane flaw in the Fourierist conception—the unacceptably high transaction costs, particularly in the absence of a powerful unifying ideology, of coordinating domestic activity within a Phalanstery building.[9]

As the Brook Farm example illustrates, basic principles of transaction-cost economics can help illuminate the dynamics of home arrangements. The theory of the firm similarly throws light on the scope and governance of domestic enterprise. These assertions should not be taken to imply that economists themselves have nothing to learn from other disciplines. Those who study the structure of business and governmental organizations can benefit from Aristotle's basic insight that social arrangements that succeed within the household commonly inspire creators of more complex human institutions. According to one estimate, family-controlled enterprises, broadly defined, are responsible for a majority of U.S. business activity conducted *outside the household*.[10] Organizers of business firms, like organizers of households, see advantages in consorting with intimates and undoubtedly apply to the workplace some of the lessons that they have learned at home.[11]

The household is an especially fruitful setting for empirical work on systems of social control within small groups—a topic of interest to, among others, game theorists, sociologists, and political scientists. While there has been much empirical work on interspousal relations, there has been far less on homeways. How commonly do participants in a household relationship employ tit-for-tat sanctions, pay money to one another, or prepare written contracts? When do co-occupants informally privatize particular spaces within their abodes? How do the participants in large households make collective decisions and when to they resort to creating a governing hierarchy?

A policy analyst, when appraising a regulatory, welfare, or taxation measure, should be alert to its possible effects on the dynamics of household formation. It has long been recognized that exclusionary zoning practices can greatly limit housing choices, especially those of poor households. Programs such as rent control and the provision of project-based housing subsidies also unnecessarily restrict individuals' choices about where and with whom to live. To pursue their personal visions of the good life, individuals must have wide berth to tailor their household institutions as they see fit. One of the Soviet Union's great sins was its suppression of freedom of household formation. Civil libertarians, take note.

Finally, study of the household promises to illuminate central positive and normative questions about the role of small-bore private law. Legal centralists assume that private law influences events not only after things go wrong, but also before they do—that is, when people prepare for that possibility. One of my central factual premises, by contrast, has been that most people, wishing to minimize involvement with lawyers, structure their household arrangements informally and beyond the shadow of private law. Some legal commentators, on the other hand, have urged participants in household relationships to enter into more written contracts with one another.* In a few domestic situations,

---

*See, for example, Martha Ertman, "Commercializing Marriage," 55–59; Marjorie Shultz, "Contractual Ordering of Marriage," 328–34; and sources cited in chapter 8 herein, notes 69 and 72. But compare Lithwick and Goldstein, *Absurd Contracts*, a collection of tongue-in-cheek contracts purportedly drafted to govern aspects of intimate relationships.

this indeed is wise counsel.[12] When household participants are intimates enmeshed in a long-lived relationship, however, formalization usually is a mistake. Attorneys who contribute to the legalization of home relations typically not only waste the fees that their clients pay them, but also debase the quality of life around the hearth.

Appendix A: Data on Intentional Communities

The Fellowship for Intentional Community, a nonprofit organization, maintains on its website a "Community List" (http://directory.ic.org/iclist/) that includes over a thousand entries. The name of each community on the list functions as a hotlink to an individual posting prepared by members of that community. These postings respond to a standardized set of inquiries that the Fellowship poses. In March 2007, these individual community postings (and, in some instances, the listed communities' own websites) were examined to generate a database on 490 intentional communities in the United States.[1] The statistics presented in this appendix are drawn from this database.

A community appearing on the Fellowship's Community List was included in the database only if it met *all* of the following criteria:

- was located within the United States;
- was already in existence (as opposed to "forming");
- operated year-round;

- had provided information sufficient for it to be affirmatively classified in each of tables A.1 to A.4;
- did not function as an auxiliary to a social services program (for example, a program of aid to the homeless);
- reported having ten or more adult residents; and
- reported that members shared at least some meals.

The last three of these requirements derive from the somewhat restrictive definition of "intentional community" offered in chapter 4, that is, "a self-governed association of ten or more adult residents, most of them unrelated, who, as a matter of ideology not only share living spaces but also dine together for some or all of their meals."[2]

Table A.1 indicates how many of the total of 490 intentional communities in the database fall into various categories. A community's classification was based on its self-description. A community was characterized as "religious," as opposed to "secular," if it reported having a non-optional "shared spiritual path." (Two co-housing communities were classified as religious organizations.) Table A.1 includes a separate row for the intentional communities affiliated with two large umbrella religious organizations, the Order of Saint Benedict and the Hutterian Brethren. These organizations each have only a single entry on the Community List, but that far understates their importance. In their various postings the Benedictines reported about 150 separate residential communities in the United States and an average community population of forty adults. The Hutterites, for their part, reported 124 communities. These are estimated to house an average of ninety total residents, about thirty of them adult.[3] The tallies in table A.1 separately count each of these distinct Benedictine and Hutterite communities. Note that of the total of 490 communities identified in table A.1, over half are Benedictine or Hutterite. Of the intentional communities that have separate descriptions on the Community List, however, more than two-thirds are secular.

The Community List undoubtedly is incomplete and thus so is the database that was derived from it. The members of an intentional community that satisfied all of the criteria for inclusion might be unaware of the existence of the List or, particularly if

TABLE A.1
Number of U.S. Intentional Communities, 2007, and
Their Median Numbers of Adult Members

	Number of Communities	*Median Number of Adult Members*
Religious Communities		
Had Separate Entry on Fellowship's List	69	24
Benedictine or Hutterite	274	40*
Total Religious	343	—**
Secular Communities		
Secular Co-Housing	65	40
Other Secular	82	18
Total Secular	147	30
All Communities	490	—**

Sources: http://directory.ic.org/iclist/; www.osb.org; www.hutterianbrethren.org.

*This figure is the self-reported *average* adult population of Benedictine communities, which are more numerous than Hutterite communities. The actual median figure for both groups is likely somewhat lower than 40, but no sources were found on the distribution of the sizes of the adult populations in these two kinds of communities.

**Given the absence of data mentioned in the prior note, no median is estimated for either the "total religious" category or the "all communities" category.

they were free-spirited or opposed to contacts with outsiders, unwilling to provide answers to all of the pertinent questions. The List appears to be quite complete for relatively mainstream intentional communities. Of the eighty-one co-housing communities separately analyzed in appendix B, for example, sixty-five satisfied all of the stated criteria and also are included in the appendix A database. Of the remaining sixteen co-housing communities, only two were excluded from the appendix A database solely because the community's name was not found on the Fellowship's List.

Assuming that the community self-postings are reliable, the figure of 490 appearing in table A.1 represents the lower bound on the total number of intentional communities in the United States in 2007. There are reasons to suppose that this figure is

significantly too low. The communities of several relatively collectivist religious organizations, such as the Bruderhof and the
Franciscans, appear to be underreported in the Community List.
And, as noted, members of the most free-spirited or withdrawn
communes may have failed to identify themselves to the Fellowship. On account of these various omissions, the round number of
1,000 can be used as a very rough estimate of the number of intentional communities in the United States in 2007.

Table A.1 also indicates the median number of adult residents
reported by the intentional communities in each category (all of
which, again, include only settlements with at least ten adult residents). In each of the varieties of community, the median number of adults present is about two or three dozen.[4] Of the 216
communities with separate descriptions on the Community List,
13 report having more than 100 adult residents. The typical intentional community thus is far smaller than the traditional kibbutz, which housed an average of four hundred persons.[5] And it
doesn't even approach the scale B. F. Skinner envisioned in
Walden Two—a community whose common cafeteria was designed to serve nearly one thousand persons.[6]

The Fellowship asks each community to report its method of
decision-making. Table A.2 indicates the percentage distribution
of the responses of the communities in each category. The differences are striking. In a religiously oriented community, a leader or
small leadership group typically has decision-making power,
while in a secular one, the members are likely to seek to make decisions solely by consensus. Only 3 percent of the intentional
communities in the database report that they govern themselves
exclusively by majority rule.

Table A.3 indicates a similar gulf in practices on the financial
front. Most intentional religious communities report that their
members tend to share some or all financial resources. In contrast,
not a single secular co-housing community reports engaging in
any financial sharing, and only 5 percent of the other secular communities report the complete sharing to which both the Benedictines and Hutterites, for example, are committed.

The discussion in chapter 4, text following note 43, refers to
an intentional community as "strongly communal" if its members

TABLE A.2

Methods of Decision-Making Used in Intentional Communities
(stated in the percentage of communities using that method)

	Solely by Consensus	Mostly by Consensus	At Least Partly by a Leader or Leadership Core Group	Solely by Majority Rule	Other Decision-Making Method
Religious Communities					
Has Separate Entry on Fellowship's List (n = 69)	25%	1%	55%	3%	16%
Benedictine or Hutterite (n = 274)	0	0	100	0	0
All Religious (n = 343)	5	0	91	1	3
Secular Communities					
Secular Co-Housing (n = 65)	83	15	0	0	2
Other Secular (n = 82)	63	6	11	16	4
All Secular (n = 147)	72	10	6	9	3
All Communities (n = 490)	25	3	66	3	3

TABLE A.3

Financial Arrangements within Intentional Communities

(stated in the percentage of communities reporting using that arrangement)

	Members Have Independent Finances	Partial Sharing	Complete Sharing	Other Financial Arrangement
Religious Communities				
Has Separate Entry on Fellowship's List (n = 69)	30%	7%	42%	20%
Benedictine or Hutterite (n = 274)	0	0	100	0
All Religious (n = 343)	6	1	88	4
Secular Communities				
Secular Co-Housing (n = 65)	100	0	0	0
Other Secular (n = 82)	73	9	5	13
All Secular (n = 147)	85	5	3	7
All Communities (n = 490)	30	2	63	5

TABLE A.4
Number of Shared Meals per Week (stated in the percentage of communities reporting that number)

	One Meal or Less	2–5 Meals	6–7 Meals	More Than 7 Meals
Religious Communities				
Has Separate Entry on Fellowship's List (n = 69)	16%	10%	25%	49%
Benedictine or Hutterite (n = 274)	0	0	0	100
All Religious (n = 343)	3	2	5	90
Secular Communities				
Secular Co-Housing (n = 65)	22	74	2	3
Other Secular (n = 82)	37	24	29	10
All Secular (n = 147)	30	46	17	7
All Communities (n = 490)	11	15	8	65

share a majority of their meals. As table A.4 indicates, religiously oriented communities are far more likely to satisfy this standard. Ninety percent of the religious collectives in the database reported that members share more than seven meals per week, whereas only 7 percent of secular communities did. All 274 Benedictine and Hutterite communities in the database were assumed to meet this standard, but only 44 of 216 of the communities with separate entries stated that they met it.

The text of chapter 4, at note 45, includes an assertion that, in 2007, it is highly unlikely that as many as 30,000 U.S. adults were living in strongly communal fashion. The figures provided in tables A.1 and A.4 undergird this assertion. Given the incompleteness of the List, it is conceivable that as many as 600 strongly communal settlements existed in that year. The data presented in table A.1 and the text following it, however, make it highly unlikely that these communities housed an average of fifty or more adult residents, the number necessary to generate a total of 30,000.

Appendix B: Data on Co-housing Communities

The Cohousing Association of the United States maintains a web-site that lists co-housing communities (http://directory.cohousing .org/us_list/all_us.php). Because the co-housing movement is self-consciously cooperative, organized, and ambitious, this list likely is quite complete. The Association's list includes hotlinks to postings in which each listed community describes itself. These postings were examined in March and April 2007 to generate a database on eighty-one co-housing communities. A community appearing on the Association's list was included in this database only if it: (1) was located in the United States; (2) reported a specific number of completed units; and (3) indicated a specific completion date prior to 2006 (or, in the case of a retrofitting community, a record of permanent occupation prior to that year). Only a handful of communities were excluded for failing the third requirement, which was imposed to enable the tabulation of the entries in table B.1. Some of the co-housing communities in-cluded in the database have attributes that disqualify them from inclusion in the appendix A database—for example, having fewer

TABLE B.1
Sizes and Completion Dates of U.S. Co-housing Communities

Date of Completion	Number of Communities Completed	Median Number of Dwelling Units
1991–1995	14	26
1996–2000	38	24
2001–2005	29	30
Total	81	26

than ten adult residents or no shared meals. As noted, sixty-five of the eighty-one co-housing communities in the appendix B database also appear in the appendix A database.

Muir Commons, the first newly built co-housing development in the United States, was completed in 1991 in Davis, California.[7] As table B.1 indicates, the annual rate of completions of co-housing ventures increased during the late 1990s, and then tapered off a bit in 2001–2005. Seven of the eighty-one co-housing communities in the database include forty or more housing units, but only one, East Lake Commons, a sixty-seven-unit development in Decatur, Georgia, has more than sixty. The table reveals no apparent trend in size.

Seventy-two of the eighty-one co-housing communities indicated their method of decision-making. Of these seventy-two, 82 percent reported making decisions solely by consensus, and another 14 percent, mostly by consensus. None reported relying exclusively on majority rule. (Not surprisingly, these results closely track those displayed in table A.2.) Several communities reported striving to seek consensus during the initial stages of deliberation, with a possible resort to voting at a subsequent stage. The Milagro Co-Housing community in Tucson, for example, states that it requires at its final stage a vote of 90 percent in favor. In their postings, a few co-housing associations noted that they were organized as a homeowners' association whose rules called for the election of a board of directors.

Notes

Chapter 1: How Households Differ from Families

1. In this book a household thus is distinguished from the dwelling unit that its participants occupy, and also is regarded as an institution that potentially has participants in addition to those who regularly reside in that dwelling unit. The U.S. Census Bureau, by contrast, equates a household with a dwelling's occupants. "A 'household' comprises all persons who occupy a 'housing unit,' that is, a house, an apartment, or other group of rooms, or a single room that constitutes 'separate living quarters'" (Statistical Abstract: 1999, 6). The Bureau in turn defines a "housing unit" as a room or rooms lived in by persons who do not live and eat with any other occupants of the same structure (ibid., 718), and thus, by implication, who do often live and eat with one another. The Bureau defines a "family" as a set of persons related by birth, marriage, or adoption who live together in the same housing unit (ibid., 6). It uses the term "group quarters" to describe the residences of persons in dormitories, jails, nursing homes, military barracks and the like (ibid.). On group quarters, see chapter 4, note 2 and notes 37–40 and accompanying text.

2. Calculated from data presented in Statistical Abstract: 2006, 51. This is the percentage of multiperson households that includes a married couple but no children of that couple under age 17.

3. In 1998, 110.6 million married Americans were living with their spouses, but 7.3 million were not (Statistical Abstract: 1999, 60).

4. These households increased in number from 1.1 million in 1970 (Statistical Abstract: 1999, 60) to 6.2 million in 2004 (Statistical Abstract: 2006, 51).

5. The total of 12.3 million was calculated from data presented in Statistical Abstract: 1999, 61; see also chapter 4, text accompanying notes 10–15, 36–46.

6. In 2000, self-identified cohabiting opposite-sex partners headed 4.9 million households (U.S. Census Bureau, *Married-Couple and Unmarried-Partner Households: 2000*, 2). For additional statistics on this population, see sources cited in Garrison, "Consent Necessary?" 817 nn.1–2, 839–48. See also Casper and Bianchi, *Continuity and Change*, 39–66 (discussing cohabitation arrangements); and Sassler, "Cohabiting Unions" (reporting the results of interviews that probed motivations for cohabitation).

The Census Bureau tallied 0.6 million self-identified same-sex partner households in 2000 (U.S. Census Bureau, *Married-Couple and Unmarried-Partner Households: 2000*, 2). Reviews of studies of cohabitation and family formation by same-sex couples include Badgett, *Money, Myths, and Change*, 142–51; and Black, Sanders, and Taylor, "Economics of Lesbian and Gay Families."

On clustering by welfare recipients, see, for example, Edin and Lein, *Making Ends Meet*, 54–55. LeDuff, "Hard Work," describes households of recent immigrants. Communes are discussed in chapter 5 below, text accompanying notes 38–65.

7. See, for example, Becker, *Treatise on the Family*; Lundberg and Pollak, "American Family and Family Economics."

8. See "Developments in the Law: The Constitution and the Family."

9. See, for example, Bowles and Garoupa, "Household Dissolution" (an article in fact about the dissolution of marriage); and Hadfield, "Households at Work."

10. Robinson and Godbey, *Time for Life*, 100, 105 (reporting

data from time diaries). Other studies, however, report significantly fewer hours for both sexes. See, for example, the Bureau of Labor Statistics's American Time Use Surveys (begun in 2003), and the sources cited in Brinig, "Unmarried Partners," 1340, and Hersch, "Marriage, Household Production, and Earnings," 201, 205. Men's and women's hours of housework became less unequal between 1965 and 1995, primarily because women's hours fell (*Time for Life*, 105; Bianchi et al., "Is Anyone Doing the Housework?" 206–19).

11. Quah, *Economics and Home Production*, 80–89; Hawrylyshyn, "Value of Household Services." Most estimates fall in the lower part of the range mentioned in the text. See also chapter 7, note 14.

12. On this evolution, see Sahlins, *Stone Age Economics* 41–148 (a discussion of the "domestic mode of production" in pre-literate societies); and Medick, "The Proto-Industrial Family Economy."

13. One significant exception is Booth, *Households*. Other works close in spirit to the present one include Ben-Porath, "The F-Connection"; and Haddock and Polsby, "Family as a Rational Classification."

14. Margaret Reid's pioneering book, *Economics of Household Production*, was published in 1934.

15. See especially Becker, *Treatise on the Household*; and Pollak, "Transaction Cost Approach." Pollak distinguishes families from households at pp. 588–89, but makes limited use of the distinction.

16. Aristotle, *The Politics*, 9.

17. See chapter 5, text accompanying notes 6–11.

18. Coase, "Nature of the Firm," 388, 394 (discussions of the boundaries of a business enterprise).

19. On the pervasive influence of love and unconditional giving in many household relationships, see chapter 2, note 43 and accompanying text; chapter 5, footnote on pages 51–52; chapter 6, footnote on page 65 and accompanying text; chapter 8, note 39 and accompanying text; and sources cited therein.

20. For example, Glenn, "Split Household"; and Tienda and Angel, "Headship and Household Composition." See also chapter

3 below, note 22, and the sources on households in other nations cited in chapter 4, notes 6–9, 15, 19, 32–35. Economists increasingly are willing to acknowledge the influence of culture. See, for example, Greif, *Path to the Modern Economy*, 269–301, discussing the effects of varying cultural beliefs on the evolution of medieval trading institutions among the Maghribis and Genoese, and Roth et al., "Bargaining and Market Behavior," tentatively attributing differences in bargaining behavior to "cultural differences."

21. Compare Brinig, *Contract to Covenant*, 83–139, analyzing "the family as firm."

22. In the corporate setting, classic analyses include Berle and Means, *Modern Corporation*; and Jensen and Meckling, "Theory of the Firm."

Chapter 2: Household Formation and Dissolution in a Liberal Society

1. When occupants formally lease their dwelling unit from a landlord, ownership relations may become multilayered. A lease confers on these prime tenants robust entitlements to control the property for the pertinent block of time and commonly empowers them to transfer some or all of these entitlements to third parties. See Merrill and Smith, "The Property/Contract Interface," 820–33. A prime tenant who makes a partial transfer to a third party is simultaneously a tenant of the prime landlord and also a sublandlord of the third party. A complex arrangement of this sort makes use of a simple property-rights regime that Merrill and Smith call an "exclusion strategy" (ibid., 790–99). In broad terms, the prime landlord delegates, for the term of the lease, his broad power to exclude to the prime tenant, who in turn transfers that power to the third party. In each instance, the transferor usually explicitly or implicitly retains, by contract, some circumscribed entry rights.

2. See chapter 1, note 1.

3. Dagan and Heller, "Liberal Commons," especially at pp. 552–53, 609–10.

4. More, *Utopia*; see chapter 5, note 7 and accompanying text.

5. On *komunalkas*, see Gerasimova, "Soviet Communal Apart-

ment"; Heller, "Tragedy of the Anticommons," 650–58; and Wines, "Tight Space."

6. A liberal state, prompted either by paternalism or concern about externalities, nonetheless typically regulates some acts by household participants. See chapter 5, text accompanying notes 17–24.

7. See Booth, *Households*.

8. These three foundational entitlements can be distinguished from "small-bore" legal policies of lesser scope or impact. See chapter 5, note 26 and accompanying text.

9. See Ellickson, "Controlling Chronic Misconduct," 1192 nn.132–33, 1193 n.134.

10. Ibid., 1189–91, a description of trends in aid to the homeless.

11. According to a National Multi Housing Council survey, the top fifty owners of apartments in the United States had an ownership interest in 2.96 million units in 2005, about 8 percent of the nationwide stock of rental housing (*Statistical Abstract: 2006*, 626; Obrinsky, "NMHC 50," 10). See also chapter 4 below, text accompanying notes 47–55.

12. See Merrill, "Right to Exclude"; and U.S. Const., Amendment 3, which limits the quartering of troops in "houses." See also Barros, "Home as a Legal Concept"; Shiffrin, "Compelled Association" (discussing associations' rights to exclude); and Strahilevitz, "Information Asymmetries" (identifying types of exclusion strategies). A private landowner's key entitlements in addition to the right to exclude are the right to control land uses and the power to transfer.

13. On exceptions to the rights of a landowner to exclude, see generally Ellickson, "Property in Land," 1382–85. In most situations, the owners of a house are entitled to exclude a sick and lonely outsider who seeks admission. If they do invite him in, however, they then may owe him a duty of care (*Depue v. Flateau*, 111 N.W.1 [Minn. 1907]).

14. Fischel, *Homevoter Hypothesis*, 80. In 2004, about 80 percent of U.S. household heads over age 45 were homeowners. The percentage peaked at 82.6 percent for those between the ages of 65 and 74 (Joint Center for Housing Studies, *Housing 2005*, 36).

Chapter 6 explains why ownership of a housing unit typically is conferred on providers of at-risk capital.

15. A slave who lacks the formal entitlement to trade labor for either monetary or in-kind compensation nevertheless may have some bargaining leverage in practice (Barzel, *Property Rights*, 109–10, 113).

16. See Aristotle, *Politics*, 7–37.

17. On the coverture system and its breakdown, see, for example, Geddes and Lueck, "Gains from Self-Ownership"; and Siegel, "Home as Work."

18. Maine, *Ancient Law*, 168–70.

19. Most commentators agree with Maine that there has been a broad historical trend toward freeing individuals from immutable blood and marriage obligations. See, for example, Friedman, *Private Lives*, 1–11; Glendon, *New Family*, 11–13, 41–46. Carole Shammas's *History of Household Government* documents the enhancement, especially between 1840 and 1880, of the rights of wives, children, and domestic workers. But compare Regan, *Pursuit of Intimacy*, expressing concern that individual autonomy in the making of household arrangements can be taken too far.

20. Dagan and Heller, "Liberal Commons," 567–77.

21. See Hirschman, *Exit, Voice, and Loyalty*, 21–25, and below, notes 44–50 and accompanying text.

22. The canonical precedent is *Lumley v. Wagner*, 42 Eng. Rep. 687 (Ch. 1852), a decision that denied the remedy of specific performance of a contract to perform as an opera singer. See also *Restatement (Second) of Contracts* § 367 (1979); *Government Guarantee Fund v. Hyatt Corp.*, 95 F.3d 291, 303 (3d Cir. 1996) (stating that specific enforcement of a personal services contract "would . . . run contrary to the Thirteenth Amendment's prohibition against involuntary servitude"); and Schwartz, "Case for Specific Performance," 297, presenting the case *against* specific performance of a personal services contract.

23. Ayres and Gertner, "Filling Gaps."

24. Calabresi and Melamed, "Property Rules."

25. Default rules authorize a co-owner in either joint tenancy with right of survivorship or tenancy in common to transfer all or a portion of an undivided interest to another (Stoebuck and

Whitman, *Law of Property*, 201). But compare Dagan and Heller, "Liberal Commons," 601, 620, an implicit endorsement of statutory conferral on the remaining co-owners, at least as a default, of a right of first refusal. A minority of states authorize spouses to co-own as tenants by the entirety. In most of these jurisdictions, a spouse, prior to divorce, cannot unilaterally exit from a tenancy by the entirety by either sale or partition (Stoebuck and Whitman, *Law of Property*, 196–97, 215).

26. On the American law of partition, see Stoebuck and Whitman, *Law of Property*, 214–24. The key English enactment was the Statute of Anne, 1704, 4 Anne c. 16, § 27. On rights of partition in other nations, see Dagan and Heller, "Liberal Commons," 618–20.

It is instructive to compare the exit systems available to investors in various forms of business enterprise. Section 31 of the Uniform Partnership Act (1914) entitles any partner to unilaterally dissolve a partnership. In a corporation, where shareholders commonly are more numerous and less personally involved, a single shareholder who wants to exit typically is unable to force dissolution, but instead must either sell off shares or else persuade the Board and a majority of the shareholders to approve a resolution dissolving the corporation. For general discussions of an investor's means of exit from a business enterprise, see Hansmann, Kraakman, and Squire, "Rise of the Firm," 1341–43, 1391, 1394–96; and Saul Levmore, "Love It or Leave It."

27. Miceli and Sirmans, "Partition of Real Estate," offers an economic analysis of the merits of these two alternatives.

28. The right of a co-owner to partition or transfer his interest generally can be waived for a period of 5–15 years in a civil-law jurisdiction and for a "reasonable period" in a common-law jurisdiction, where the legal issue typically is seen as whether the waiver is a permissible restraint on alienation (Stoebuck and Whitman, *Law of Property*, 214; Dagan and Heller, "Liberal Commons," 616 and n.258). See ibid., 596–601, for a stimulating discussion of other possible limitations on owner exit, such as mandatory cooling-off periods. For behavioral-economic justifications of cooling-off periods in some contexts, see Camerer et al., "Regulation for Conservatives," 1238–47.

29. See generally Stoebuck and Whitman, *Law of Property*, 389–96, a survey of the law governing the termination of interests in leases.

30. A participant in a landlord-tenant relationship may be able to exit from it by transferring his interest to a third party. Although default liberal principles generally support free alienability, a lease may contain provisions that limit transfer rights (ibid., 379–88). Partly because an abusive occupant can inflict massive damage on a dwelling unit, lease provisions are more likely to constrain transfer of the tenant's interest than sale of the landlord's interest.

31. In contrast to the United States, many nations that are predominantly liberal in most other respects impose rent controls, good-faith eviction requirements, and other potent restrictions on a landlord's power to terminate a residential tenancy. See, for example, Arnott, "Rent Control," 206–09.

32. On the implications of the permanence of parental ties, see Alstott, *No Exit*.

33. For a fuller discussion of limitations on freedom of contract, see chapter 5, text accompanying notes 17–24.

34. See, for example, Dagan and Heller, "Liberal Commons," 596, endorsing freedom of contract among co-owners as long as exit is available and third-party interests are not jeopardized; and Karst, "Freedom of Intimate Association," 686–89, arguing that, as a constitutional matter, a government must have a substantial justification for interfering with co-occupants' arrangements.

35. See, for example, *California Family Code* § 308.5 ("Only marriage between a man and a woman is valid or recognized in California"); *New York Domestic Relations Law* § 5 (barring marriages between close relatives); ibid., § 6 (forbidding bigamy); ibid., § 15a (prohibiting a marriage in which either party is under age 14); ibid., §§ 13, 13b (requiring persons intending to marry to obtain a license and, in the absence of court order, then to wait at least 24 hours); ibid., § 170 (specifying permissible grounds for divorce, many of which require the parties to wait at least one year). But see, for example, *Goodridge v. Department of Public Health*, 798 N.E.2d 941 (Mass. 2003), which held that the denial of a marriage license to a same-sex couple violated equal protection principles embodied in the state constitution.

36. See chapter 5, note 39 and accompanying text; and chapter 8, notes 96–97 and accompanying text.

37. Wax, "Bargaining in the Shadow," 529–31; Scott and Scott, "Marriage as Relational Contract," 1270–80.

38. It is regarded as axiomatic that, absent other, conflicting interests, parties to any sort of contract can be expected to seek to maximize their joint gains (Schwartz and Scott, "Contract Theory," 552–54).

39. See Coase, *The Firm, The Market*, 6.

40. These bounds on capacities are lucidly assessed in Jolls, Sunstein, and Thaler, "Behavioral Approach."

41. See Lundberg and Pollak, "Bargaining and Distribution."

42. In 1974, in "A Theory of Social Interactions," Gary Becker advanced a "Rotten Kid Theorem" that predicts, under the conditions of the model, that the altruistic household head would be able to induce kids never to engage in rotten behavior. Becker later conceded that his model was implausible even when applied to a kinship-based household. See Becker and Murphy, "The Family and the State," 4–5.

43. See Regan, *Alone Together*, 15–22, 33–86. See also Brinig, *Contract to Covenant*, 83–84, highlighting the role of love in family relations. But contrast, for example, Hasday, "Intimacy and Economic Exchange," 492–93; and Hill, "Personal Sphere." See generally Silbaugh, "Marriage Contracts," 111–22, an assessment of objections to viewing interactions among intimates as exchange relationships.

44. See, for example, Browning et al., "Incomes and Outcomes"; Lundberg and Pollak, "Bargaining and Distribution"; Lundberg, Pollak, and Wales, "Do Husbands and Wives Pool?" Amy Wax's "Bargaining in the Shadow" provides a comprehensive review of the legal and social scientific literatures on bargaining within marriage. See also Grossbard-Shechtman, *Economics of Marriage*, 25–83 (developing a model of husband-wife exchange); Lennon and Rosenfield, "Relative Fairness" (articulating an analogous approach within sociology). A bargaining model, which typically assumes that individuals possess both legal and mental capacity, may apply poorly when a child or incompetent adult is involved in a relationship.

45. Lundberg and Pollak, "Bargaining and Distribution," 146–49. To reduce the risk that a particular member will exit, the other participants may strive to induce that person to invest in household-specific human capital. See chapter 6, notes 32–38 and accompanying text.

46. See Lundberg and Pollak, "Separate Spheres Bargaining"; and Bergstrom, "Family Way," 1926. For a concise review of various models of interspousal bargaining, see Pollak, "Bargaining Around the Hearth."

47. Pollak, "Transaction Cost Approach," 603–04 (drawing this example from Greven, *Four Generations*).

48. See, for example, Blumstein and Schwartz, *American Couples*, 53–56, 309–10; Wax, "Bargaining in the Shadow," 547–51.

49. Nock, "Married Spouses," 49–50.

50. Brinig and Allen, "These Boots," 136–37, 146–47, 154–60.

Chapter 3: The Predominant Strategy: Consorting with Intimates

1. Scott, "Self-Enforcing Indefinite Agreements," 1663–72, provides an overview of the literature; see also Benkler, "Sharing Nicely."

2. See chapter 8, text accompanying notes 30–60.

3. A person cooperates with other group members when his actions serve to maximize the aggregate welfare of all members. See chapter 8, text accompanying notes 4–9. See also Axelrod, *Evolution of Cooperation*, 3–11 (implicitly adopting this definition).

4. Many studies indicate that cooperative behavior becomes more likely as social distance narrows. See, for example, Buchan, Croson, and Dawes, "Swift Neighbors"; Macy and Skvoretz, "Evolution of Trust."

5. See chapter 8, text accompanying notes 35–51.

6. Trust is conventionally defined as the expectation that another person will act cooperatively, instead of opportunistically, when both options are available (Blair and Stout, "Trust, Trustworthiness," 1745–46). On how a past history of successful gift exchange can deepen trust, see Leslie, "Enforcing Family Promises,"

575–78; Posner, "Gifts and Gratuitous Promises," 577–82, 591, 603–06; and Rose, "Giving, Trading, Thieving," 316–17. See also Caplow, "Kin Networks," 391–92 (discussing how the giving of Christmas gifts solidifies family relationships). General discussions include James Coleman, *Foundations of Social Theory*, 91–116; Fukuyama, *Trust*; and Glaeser et al., "Measuring Trust."

7. McAdams, "Origin, Development," 386–90.

8. Other attributes, such as a shared sense of group identity, also may be helpful. See Dawes, van de Kragt, and Orbell, "Cooperation for the Benefit of Us"; Hogg and Abrams, *Social Identifications*; and Tajfel, *Human Groups*. General overviews of the conditions that foster cooperative behavior include Blair and Stout, "Trust, Trustworthiness," 1759–80; Sally, "Conversation and Cooperation"; and Taylor, *Community, Anarchy and Liberty*, 104–29.

9. Axelrod, *Evolution of Cooperation*, 124–29; Dixit, *Lawlessness and Economics*, 12–13, 59–65; see also Keser and van Winden, "Conditional Cooperation," 31–33.

10. Pollak, "Transaction Cost Approach," 585–88. See also Haddock and Polsby, "Family as a Rational Classification," 19–20, 24, 33–35. A family can be envisaged as a naturally existing interpersonal network that typically is especially capable of generating and enforcing norms. Compare Aviram, "Private Legal Systems," stressing the importance of networks but not of families as such.

11. Netting, "Smallholders, Householders, Freeholders"; Pollak, "Transaction Cost Approach," 591–93. But compare Bernheim and Stark, "Altruism Within the Family," offering caveats about the helpfulness of altruism in these contexts.

12. For discussion of how these first-party systems mesh with other social controls, see chapter 8, text accompanying notes 30–33.

13. Pollak also notes some disadvantages of kinship-based households. The multiplex nature of kinship ties poses risks that conflict will be imported into the household from an external strand of the kinship relationship, for example, a sibling rivalry. Members who are added to a household mainly for kinship reasons are not likely to possess the labor skills the household most

needs, and also may make the household expand to beyond its most efficient size ("Transaction Cost Approach," 587–88).

14. For real-world examples, see *In re Marriage of Owen*, 797 P.2d 226, 228 (Mont. 1990) (mentioning an eviction notice that parents who owned a house had delivered to a son who was occupying it); *Esteves v. Esteves*, 775 A.2d 163 (N.J. Super. Ct. App. Div. 2001) (involving a suit by parents against their son over the division of proceeds of the sale of a house that the three had owned as tenants in common).

15. See Gautschi, "History Effects in Social Dilemma Situations."

16. On the advantages of smaller group size, see Dixit, *Lawlessness and Economics*, 65–76; Axelrod and Dion, "Further Evolution of Cooperation," 1389; Molander, "Prevalence of Free Riding," 766–68. It should be noted that in some experimental multiperson games, however, the level of cooperation has proved not to depend much on the number of players (Sally, "Conversation and Cooperation," 77).

17. See chapter 4, table 4.2 on page 37.

18. Blau, *Exchange and Power*, 69–70; compare Becker, *Treatise on the Family*, 108–34 (discussing "assortative mating").

19. There is some experimental evidence that individuals tend to be more trustworthy when they deal with persons of the same race and nationality (Glaeser et al., "Measuring Trust," 814).

20. Becker, *Treatise on the Family*, 30–53, 57–64.

21. On various conceptions of equality within marriage, see Frantz and Dagan, "Properties of Marriage," 91–94; and Wax, "Bargaining in the Shadow," 533–37. Hochschild, "Economy of Gratitude," documents the increasingly egalitarian nature of interspousal relations.

22. Compare McAdams, "Cultural Contingency," 223–25, a discussion of how cultural influences can make certain equilibria particularly salient. In the United States, about two-thirds of parents' wills bestow equal bequests on surviving children (Bernheim and Severinov, "Bequests as Signals," 733–34).

23. See Boehm, *Hierarchy in the Forest*.

24. McKean, "Success on the Commons," 262–72, discusses

the extent of egalitarianism among co-owners of common property resources.

25. For discussions of the advantages of equality by a sociologist of law and a scholar of law and economics, see, respectively, Black, *Behavior of Law*, 11–36; and Hansmann, *Ownership of Enterprise*, 39–44.

26. ScottHanson and ScottHanson, *Cohousing Handbook*, 168; Ellickson, "Property in Land," 1351. In many intentional communities, however, the reality is a status hierarchy headed by a charismatic leader (Zablocki, *Alienation and Charisma*, 290–320).

27. On the rebuttable presumption of equal ownership of shares, see, for example, *Lemay v. Hardin*, 48 S.W.3d 59 (Mo. Ct. App. 2001); *Bryan v. Looker*, 640 N.E.2d 590 (Ohio Ct. App. 1994); and Stoebuck and Whitman, *Law of Property*, 179–80, 221–22. Traditionally, co-owners in joint tenancy could only own in equal shares (the so-called unity of interest; ibid., 183). Ihara, Warner, and Hertz, *Living Together*, offers a form contract that provides for equal ownership of a home (pp. 3/9, 6/17–/18).

28. See, for example, *California Civil Code* § 1946 (West 1998) (30 days); *Florida Statutes Annotated* § 83.57(3) (West 2004) (15 days).

Chapter 4: A Historical Overview of Household Forms

1. Household size in the United States varies slightly by state. In 1996, the average number of persons per household (including single-person households) ranged from a low of 2.49 in Colorado to a high of 3.08 in neighboring Utah (*Statistical Abstract: 1999*, 63).

2. According to the U.S. Census Bureau, in 1999 there were 1.3 million households with seven or more occupants, and together they included a population of 10,219,000 (calculated from data presented in *American Housing Survey: 1999*, 62). It is important to note, however, that during the 1990s the Census Bureau placed all households occupied by ten or more unrelated per-

sons in the "group quarters" category (ibid., appendix A, A-9). In 2000, when the Bureau was no longer classifying these households in this fashion, it tallied a total of 7.8 million people living in a group quarters of some sort. About half of these individuals were in institutions formally authorized to provide supervised care or custody, and about another quarter were residents of college dormitories (U.S. Census Bureau, *2000 Census of Population and Housing: Summary File 1; Technical Documentation* 6-84 to -88, Mar. 2005). For more on the group quarters population, see chapter 1, note 1, and below, text accompanying notes 37–40.

3. For discussion of how the demographics of U.S. households changed between 1940 and 1980, see Sweet and Bumpass, *American Families and Households.*

4. The figures for 1790 and 1900 are from U.S. Census Bureau, *Historical Statistics* (1975) 41; the figure for 2004 is from *Statistical Abstract: 2006*, 51.

5. Ibid.

6. United Nations, "Human Settlements Data Bank." See also Angel, *Housing Policy Matters*, 351 (reporting World Bank data for 1990). In *Treatise on the Family*, 46–47, Becker reports data from over a dozen surveys of household size in different societies in different eras. See also chapter 7 below, text accompanying notes 12–37.

7. Laslett, "Mean Household Size in England," 138.

8. Ibid.

9. See Nakane, "Japan over Three Centuries," 531 (providing an estimate of 4.9 for preindustrial Japan); and Läfgren, "Family and Household," 466 (reporting that in 1890 Sweden's average household size was 4.56).

10. Unless otherwise indicated, the data in this paragraph are drawn from *Statistical Abstract: 1999*, 60–62. The Census Bureau defines a householder as an occupant whose name either appears on the deed or lease to the dwelling unit, or, when there is an oral lease, is responsible for paying rent (U.S. Census Bureau, *American Housing Survey: 1999*, appendix A, A-8).

11. The fraction of households consisting of a single person rose from 5 percent in 1900 (U.S. Census Bureau, *Historical Statistics*, 42) to 26 percent in 2004 (*Statistical Abstract: 2006*, 52).

The likelihood of living alone increases with age. In 1998, of those aged 20 to 24, 6 percent lived singly, compared to 31 percent of those over age 64 (*Statistical Abstract: 1999*, 57). See also chapter 7 below, text accompanying notes 18–25.

12. Calculated from data reported in *Statistical Abstract: 1999*, 62.

13. In 1940, 2.8 percent of nonfamily households contained four or more members (Sweet and Bumpass, *American Families and Households,* 349). As table 4.2 indicates, by 1998 the figure had fallen to 1.1 percent.

14. Ellickson and Thorland, "Ancient Land Law," 354–57.

15. Notable sources on the history of households in Europe include Herlihy, *Medieval Households*; and Laslett and Wall, eds., *Household and Family in Past Time.* On Asia and the Arab world, see sources cited below in notes 32–35 and footnote on page 39. On Ghana, see Goody, "Evolution of the Family."

16. See Stack, *All Our Kin*; and Scannapieco and Jackson, "Kinship Care."

17. The portion of Rhode Island households that included one or more nonrelatives declined from 24 percent to 2 percent between 1875 and 1960 (Pryor, "Rhode Island Family Structure," 586).

18. According to the U.S. Census Bureau, *American Housing Survey: 1999*, 62–4, 1 percent of households include lodgers and 4 percent include unrelated adults who are neither co-owners nor co-renters.

19. Ellickson and Thorland, "Ancient Land Law," 354–57. Partly because the evidence is thin, historians' portrayals vary. Compare, for example, Diakonoff, "Structure of Near Eastern Society," 42–43 (arguing that ancient man knew only communal property), with Postgate, *Early Mesopotamia* 91–93 (stating that, at least in cities, ancient Mesopotamian households rarely included more than one conjugal unit).

20. Booth, *Households*, 15–34.

21. Ellickson and Thorland, "Ancient Land Law," 355.

22. Booth, *Households*, 34–93. On the Classical Greek household, see also Cox, *Household Interests*; Hunter, *Policing Athens*, 9–95; and Pomeroy, *Classical and Hellenistic Greece.* The occupants

of an *oikos* commonly included slaves, a feature that Aristotle emphasized. See chapter 2, text accompanying note 16.

23. Xenophon, *Oeconomicus*, 58–61, 137–59. On the possibility that Xenophon was being more normative than descriptive, see Cox, *Household Interests*, 132–35.

24. Herlihy, *Medieval Households*, 58–59.

25. Laslett, "Introduction." Subsequently, in "Family and Household," Laslett restricted the scope of this thesis to northwestern Europe. For a review of the debate among historians over trends in household size, see Kertzer, "Household History."

26. Hanawalt, *Ties that Bound*, 5, 103–4. Herlihy, *Medieval Households*, 62–72, reports the results of an early ninth-century survey of rural lands in St. Germain, where median household size was six.

27. Hajnal, "Pre-Industrial Household Formation," 65.

28. *Statistical Abstract: 1999*, 60.

29. Angel and Tienda, "Cultural Pattern or Economic Need?" See also Pasternak, Ember, and Ember, "Extended Family Households."

30. Ruggles, "American Family Structure."

31. U.S. Census Bureau, *American Housing Survey: 1999*, 62, 64. See also chapter 7, text accompanying notes 21–25.

32. On Japanese traditions, see Morgan and Hirosima, "Extended Family Residence in Japan." Sources on Chinese household and familial traditions include Hsieh and Chuang, eds., *Chinese Family*; and Ruskola, "Corporations and Kinship," 1622–56. Household forms in Egypt in 1976 are described in Fargues, "Arab World," 356–57, which reports that a majority of urban households, but not rural households, were nuclear.

33. Mason, Lee, and Russo, "Population Aging in Asia," 70.

34. Ibid.

35. The figures on average household sizes in India and among Indian-Americans are drawn, respectively, from United Nations, "Human Settlements Data Bank," and U.S. Census Bureau, *We the People: Asians in the United States*, 8.

36. *Statistical Abstract: 1999*, 61.

37. U.S. Census Bureau, *Total Population in Households for 2000*. For the Bureau's technical definitions of "housing units" and

"group quarters," see U.S. Census Bureau, *American Housing Survey: 1999*, appendix A, A-9 to A-10; chapter 1 above, note 1.

38. U.S. Census Bureau, *Total Population in Households for 2000*.

39. See chapter 7, text accompanying notes 1–25.

40. Calculated from figures provided in U.S. Census Bureau, *Total Population in Households for 2000*.

41. Benjamin Zablocki, the leading scholar of American intentional communities, has offered a definition of a "commune" that is more restrictive in some ways, but also more expansive in that it only requires the presence of five or more adults (*Alienation and Charisma*, 7). The Census Bureau has not attempted a tally of intentional communities. On the Bureau's historic difficulties in dealing with communities of this sort, see ibid., 72 n.†.

42. Sutton, *Modern American Communes*, profiles many of the most prominent.

43. For details, see appendix A, table A.1 and the text accompanying notes 4–5.

44. See appendix A, tables A.3 and A.4.

45. See appendix A, table A.4, and page 144.

46. *Statistical Abstract: 2006*, 52. The allusion in the text is to Putnam's *Bowling Alone*, which famously asserts that social capital in the United States is in decline.

47. This is the U.S. Census Bureau's definition (*American Housing Survey: 1999*, appendix A, A-8, A-25). It is also the usual legal definition. See, for example, Stoebuck and Whitman, *Law of Property*, 779–84, for a discussion of the key role of deeds and other documents in proving marketability of title. On why the owners identified in this manner are almost always contributors of at-risk capital, see chapter 6 below, text accompanying notes 9–39.

48. The National Association of Realtors (NAR) periodically mails out a questionnaire that asks a large sample of homebuyers nationwide to identify themselves. In 2005, 30 percent of respondents reported that they were single buyers; 61 percent, married couples; 7 percent, "unmarried couples"; and the remaining 2 percent, "other" (Rosenbloom, "A Fear of Commitment," citing National Association of Realtors, "2005 Profile of Home Buyers &

Sellers"). Although these findings support the assertions in the text, the response rate to NAR's 2005 survey was 5.4 percent, which makes it less credible than the sources cited in the text that follows.

49. Shammas, Salmon, and Dahlin, *Inheritance in America*, 172. Historical trends in how spouses have taken title to their houses is a fertile topic for additional research. The Shammas et al. and Hines studies mentioned in the text hint that married couples nationwide tended to shift, between 1890 and 1960, away from vesting title in name of the husband alone and toward some form of concurrent ownership. If able to corroborate this fundamental shift, future researchers might seek to determine to what extent it can be attributed to wives' improved access to capital, the strengthening of wives' "threat points" (see chapter 2, text accompanying notes 44–50), emerging norms of spousal equality, or other causes.

50. The percentages in the text were computed from data presented in Hines, "Real Property Joint Tenancies," 617. (A caveat: Hines included in the single-grantee category not only individuals but also corporations, trusts, and estates.) See also Cooper, "Continuing Problems," 966 n.3, which indicates that, in a sample of 300 deeds to one or more individuals in 1989 in Wayne County, Michigan, 158 involved grants to single individuals, 114 to married couples in tenancy by the entirety, 24 to joint tenants, and 4 (all by operation of law) to tenants in common. And see the sources cited in Lewis, "Struggling with Quicksand," 398 n.204.

51. U.S. Census Bureau, *POMS*. In this book, all percentage figures derived from the POMS data exclude from the denominator the number of units that the Census Bureau included in the "not reported" category. It is likely that forms of ownership that respondents declined to report were of greater than average complexity. As a result, the exclusion of the unreported category from the denominator probably biases upward the percentages reported here for the simpler forms of ownership and biases downward those reported for the more complex forms.

52. Ibid., table 97. Four percent of the single-family rental properties were owned by three or more participants either in co-tenancy or in partnership (ibid.). For-profit corporations owned another 4 percent (ibid., table 96).

53. Ibid., table 97.

54. Ibid. These figures include owners of beneficial interests held either in cotenancy or partnership, and also fiduciary ownership by the trustees of an estate. The figures exclude, however, ownership by a corporation with only one or two shareholders.

55. Ibid., table 96. The share of ownership by large business entities probably has risen a bit since the mid-1990s (the time of the POMS survey). See chapter 2 above, note 11.

56. Williamson, *Markets and Hierarchies*, 82–131, is a classic source on vertical integration in the business context.

57. *Statistical Abstract: 2006*, 630; Hughes, "Changing Homeownership Trajectory." Eighty-four percent of single-family dwellings, detached or attached, are owner-occupied (*Statistical Abstract: 1998*, 729). See also chapter 2 above, note 14, reporting that about 80 percent of U.S. household heads eventually own a home.

58. U.S. Census Bureau, *American Housing Survey: 1999*, 76.

59. Bowman, "The Good Life," 60.

60. United Nations Economic Commission for Europe, *Bulletin of Housing Statistics*, table A. According to this source, the rate of homeownership in Western Europe ranges from a low of 39.9 percent in Sweden to a high of 80 percent in Ireland.

61. Ellickson and Thorland, "Ancient Land Law," 337 n.80, 338.

62. On the privatization, after 1989, of apartments in Russia and elsewhere in the former Soviet Bloc, see sources cited in Heller, "Tragedy of the Anticommons," 647–50.

63. RAND, *First Annual Report*, 53.

64. This fact can be deduced from the following Census data: Owners inhabit one out of five dwelling units in residential structures that contain two to four units (*Statistical Abstract: 1999*, 729). Assuming that owners occupy a maximum of one unit per structure, if these structures were to contain 2.5 units on average, a conservative assumption, it would follow that 50 percent (one-fifth of 2.5) of the structures would be owner-occupied. If these structures were to contain 3.0 units on average, 60 percent (one-fifth of 3.0) of them would be owner-occupied.

65. The residency of an owner in a multifamily structure with

two to four units is associated with better building maintenance, particularly of common areas. See Porell, "One Man's Ceiling." Fair housing laws commonly grant a landlord who lives in a structure of this type more leeway in tenant selection. See, for example, the so-called "Mrs. Murphy" proviso of the federal Fair Housing Act, 42 U.S.C. § 3603(b)(2) (2000), which exempts most owner-occupied structures of four or fewer units from coverage of the Act (except its advertising provisions). On the dynamics of land-lord-tenant relationships of all types, see chapter 8, text accompanying notes 127–140.

Chapter 5: Are the Household Forms that Endure Necessarily Best?

1. For guarded discussions of the inferences that can be drawn from the survivorship of an ownership form, see Hansmann, *Ownership of Enterprise*, 22–23; and Bebchuk and Roe, "Theory of Path Dependence." See generally Roe, "Chaos and Evolution," 647–52, an analysis of the potential perversities of path dependence.

2. But compare Bryan Ellickson et al., "Clubs and the Market," presenting a stylized model of a group formation process that leads to Pareto-optimal results.

3. On utopian thought, see generally Kumar, *Utopia and Anti-Utopia*; and Manuel and Manuel, *Utopian Thought*.

4. See Boehm, *Hierarchy in the Forest*; and Buss, *Evolutionary Psychology*.

5. Maryanski and Turner, *The Social Cage*, 81–89.

6. Plato, *The Republic*, bk. 3, *416d–e; bk. 4, *419–420c.

7. More, *Utopia*, 47, 55–60. More's volume depicts even larger rural households containing a minimum of forty adults (ibid., 44). More himself probably regarded Utopia's scheme as unworkable. See Ackroyd, *Life of Thomas More*, 169–75.

8. See Engels, *Origin of the Family*, 138–39, for the prediction that, after the demise of capitalism, "social industry" would supplant the role of the private household. Fourier and Owen are discussed in Reva Siegel, "Home as Work," 1094–96. See also ibid., 1198–1205, for a description of the post–Civil War cooperative housekeeping movement, whose adherents aspired to create meta-households.

9. The United States has also been a hotbed of actual experiments with intentional communities. See text accompanying notes 38–65 below.

10. Bellamy, *Looking Backward*, 161–62, 168–69, 262–63.

11. Skinner, *Walden Two*, 18–20, 40–44, 48.

12. See Heller, "Tragedy of the Anticommons," 650–58; and Wines, "Tight Space."

13. See Ellickson, "Property in Land," 1393–94, and sources cited therein.

14. See "Developments in the Law: Legal Responses to Domestic Violence," 1501–02.

15. Those who exit from a co-ownership or a landlord-tenant relationship similarly incur transaction costs when they sever ties and establish a successor arrangement.

16. See generally Flache, "Individual Risk Preferences," offering a model of the effects of risk aversion on partner selection.

17. Within the liberal paradigm, externalities and paternalism are the basic rationales for constraining individual choices (Ayres and Gertner, "Filling Gaps," 88). Margaret Brinig, *Contract to Covenant*, 8–10, also notes the possibility of justifiable interventions based on incomplete information and monopoly.

18. See, for example, *People v. Wheeler*, 106 Cal. Rptr. 260 (Ct. App. 1973), authorizing a county to abate a commune's unsanitary conditions that posed risks of internal and external epidemics.

19. Most states deny the owner of a condominium unit the powers both to partition common areas held in tenancy in common, and to sell an undivided interest in those common areas to a transferee other than a transferee of the condominium unit itself. See, for example, *Uniform Condominium Act* § 2–107(e).

20. See, for example, *State v. Green*, 99 P.3d 820 (Utah 2004), which upheld the conviction of a man who had been living with several women he regarded as wives, even though at no time was he ever formally married to more than one of them. See generally Altman and Ginat, *Polygamous Families*. For the assertion that the structuring of intimate relationships commonly has broad social effects, see Hafen, "Constitutional Status of Marriage." And compare "Developments in the Law: The Constitution and the Family," 1198–1242, an overview of state interests in how families are organized.

21. See Brandon, "State Intervention in Imperfect Families."

22. Becker and Murphy, "The Family and the State," 1.

23. See generally Camerer et al., "Regulation for Conservatives," advocating selectively paternalistic regulation to counter human errors in decision-making. See also Jolls, Sunstein, and Thaler, "Behavioral Approach."

24. See chapter 2 above, text accompanying notes 23–24, and chapter 2, note 28 (discussing limitations on a co-owner's waiver of partition rights).

25. Katharine Silbaugh, "Housework and the Law," provides a particularly useful overview of pertinent small-bore policies. See also Barros, "Home as a Legal Concept."

26. See chapter 2, text accompanying note 8. The right to exit from a household relationship is a foundational rule. The examples that immediately follow in the text illustrate small-bore rules.

27. Because most people strive to avoid co-owning real estate with more than one or two others, these heirs might be expected either to buy one another out promptly or to agree to sell all their interests to a third party. Nonetheless, many observers contend that intestate succession contributed to the excessive fractionalization of ownership of many African-American farms in the rural South and to the eventual transfer of too many of these farms to non-black owners. See, for example, Dagan and Heller, "Liberal Commons, 551, 603–09; Mitchell, "Undermining Black Landownership," 517–23.

28. Arnott, "Rent Control," 209; Glaeser and Luttmer, "Misallocation of Housing."

29. On the influence of various government spending programs, see Ellen and O'Flaherty, "Evidence from New York." These authors assert that housing and income maintenance policies—particularly Section 8 housing allowances, public housing, and food stamps—tend to reduce the average number of adult occupants in New York City households, and for no good reason. On the influence of taxation policy, see, for example, Alstott, "Tax Policy and Feminism"; Kornhauser, "Love, Money, and the IRS"; and Smith, "Household Taxation." On creditors' rights policies, see, for example, Morantz, "Homestead Exemption."

30. See, for example, Fox, *If Americans Really Understood,*

177–200; Bourassa and Grigsby, "Income Tax Concessions"; and Hansmann, "Condominium and Cooperative Housing," 39–56. Some policy analysts, however, defend the Code's favoritism toward homeowners on the ground that homeownership has positive social consequences. See, for example, Weicher, "Comment." These social benefits are reviewed in Dietz and Haurin, "Micro-Level Consequences of Homeownership."

31. See Kennedy, "Limited Equity Coop"; and Simon, "Social-Republican Property," both of which advocate the creation of limited-equity housing cooperatives from which owner exit is constrained.

32. Hirschman, *Exit, Voice, and Loyalty*, 33–36, 76–77.

33. See Dagan and Heller, "Liberal Commons," 574–77, 596–602; and Ellickson, "Property in Land," 1375–80. Compare McKean, "Success on the Commons," 261–62, identifying social advantages of limiting the transfer of interests in common-property resources. See generally Walzer, "Communitarian Critique of Liberalism." Walzer asserts that these sorts of communitarian critiques, although eternally relevant, are substantively weak.

34. See chapter 2 above, text accompanying note 24.

35. Frantz and Dagan, "Properties of Marriage," 87; Karst, "Freedom of Intimate Association," 637–38.

36. See Green, "Rights of Exit," 171; and chapter 2 above, notes 44–50 and accompanying text.

37. On the adverse social consequences of rent controls, see chapter 8, notes 139–40 and accompanying text.

38. For a historical overview of intentional communities, particularly in the United States, see Zablocki, *Alienation and Charisma*, 19–80; see also Ellickson, "Property in Land," 1357–62.

39. See ScottHanson and ScottHanson, *Cohousing Handbook*, 237–50; Sandelin, "Dealing with Government Agencies" (offering legal advice to the founders of an intentional community of any form). As the text explains, a new intentional community's problems tend to lie not on the supply side but on the demand side.

40. In the United States, the portion of the population involved in intentional communities has "never much exceeded one per one thousand" (Zablocki, *Alienation and Charisma*, 31). See also the data provided in appendixes A and B of this book. More-

over, large nonfamily households are unusual and becoming more so. See chapter 4 above, table 4.2 on page 37 and note 13.

41. Zablocki and Kanter, "Differentiation of Life-Styles," 290–91.

42. On the contribution of rituals to bonding, see Sosis and Ruffle, "Religious Ritual and Cooperation." On the longer life expectancy of a religious community, see Zablocki, *Alienation and Charisma*, 37, 151. John Noyes's faith-based Oneida community, for example, endured from 1848 to 1881, when its members implemented a sweeping privatization program. See Carden, *Oneida*, xiii–xiv, 113–16. A prominent counterexample was the spiritually oriented Rajneeshpuram, whose rapid rise and rapid fall in central Oregon in 1981 to 1986 is depicted in Gordon, *Golden Guru*, 99–207.

43. Acts 2:44. See generally Hengel, *The Early Church* 8–9, 31–34, describing the communal sharing of goods in early Christian societies.

44. On July 20, 2007, the sect's own website, www.hutterian brethren.org, asserted the existence of 124 Hutterite communities in the United States. On the same date, another Hutterian Brethren posting, this one linked to the Fellowship for Intentional Community's Communities Directory, reported a lower total (89 U.S. communities), evidently because it excluded 35 Lehrerleut colonies in Montana.

45. Kraybill and Bowman, *On the Backroad to Heaven*, 23. The total population of Hutterite communities has been mounting, almost entirely because of the sect's extraordinarily high birthrates. See Ellickson, "Property in Land," 1360. For a more extended discussion of Hutterite settlements, see ibid., 1346–7, 1350–61; Kraybill and Bowman, 20–59; and Hostetler and Huntington, *Hutterites in North America*. On a severe schism within the sect, arising out of its system of governance by elders, see *Decker v. Tschetter Hutterian Brethren, Inc.*, 594 N.W. 2d 357 (S.D. 1999).

46. On July 20, 2007, a search based on the entry of "U.S.A." on the Order of Saint Benedict's Geographic Search Form yielded a list of 173 institutions. Approximately 23 of these were identified as schools, universities, libraries, or other nonresidential institutions.

47. Fellowship for Intentional Community, "Communities Directory: Order of Saint Benedict." The Benedictines have had their ups and downs over the centuries. See Catholic University of America, *New Catholic Encyclopedia*, 2:272–74, a recounting of the Order's major reversals in England and France after the Middle Ages.

48. Brook Farm, a going concern in West Roxbury from 1841 to 1847, wholly expired in 1849 with a liquidation of assets (Delano, *Brook Farm*, 40, 310–12). Robert Owen's collectivist experiment at New Harmony lasted only from 1825 to 1827, when he deeded the property to his sons (Wilson, "Utopia, Limited"; Bushee, "Communistic Societies," 628). The Icarian Colony at Nauvoo, established in 1849, suffered from major defections in 1858 and was liquidated in 1860 (ibid., 648).

49. Zablocki, *Alienation and Charisma*, 148–51.

50. Sosis and Ruffle, "Religious Ritual and Cooperation," 714.

51. This figure is derived from numbers provided in Pavin, "Kibbutz Movement," 57.

52. On the consequences of these financial adversities, see Brinkley, "Debts Make Israelis Rethink."

53. Muravchik, "Socialism's Last Stand," 47, 50–53.

54. See ibid., 51. See also Leggett, "Pay-as-You-Go Kibbutzim."

55. Russell, Hannemann, and Getz, "Processes of Deinstitutionalization," 12. See also Pavin, "Perceptions of Kibbutz Reforms," 59, reporting that most kibbutz members responding to a survey thought that these privatization reforms had enhanced "members' freedom and autonomy" but also diminished "trust between members."

56. According to the definition offered in chapter 4, text accompanying note 44, a community is "strongly communal" only if its members dine together for a majority of their meals.

57. E-mail message to the author from Professor Amnon Lehavi of the Radzyner School of Law, Herzliya, Israel.

58. See Kershner, "Kibbutz Sheds Socialism."

59. See generally ScottHanson and ScottHanson, *Cohousing Handbook*; Fenster, "Community by Covenant."

60. This "common house" is the principal physical feature

that distinguishes a co-housing development from a subdivision governed by a conventional homeowners' association. A conventional association may have a community room of some sort, but it is likely to be more modestly sized and equipped.

61. See appendix A, table A.4.

62. Ibid.

63. Cohousing Association of the U.S., Frequently Asked Questions (FAQ), http://www.cohousing.org/resources/faq.html #kitchen (visited Oct. 10, 2005).

64. The pioneering venture was Muir Commons, in Davis, California (McCamant and Durrett, *Cohousing*, 208).

65. During 1991–2005, about 21 million new private housing units were produced in the United States (*Statistical Abstract: 2006*, 619).

66. See, for example, Calthorpe, *Next American Metropolis*, 65, 84; and Duany, Plater-Zyberk, and Speck, *Suburban Nation*, 205–07. Brown, Burton, and Sweaney, "Neighbors, Households," provides data on the actual use of front porches.

67. Kennedy, "Limited Equity Coop"; Simon, "Social-Republican Property," 1361–66.

68. Brozan, "Co-op Complexes." See also Kennedy, "Limited Equity Coop," 97: "The private housing market does not generate a limited equity [cooperative housing] sector."

Chapter 6: Choosing Which of a Household's Participants Should Serve as Its Owners

1. See chapter 4, note 47 and accompanying text. Except in rare instances, such as those involving adverse possession (see note 2 below), the grantees listed in the deed are the only persons legally empowered to transfer the premises and offer it as security for a mortgage loan. Contractors therefore much prefer to deal with the record owners of a building than with, say, the building's occupants. If unpaid, a contractor is unlikely to be able to impose a mechanic's lien on the improved premises unless the record owners, or their agents, had explicitly or implicitly authorized the work. See, for example, *Young Kim v. JF Enterprises*, 50 Cal. Rptr. 2d 141 (App. 1996) (freeing record owner from mechanics' liens filed by contractors who had performed work for tenant without

owner's knowledge); *Grube v. Nick's No. 2*, 278 S.W.2d 252 (Tex. Civ. App.-El Paso 1955) (similar). See generally Nelson and Whitman, *Real Estate Finance Law*, 982–83.

2. The donee of a dwelling conveyed as a gift (or the devisee of an inherited dwelling) initially invests nothing but typically does make later monetary infusions. When an owner has been exceptionally passive, the doctrine of adverse possession may confer ownership on a house's long-time occupants, including ones who previously had not contributed capital. Once adverse possessors obtain ownership, however, they are likely to become capital providers.

3. For a lucid explanation of residual control decisions and residual financial flows, see Milgrom and Roberts, *Economics, Organization and Management*, 289–90. The theory derives from Grossman and Hart, "Costs and Benefits of Ownership."

4. See chapter 2 above, notes 12–13, 25, and accompanying text. On why rights to control access to a parcel of real property should belong to the owners of that property and not to the owners of personal property located there, see Merrill and Smith, "What Happened to Property," 390–91.

5. But compare Schwarz, Troyer, and Walker, "Animal House," which implicitly envisions that household occupants solely control pet ownership and spending decisions, and neglects the potential influence of the household's owners.

6. See chapter 8, text accompanying notes 30–51.

7. The market value of a dwelling unit can be negative if it is burdened by excessive mortgage debt, confiscatory property taxes, or unfavorable long-term leases.

8. See, for example, Hansmann, *Ownership of Enterprise*, 11–12; and Milgrom and Roberts, *Economics, Organization, and Management*, 289–93.

9. Hansmann uses "patron" to describe any party who transacts with a business firm (*Ownership of Enterprise*, 12). Robert Pollak has privately indicated a preference for "stakeholder."

10. See chapter 1, text accompanying note 1.

11. See, for example, Cott, *Bonds of Womanhood*, 35–39, a description of the shift of yarn-spinning from the home to the factory.

12. See Garnett, "On Castles and Commerce."

13. See U.S. Census Bureau, *Home-Based Workers*, 3, estimating that, in 1997, 4.8 percent of the workforce was working exclusively at home.

14. Hansmann, *Ownership of Enterprise*, 21–22.

15. On the agency costs of 100 percent debt financing in the corporate context, see ibid., 53–56; and Romano, *Foundations of Corporate Law*, 120 (noting that "we do not see 100 percent debt-financed firms").

16. See Nelson and Whitman, *Real Estate Finance Law*, 850. The most junior mortgage lender has an increasing incentive to monitor the behavior of the mortgage borrower (or indeed to take over ownership of the dwelling) as the total loan-to-value ratio climbs toward 100 percent.

17. See notes 27–31 below and accompanying text.

18. See chapter 4, text accompanying notes 47–55. Compare the figures on the sizes of co-occupant clusters presented in chapter 4, table 4.1 on page 36.

19. In 1999–2000, 31 percent of the residents of rental units, and 9 percent of residents of owner-occupied housing units, had moved to their present dwelling during the course of the past year (*Statistical Abstract: 2001*, 28). In 1999, 7 percent of existing single-family dwellings, detached and attached, were sold to a new set of owners (computed from data reported in ibid., 599, 604). The turnover rates of both investors and occupants, of course, are probably not entirely independent of their rights of ownership.

20. An occupant's ownership rights conceivably could be limited to the time period of personal occupation. The obvious drawback of that system, however, is that an occupant about to depart likely would adopt an overly shortsighted perspective on a management decision with long-term consequences, such as whether a roof should be replaced.

21. Hansmann regards risk-bearing considerations as a relevant, but often exaggerated, influence on ownership forms. See *Ownership of Enterprise*, 44–45, 57.

22. Ibid., passim.

23. Dad's role as an occupant as well as a partial owner, however, could give rise to complications. If Dad were occupying the

Sitcom House at a favorable (implicit) rent, he personally would reap more benefits from the repair than Aunt Audrey would. In addition, Dad's particular interest in, for example, the bedroom he occupies conceivably might influence his evaluation of roof repair alternatives.

24. Household-specific human capital, however, is not portable. On the complications this potentially poses, see below, text accompanying notes 32–38.

25. Williamson, "Corporate Governance," 1210.

26. See, for example, *Sack v. Tomlin*, 871 P.2d 298, 303 (Nev. 1994); *Spector v. Giunta*, 405 N.E.2d 327, 330 (Ohio App. 1978). The traditional default rules of partnership law are similar. When a partnership is dissolved, partners' contributions of capital are paid back before profits are distributed (*Uniform Partnership Act* §§18(a), 40(b)). This rule helps protect passive equity investors who have awarded a larger partnership share in advance to a coventurer who has volunteered to assume prospective management duties. Compare *Meinhard v. Salmon*, 164 N.E. 545 (N.Y. 1928), a famous decision involving a partnership organized along these lines.

27. ScottHanson and ScottHanson, *Cohousing Handbook*, 167–78, 269. After completion, the participants in a co-housing venture sometimes reorganize themselves into a condominium association (ibid., 170–71). This organizational form entails control by investors, not occupants.

28. Benjamin Zablocki argues that the trust form best assures that the ideals of a community's founders will be respected (*Alienation and Charisma*, 64–65).

29. Brook Farm's assets initially were vested in an unconventional association, directed by four trustees, which borrowed capital from a separately organized joint-stock company (Delano, *Brook Farm*, 68–72, 97). Delano mentions that these trustees were elected annually, but does not identify who the electors were (ibid., 68). See also Zablocki, *Alienation and Charisma*, 64, reporting that trusts owned the sites of 12 percent of the rural communes in his Woodstock-era sample.

30. See Delano, *Brook Farm*, 96–97, 184–85, 413 n.11. In 1845, the legal conversion of the community into a "phalanx,"

structured as a more conventional corporation, prompted new infusions of equity (ibid., 207).

31. See ibid., 55, 69–70, 97, 102, 249–50, 263, 361 n.27.

32. On the analogous problem of inducing a worker to invest in skills specific to a particular employer, see, for example, Donaldson and Eaton, "Firm-Specific Human Capital."

33. Compare Grossbard, "Repack the Household," 346–47, stressing the need of household participants to motivate contributions by home workers.

34. Similarly, some observers have contended that a corporate employee with firm-specific human capital may merit a share of corporate ownership. See, for example, Blair, *Ownership and Control*, 238–74.

35. On the high incidence of husband-wife co-ownership of real estate, see chapter 4 above, text accompanying notes 49–50.

36. Recognition of this risk underlies the default legal presumption that co-owned real estate is to be partitioned in shares proportionate to capital contributed. See above, text accompanying note 26.

37. See chapter 3 above, text accompanying notes 16–28. See also Ihara, Warner, and Hertz, *Living Together*, 6/17, 6/22–/25, offering form contracts that allocate ownership shares in proportion to equity contributions, and ibid., 10/16, advising that, at time of breakup, an occupant who had contributed labor to make physical improvements to a house should be awarded compensation for that labor, but not an ownership share. But compare ibid., 6/21–/22, discussing the possibility of a contract conferring a partial share of house ownership on someone who will contribute labor to improve the house.

38. On the role of gift exchange among household participants, see chapter 8 below.

39. See Ellickson and Thorland, "Ancient Land Law," 337–38, 355–57, drawing on sources on household organization in ancient Mesopotamia, Egypt, and Israel.

Chapter 7: The Mixed Blessings of Joining with Others

1. Perhaps the most prominent overviews are Reid, *Economics of Household Production*; and Gronau, "Home Production." See

also Bryant and Zick, *Economic Organization of the Household*; Kooreman and Wunderink, *Economics of Household Behavior*; and the sources cited in the notes that follow.

2. Lazear and Michael, "Family Size," 97; Nelson, "Household Economies of Scale," 1308. But compare Deaton and Paxson, "Economies of Scale," reporting that per capita food consumption declines in large households.

3. Hersch and Stratton, "Male Marriage Wage Premium." See also Loh, "Marriage Premium."

4. See, for example, Mertes, *English Noble Household*, 73–74, a discussion of English lords' systems of providing social insurance to elderly servants within their households; and Dercon and Krishnan, "Risk Sharing within Households in Rural Ethiopia." Compare Pollak, "Transaction Cost Approach," 589–91, an assessment of the merits and demerits of the family as an insurance provider.

5. For analysis of why there are many large business enterprises but few large households, see Becker, *Treatise on the Family*, 51–53. Becker stresses the tendency of firms to be more capital-intensive than households. Another possibility is that individuals' preferences for autonomy and privacy are much more pronounced within home settings than at workplaces.

6. See chapter 3, text accompanying notes 16–17; and chapter 8, text accompanying notes 52–54, 74–90.

7. See Strahilevitz, "Theory of Privacy."

8. See chapter 4, table 4.2 on page 37.

9. Coase, "Nature of the Firm."

10. Reid, *Economics of Household Production*, 219–23.

11. On patterns of domestic outsourcing, see De Ruijter, van de Lippe, and Raub, "Trust Problems," and sources cited therein.

12. See chapter 4, text accompanying notes 3–9.

13. De Tocqueville's characters also owned books and kitchenware, items presumably acquired through trade with outsiders (de Tocqueville, *Democracy in America*, 731–33).

14. According to one estimate, between 1930 and 1985, the output of households in the United States fell from 73 percent to 28 percent of the output of the external market sector (Devereux and Locay, "Specialization, Household Production," 402). But see Hawrylyshyn, "Value of Household Services," 124–28, for the assertion that home production's share of the national economy de-

creased only modestly during the first three-quarters of the twentieth century.

15. See Reid, *Economics of Household Production*, 47–72, 362–68.

16. See Locay, "Economic Development," attributing the shift away from household production mainly to economies of scale in firm production. For analysis of how occupants of a multiperson household decide how to divide their labor between internal and external production, see Apps and Rees, "Collective Labor Supply."

17. But compare Ben-Porath, "The F-Connection," 19–23, an argument that the effects of wealth on household size are mixed.

18. Posner, *Overcoming Law*, 536. On the increasing role, since the mid-nineteenth century, of the home as a center of privacy, see Hareven, "Home and Family"; and Solove, "Conceptualizing Privacy," 1137–40.

19. See Michael, Fuchs, and Scott, "Propensity to Live Alone," finding that rising incomes prompt more young single adults and elderly widows to live singly; Johnson and DaVanzo, "Decision to Leave Home," finding a strong trend toward earlier homeleaving in Malaysia; and Whittington and Peters, "Residential Independence," asserting that children with higher earning potential are more likely to exit from their parental home.

20. Rosenfeld and Kim, "Independence of Young Adults," 548–49. These authors do not indicate how they treated, in their calculations, cohabitation with just one parent.

21. Steven Ruggles's "American Family Structure" is a leading historical study of trends in the living arrangements of the elderly.

22. Kramarow, "Elderly Who Live Alone."

23. Costa, *Evolution of Retirement*, 108, 130. The percentages reported in the text refer only to the living accommodations of noninstitutionalized men.

24. Ibid., 114–30. "Increases in income have always been associated with an increased demand for the privacy and autonomy provided by separate living arrangements. Rising incomes therefore contributed enormously to the increase of well-being among the elderly" (ibid., 128). But compare Posner, *Aging and Old Age*, 285–86, noting the desire of many seniors not to be a burden on their children.

25. In 2000, of Americans of both sexes age 65 or over who were not living with a spouse, 66 percent were living alone (*Statistical Abstract: 2001*, 42).

26. See generally U.S. Census Bureau, "America's Families and Living Arrangements," 5–6; and Santi, "Size of American Households."

27. The estimate of life expectancy in 1900 is based on reports from the limited number of states then collecting death statistics (*Statistical Abstract: 1999*, 874). The source of the figure for 2000 is *Statistical Abstract: 2006*, 76. For an individual who survives childhood, the increase in life expectancy has been less pronounced. Steven Ruggles asserts, without citing authority, that the life expectancy of those at age 30 was age 60 in 1850, and age 76 in 1980. See "American Family Structure," 111. Compare Lundberg and Pollak, "American Family and Family Economics," 6, an article published in 2007 that states that the remaining life expectancy of both American men and women at age 65 had risen by about four years since 1950. *Statistical Abstract: 1999*, 874, reports that the birthrate dropped by slightly over half between 1910 and 1997.

28. See chapter 5, text accompanying notes 25–30.

29. On these changes, see chapter 2, notes 17–19 and accompanying text, and chapter 8, text accompanying notes 87–90.

30. Pollak, "Transaction Cost Approach," 593–94, discusses the comparative advantages of family production in a low-trust neighborhood environment.

31. Sobel, "Can We Trust Social Capital?" provides a review of some of the pertinent literature. See also Putnam, *Making Democracy Work*, which asserts the importance, for economic development, of the presence of civic associations based on horizontal social ties.

32. See Hunter, *Policing Athens*, 78, noting the responsibility of slaves to do the "shopping." See also chapter 4 above, text accompanying notes 19–23 (discussing the downsizing of the ancient Greek household).

33. Mertes, *English Noble Household*, 185–88 and app. C. See also Woolgar, *Great Household*, 9–16, 39.

34. On the communal dining practices within these noble

households, see Woolgar, 145–49, 157–58, 161–62. Even these huge households were far from autarkic. Their financial records reveal incessant purchases of wines, foodstuffs, and other supplies and services from outside vendors (Mertes, 102–20).

35. Ibid., 185–87. Mertes also attributes the burgeoning size of these households to a noble's increased ability to administer a feudal domain from a central place and to statutory changes that made appointment to a household position a noble's preferred method of compensating a loyal follower (ibid).

36. See ibid., app. C. Compare Greif, "Family Structure, Institutions, and Growth," a discussion of the rise of corporate organizations and the decline of the role of extended kinship groups in late medieval Europe.

37. See chapter 5, text accompanying notes 50–56. Modern Italy offers yet another illustration of how the characteristics of an external trading environment can affect household structure. Households traditionally have been smaller and less self-sufficient in northern Italy than in southern Italy, where norms historically have been less liberal and non-kin less trusted. See Sgritta, "Italian Family," 377–78; and Ginsborg, *Italy and Its Discontents*, 69, 82, 97–98, 106–07. But compare ibid., 124–26, describing the growth of civic institutions in southern Italy after 1980.

38. See Fleishman, "Buddy System"; and Rendon, "Splitting the Cost," a description of instances in which buyers had pooled capital in order to expand their range of housing choices.

39. On the headaches that can arise when two or more married couples share ownership of a vacation home, see Kaufman, "House Divided."

40. U.S. Census Bureau, *American Housing Survey: 1999*, 76. In over 80 percent of the instances in which some owners were not occupants, the absentee owners did not bear any ongoing ownership costs (ibid.). But compare Caplin et al., *Housing Partnerships*, urging the sale of home equity to nonoccupying limited partners.

41. See chapter 4, text accompanying note 55.

42. See chapter 4, text accompanying notes 49–50.

43. To avoid having their house caught up in a probate proceeding, a couple can own it in a form, such as joint tenancy or tenancy by the entirety, that immediately devolves full ownership

on the survivor. See Stoebuck and Whitman, *Law of Property*, 182–98. When a married couple owns a house as community property, upon the death of the first spouse, the basis of the entire house steps up to its value on that date (*Internal Revenue Code* §§ 1014(a), 1014(b)(6)).

44. Cooper, "Continuing Problems."

45. See, for example, Hansmann, "Condominium and Cooperative Housing," 30–39; Henderson and Ioannides, "Model of Housing Tenure Choice"; Henderson and Ioannides, "Owner Occupancy"; and the sources cited in the notes that follow.

46. Varady and Lipman, "What Are Renters Really Like?" 501. Wealthier people are somewhat more likely to be homeowners, indicating that a home is either a normal or superior good. For a debate over why the wealthy buy, compare Henderson and Ioannides, "Owner Occupancy," with Fu, "Model of Housing Tenure Choice."

47. See Hansmann, *Ownership of Enterprise*, 201–02; and Wolfson, "Generalized Lease-or-Buy Problem."

48. Lea and Wasylenko, "Tenure Choice," 135.

49. Housing was an extraordinarily good investment in some U.S. metropolitan areas between 1995 and 2004. See Himmelberg, Mayer, and Sinai, "Assessing High House Prices." But compare Shiller, *Irrational Exuberance*, 11–27, asserting that U.S. home prices increased, in real terms, only 0.4 percent per annum between 1890 and 2004.

50. See Bourassa and Grigsby, "Income Tax Concessions"; and Hansmann, "Condominium and Cooperative Housing," 39–56. These tax benefits may be partially capitalized into higher purchase prices.

51. See chapter 4, text accompanying note 57.

52. In many contexts, freeing land from a long-term lease therefore increases its aggregate value. See, for example, Asabere, "Estates of Ghana"; and Capozza and Sick, "Valuing Long Term Leases." This fact casts doubt on the merits of "community land trusts" that involve the long-term ground leasing of house sites. On these arrangements, see Abromowitz, "Community Land Trusts," and the website of the Institute for Community Economics, http://www.iceclt.org/.

53. Hansmann, *Ownership of Enterprise*, 197–99.

54. The full history is narrated in Hansmann, "Condominium and Cooperative Housing," 28–30, 61–62.

55. *Ownership of Enterprise*, 195–223.

56. "Condominium and Cooperative Housing," 56, 63, 67–68. But compare ibid., 32–33, Hansmann's discussion of the difficulties between landlords and tenants that can arise because of "lock-in" and "moral hazard" problems.

57. Transaction-cost considerations also underlie the relative paucity of commercial, as opposed to residential, condominium complexes. Hansmann offers reasons for this disparity in "Condominium and Cooperative Housing," 64–67. As he stresses, federal income tax considerations strongly favor the purchase of a residence, but the rental of commercial real estate. In the eyes of a business executive, these tax advantages of renting business space may swamp the transaction-cost disadvantages of not owning it. In addition, however, commercial leasing customs have evolved to reduce the transaction costs of landlord-tenant coordination. Commercial leases tend to be much longer than residential leases. See Lefcoe, *Real Estate Transactions*, 850, indicating that many commercial leases have terms of 5–25 years. Modern commercial space also tends to be designed to be readily adapted to an incoming tenant's tastes. A commercial tenant who has a long-term lease and broad authority to install and remove trade fixtures therefore may not be much concerned about possible entanglements with the landlord over proposed improvements.

58. See Goodman and Goodman, "Co-op Discount," 232, finding a condominium premium of 12 percent; and Schill, Voicu, and Miller, "Condominium versus Cooperative Puzzle," 312, finding a condominium premium of 8.8 percent.

59. For further elaboration, see chapter 5 above, text accompanying notes 25–30 and the full paragraph on page 59.

60. On the impact of mortgage finance systems, see Chiuri and Jappelli, "Financial Market Imperfections."

61. United Nations Economic Commission for Europe, *Bulletin of Housing Statistics*, table A.

62. Caldwell, "Islam on the Outskirts," 55, 56; Wikipedia, Million Programme. More generally, a nation's rate of homeown-

ership is negatively correlated with the magnitude of its welfare expenditures (Angel, *Housing Policy Matters*, 330–39).

63. But compare Saunders, *Nation of Home Owners*, 29–41, a highly skeptical assessment of Marxist scholars' assertions that capitalist regimes promote homeownership in order to dampen revolutionary sentiment.

64. Fischel, *Homevoter Hypothesis*, 4, 81–82.

65. See Cole and Furbey, *Eclipse of Council Housing*, 172, 196–98; see also Salsich, "Perspectives on Privatization," 277–78.

Chapter 8: Order without Law in an Ongoing Household

1. Bernstein, "Merchant Law," 1796–98.

2. The obligatory reference is Mnookin and Kornhauser, "Bargaining in the Shadow of the Law."

3. See Pollak, "Bargaining Around the Hearth," 355; and chapter 9 below, text accompanying notes 1–4.

4. See also chapter 6, text accompanying note 14; and chapter 7, text following note 50. This prediction is consistent with the hypothesis of welfare-maximizing norms developed in Ellickson, *Order Without Law*, 167–83.

5. On the many potential complications, see generally Adler and Posner, "Cost-Benefit Analysis."

6. On the importance of social aspects of land institutions, see Ellickson, "Property in Land," 1344–62. See also Dagan and Heller, "Liberal Commons," 572–74, discussing methods of reconciling the economic and social aspects of domestic life.

7. The prediction is restricted to "low-level rules," that is, those governing everyday matters whose resolution has relatively minor consequences. Household participants also may have to deal with momentous matters, for example, a co-occupant's obligations to render care to another co-occupant who has encountered a catastrophic health problem. Participants' rules addressing these momentous issues may include an element of interpersonal insurance and not satisfy Kaldor-Hicks criteria.

8. Compare Polinsky, "Probabilistic Compensation Criteria," asserting that individuals focus on the aggregate impact of bundles of decisions, not on the impact of an isolated decision.

9. For a richer taxonomy of rules, see Ellickson, *Order Without Law*, 132–36. See also Ostrom, *Governing the Commons*, 52–54, a categorization of rules used by commoners.

10. Compare Posner, *Economic Analysis of Law*, 72–73, proposing an analogous rule when ownership is divided between holders of present and future interests.

11. Calabresi and Hirschoff, "Strict Liability in Torts," 1060.

12. Ellickson, *Order Without Law*, 278–79.

13. Compare ibid., 162–64, 210–11, 224–29, discussing norms when labor is specialized.

14. See sources cited in note 91 below.

15. Bernstein, "Merchant Law," 1796.

16. Compare ScottHanson and ScottHanson, *Cohousing Handbook*, 25–29, 172, 269–70, passages that urge the members of co-housing communities to employ agendas, written minutes, and similar formalities.

17. RAND, *Housing Assistance Supply Experiment*, 55.

18. See Mansbridge, *Beyond Adversary Democracy*, 32–33; Davis, "Group Consensus Decisions," 26–27. For simplicity, the discussion in the text assumes that the group has a discussion leader. This assumption sidesteps two intriguing empirical questions. First, under what circumstances do the members of a group devoted to consensual decision-making formally designate a discussion leader? Second, when they do choose to designate one, do they select that leader by consensus or by another procedure such as majority vote?

19. Dagan and Heller, "Liberal Commons," 590–95. Dagan and Heller note the advantages of consensual decision-making (see ibid., 594), but regard majority rule and unanimity to be the main candidates for a default decision rule. They also recommend that lawmakers require commoners to unanimously approve some measures—for example, a program that would be purely redistributive (ibid., 592–93); see also Ellickson, "Cities and Homeowners Associations," 1532, embracing the same position.

20. Many kibbutzim now authorize members to decide selected issues by referendum. Ben-Rafael, *Kibbutz at Century's End*, 58, 89, 181.

21. Groups as diverse as tribes of foragers and corporate boards

of directors similarly prefer to decide by consensus (Boehm, *Hierarchy in the Forest*, 113–17; Bainbridge, "Group Decisionmaking in Corporate Governance," 45).

22. See the final paragraph of appendix B and compare appendix A, table A.2. See also Fenster, "Community by Covenant," 13–14; Moench, "Decision-making," 30–31.

23. See Lewis, "Struggling with Quicksand," 388–89, describing decision-making by three sisters who had inherited properties from their intestate mother. Dagan and Heller, "Liberal Commons," 615 and nn.254–55, 616, provide a useful summary of the significant variations among the statutes of several industrialized nations that have attempted (not necessarily with success) to prescribe default decision rules for co-owners.

24. See the sources on civic republicanism cited in Block, "Evolution of Social Choice Theory," 983 n.29.

25. ScottHanson and ScottHanson, *Cohousing Handbook*, 266–67; Moench, "Colors of Empowerment," 26–27. In practice, of course, participants may choose to use words, not colored cards, to communicate the depth of their sentiments.

26. On Condorcet's and others' insights into possible shortcomings of majoritarian procedures, see Block, "Evolution of Social Choice Theory," 981–84. See also Buchanan and Tullock, *Calculus of Consent*, 131–45, a critical inquiry into the operation of majority rule.

27. Norbert Kerr, "Group Decision Making," 90–92.

28. For example, the sample document in ScottHanson and ScottHanson, *Cohousing Handbook*, 176, states: "In order to promote a feeling of community, caring and trust among all members of the group a consensus-seeking process will be used." See also Mansbridge, *Beyond Adversary Democracy*, 8–10, 252–60. Compare Diamond, Rose, and Murphy, "Behavior of the Non-Unanimous Civil Jury," reporting that jurors operating under a unanimity requirement in fact try to achieve consensus and report greater satisfaction with their deliberations than jurors who decide by supermajority, with Nemeth, "Majority vs. Unanimity Decision Rules," finding that a unanimity rule made members of mock juries more unfriendly toward one another.

29. See ScottHanson and ScottHanson, *Cohousing Handbook*,

176; Fenster, "Community by Covenant," 29–30, 34–35, 42–43; and the final paragraph of appendix B.

30. These self-restraints, while crucially important, operate within the household much as they do beyond it. For this reason, the analysis in this chapter rarely refers to this form of social control.

31. On methods that parties may use, in the absence of a state, to make promises credible, see Dixit, *Lawlessness and Economics*; and Kronman, "State of Nature," 11–24.

32. I present a slightly different taxonomy of rules in *Order Without Law*, 123–36.

33. Ibid.

34. Compare Singer, "Privatization of Family Law," describing both individuals' desires to customize domestic rules and legal systems' increasing toleration of such efforts.

35. Compare Scott and Scott, "Marriage as Relational Contract," 1285–88, an analysis of the evolution of norms between particular spouses.

36. See chapter 6, footnote on page 65 and accompanying text.

37. See Blackstone, *Commentaries* 1: *74–75. Contrary to Henry Maine's renowned assertion of a trend from status to contract (see chapter 2 above, text accompanying note 18), when household-specific norms are the predominant form of coordination, household relations are determined neither by status nor by contract.

38. Compare Ellickson, *Order Without Law*, 55–56, a discussion of the mental accounting of inter-neighbor debts.

39. Nock, "Time and Gender in Marriage," 1981. Compare Murstein, Cerreto, and MacDonald, "Effect of Exchange-Orientation," marshaling evidence that an exchange-orientation is generally inimical to a relationship, with Sprecher, "Effect of Exchange Orientation," reporting data inconsistent with that thesis. See generally Regan, *Alone Together*, 41–42, 71–73, and sources cited therein.

40. For evidence from a variety of contexts of the application of escalating self-help sanctions to control deviants, see Dixit, *Lawlessness and Economics*, 61; and Ellickson, *Order Without*

Law, 56–64. Compare chapter 2, text accompanying notes 44–46.

41. On the role of express contracts in relatively intimate settings, see Schneider and Brinig, *Invitation to Family Law*, 427–75; and Ellickson, *Order Without Law*, 246–48, 253, 274.

42. For discussion of when merchants choose to put their agreements in writing, see Johnston, "Business Norms."

43. On the advantages that spouses may obtain by coordinating via gift exchange as opposed to express contract, see Ellman, "*Marvin's* Fatal Flaw," 1373–79; and Pollak, "Transaction Cost Approach," 595–97. As just noted, however, those opting to use gift exchange to resolve most issues would not necessarily be averse to occasionally using oral contracts to resolve some challenges, such as how to split the work of an unusual event such as hosting a large dinner party. See also text accompanying notes 61–73 below.

44. See Ben-Porath, "The F-Connection," 5–8, 18, discussions implying that gift exchange among intimates is a relatively cheap mechanism.

45. When parties who are somewhat trusting negotiate a written contract, they commonly choose to keep many of its terms indefinite (Scott, "Self-Enforcing Indefinite Agreements"). Labor contracts, for example, tend to be quite incomplete and, as a result, an employment relationship typically involves significant elements of gift exchange (Akerlof, "Labor Contracts as Partial Gift Exchange"). This occurs in part because a worker's exact contributions may be too subtle to be objectively measured (Baker, Gibbons, and Murphy, "Optimal Incentive Contracts").

46. See Cowen, *Discover Your Inner Economist*, 13–16 ("The Dirty Dishes Parable"), 24–25. See also Camerer and Hogarth, "Effects of Financial Incentives"; and Gneezy and Rustichini, "A Fine Is a Price."

47. See Ellickson, *Order Without Law*, 234–35, and chapter 3, note 6 and accompanying text.

48. In some nations, participants in a household relationship conceivably might also refrain from transferring cash in order to reduce the recipient's income tax liabilities or to enhance the recipient's eligibility for welfare benefits.

49. See Sobel, "Interdependent Preferences and Reciprocity," a review of the relevant literature. A kindred proposition holds that an actor who receives extrinsic rewards for an action derives less intrinsic satisfaction from performing that action. See, for example, ibid., 416–17; and Titmuss, *Gift Relationship*, a famous analysis of the motivations of blood donors.

50. Fehr, Fischbacher, and Kosfield, "Neuroeconomic Foundations of Trust." See also Rabin, "Incorporating Fairness into Game Theory," arguing that individuals enjoy being nice to those who have been nice to them.

51. Molm, Peterson, and Takahashi, "Procedural Justice in Social Exchange." Compare Mahar, "Prenuptial Agreements," reporting that about 60 percent of survey respondents regarded a request for a prenuptial agreement as a reason for raising their estimates of the probability of divorce.

52. The formula is $n(n-1)/2$, where n is the number in the group.

53. Foundational works on the role of hierarchies include Dahl and Lindblom, *Politics, Economics and Welfare*; and Williamson, *Markets and Hierarchies*. See also Bainbridge, "Privately Ordered Participatory Management," 1004–14; and Smith, "Modularity in Contracts," 1182–85 (offering diagrams that portray alternative forms of hierarchy).

54. See, for example, *Florida Statutes Annotated* § 721.13(1)(a). On timeshare entities, see generally chapter 7 above, footnote on pages 85–86.

55. In interviews most Americans express broad tolerance toward others' modes of living (Wolfe, *One Nation, After All*, 108–11, 129–31).

56. See chapter 5, text accompanying notes 18–24. But compare McAdams, "Origin, Development," 412–19, a discussion of the possibility of "nosy norms."

57. See chapter 2, text accompanying notes 4–36.

58. See chapter 5, text accompanying notes 25–30; and chapter 7, text accompanying notes 59–65.

59. See Macaulay, "Non-Contractual Relations in Business"; Ross, *Settled Out of Court*; and the other sources cited in Ellickson, *Order Without Law*, 141–47, 256–57.

60. See Ellickson, *Order Without Law*, 250–52.

61. On the role of money within the marriage relationship specifically, see generally Blumstein and Schwartz, *American Couples*, 51–111; and Pahl, *Money and Marriage* (analyzing spousal relations in the United Kingdom).

62. Warton and Goodnow, "Money and Children's Household Jobs," 343.

63. See notes 65–73 below and accompanying text. Scholars of domestic relations appear to have done little empirical work on the frequency of oral and written contracting.

64. Kimel, "Neutrality, Autonomy and Freedom of Contract," 490–93; see also text accompanying notes 49–51 above. But compare Bellia, "Promises, Trust, and Contract Law," critiquing Kimel's behavioral assumptions.

65. See, for example, *Minnesota Statutes Annotated* § 513.075, which states that a court is to enforce a cohabitation agreement between an unmarried man and woman only if it is in writing and only after termination of their relationship. Compare *Morone v. Morone*, 413 N.E.2d 1154 (N.Y. 1980), allowing an ex-cohabitant to pursue recovery based on an oral contract, but not on an implied contract theory. But see *Marvin v. Marvin*, 557 P.2d 106 (Cal. 1976), permitting an ex-cohabitant to proceed on both oral-contract and implied-contract theories. See also text accompanying notes 111–113 below.

66. See, for example, American Jurisprudence Legal Forms, 9B: §§ 139:135–:159 (Nonmarital Cohabitation Agreements); Ihara, Warner, and Hertz, *Living Together*; and Solot and Miller, *Unmarried to Each Other*, 137–41.

67. Ihara, Warner, and Hertz, *Living Together*, 3/3. See also Stoner and Irving, *Prenuptial Agreements*, 2/7: "[A] prenup isn't the best place to address lifestyle agreements—that is, matters such as who's responsible for taking out the garbage and what kind of schedule you will keep. . . ."). But compare Ihara, Warner, and Hertz, 3/20, providing a sample agreement that requires the breadwinner to pay a weekly salary to the homemaker.

68. Ira Ellman, "*Marvin's* Fatal Flaw," 1367 n.17, reporting Hertz's admission that co-occupants who request that documents be drafted typically end up not signing them. But see *Posik v.*

Layton, 695 So.2d 759 (Fla. Dist. Ct. App. 1997), enforcing, after breakup, the terms of a lesbian couple's written cohabitation agreement that had required one partner to do the cooking, housework, and yard work.

69. Sources advocating, and offering examples of, written roommate agreements include Portman and Stewart, *Renters' Rights*, 6/6–/9; and Ellin, "Taming Roommate Chaos."

70. In neighborhoods of New York City where apartments are unusually expensive, about two dozen companies, some of them less than reputable, advertise that they specialize in helping total strangers arrange for co-rentals (Hevesi, "Making Roommates of Perfect Strangers"). Hevesi's article makes no mention, however, of written housemate agreements.

71. *Ganson v. Goldfader*, 561 N.Y.S.2d 366 (Sup. Ct. 1990), exemplifies how rent control tends to raise stakes. The case involved a battle among a series of contract-writing occupants of a rent-stabilized Manhattan apartment over which of them would be entitled to buy the unit at the insider price when the building was converted to a cooperative.

72. See, for example, Baylor University, Off Campus Housing Guide; Swarthmore Student Housing, RA Resources; University of Iowa Tenant Landlord Association, Roommate Issues.

73. See, for example, University of Massachusetts Amherst, Housing and Residence Life, (encouraging freshmen at UMass Amherst to sign roommate agreements). But cf. Lewin, "First Test for Freshmen" (reporting that some universities encourage entering students to use an online matchmaking service to find roommates).

74. See ScottHanson and ScottHanson, *Cohousing Handbook*, 167–78.

75. See Zablocki, *Alienation and Charisma*, 250–55. See also appendix A, table A.2.

76. See ScottHanson and ScottHanson, *Cohousing Handbook*, 267–69; Fenster, "Community by Covenant," 13–14. The occupants of a voluntary group quarters, such as a retirement home or college dormitory, similarly may elect an advisory governing board.

77. See Zablocki, *Alienation and Charisma*, 46–47, a discussion of the tendency of communes to drift toward charismatic authoritarian leadership.

78. See Ben-Rafael, *Kibbutz at Century's End*, 107–11, 181, 184. But compare ibid., 58, 89, 181, noting that some kibbutzim make use of referenda. On the size of kibbutzim, see chapter 5, text accompanying note 51.

79. See appendix A, table A.1. See also ScottHanson and ScottHanson, *Cohousing Handbook*, 128 (advocating communities of between 12 and 36 dwelling units); Zablocki, *Alienation and Charisma*, 43, 83 (asserting that the average number of residents of a U.S. commune fell from over 100 before 1820 to about 25 in 1965–1975). Because privacy and autonomy are superior goods (see chapter 7 above, text accompanying note 57), a society's intentional communities are likely to become smaller as its wealth increases.

80. See appendix A, table A.3.

81. Peter, *Hutterite Society*, 61, 81.

82. See Zablocki, *Joyful Community*, 201–05.

83. Carden, *Oneida*, 85–88.

84. See Ellickson and Thorland, "Ancient Land Law," 355–57, a discussion of hierarchically organized households in the earliest historical periods.

85. Aristotle, *The Politics*, 9.

86. Mertes, *English Noble Household*, 6–7, 17–18, 22, 25, 177–80.

87. See chapter 4, text accompanying notes 19–20.

88. See generally Buchanan, "Laws of Succession," 78–79, identifying some advantages of mechanical rules of inheritance.

89. Booth, *Households*, 19–21, 38–39. A Roman *paterfamilias* was similarly constrained by a duty of *pietas*. See Saller, *Roman Family*, 105–14.

90. See chapter 4, text accompanying notes 21–35.

91. See Scott, "Social Norms," 1914–16. On the inclinations of most men and women to adhere to traditional gender roles within a household setting, see Berk, *Gender Factory*, 164–65, 201–11; and Nock, *Marriage in Men's Lives*, 37–62. See also Goffman, "Arrangement Between the Sexes."

92. Lundberg and Pollak, "Separate Spheres Bargaining," 993–94.

93. Zablocki, *Alienation and Charisma*, 318–20.

94. See Hadfield, "Sexual Division of Labor."

95. See chapter 5, notes 17–24 and accompanying text. See generally Barros, "Home as a Legal Concept," a review of the ways in which the law is more protective of the home than of other types of property; and Teitelbaum, "Family History and Family Law," an overview of the history of government involvement in family arrangements. Some commentators favor more state involvement. See, for example, McClain, "Families, Schools, and Sex Equality," 1646–53: "Government does have an interest in who does the dishes. . . ."

96. *Lawrence v. Texas*, 539 U.S. 558 (2003).

97. *Moore v. City of East Cleveland*, 431 U.S. 494 (1977). But compare *Village of Belle Terre v. Boraas*, 416 U.S. 1 (1974), which upheld, against a wide-ranging constitutional attack, an ordinance that limited the composition of nonfamily households to a maximum of two adults. For criticism of *Belle Terre*, see Karst, "Freedom of Intimate Association," 686–89. Some states, however, have been more protective of domestic freedom. See, for example, *City of Santa Barbara v. Adamson*, 610 P.2d 436 (Cal. 1980), where the Supreme Court of California struck down, as a violation of a state constitutional provision, an ordinance that restricted the creation of households of more than five unrelated persons. On why lawmakers might have greater solicitude toward family households than nonfamily households, see Haddock and Polsby, "Family as a Rational Classification."

98. See text accompanying note 67 above, which identifies the risk that a court would deem such a complaint legally frivolous.

99. See, for example, *Kilgrow v. Kilgrow*, 107 So.2d 885 (Ala. 1958) (refusing to adjudicate suit between cohabiting spouses over where their seven-year-old child should attend school); *McGuire v. McGuire*, 59 N.W.2d 336 (Neb. 1953) (rejecting, for reasons of public policy, suit by wife for support payments from husband who lived with her); *Miller v. Miller*, 42 N.W. 641 (Iowa 1889) (declining to enforce a written interspousal contract in an intact marriage on grounds of public policy and stating, at 643: "That which should be a sealed book of family history must be opened for public inspection or inquiry. The law, except in cases of necessity, will not justify it."). But see, for example, *Miller v. Miller*, 30 N.W.2d 509 (Mich. 1948) (granting wife support pay-

ments, on ground of extreme cruelty, against cohabiting husband). See generally Hasday, "Intimacy and Economic Exchange," 499–507; and Shultz, "Contractual Ordering of Marriage," 232–37. Defenders of this tradition of judicial noninvolvement in ongoing marriages include Levmore, "Love It or Leave It," 244–48; and Scott and Scott, "Marriage as Relational Contract," 1294–95. See also Cohen, "Marriage, Divorce, and Quasi Rents," 300–02, on the futility of specifically enforcing intimate obligations. Among the commentators who urge greater judicial oversight of ongoing marriages are Olsen, "Myth of State Intervention"; and Rasmusen and Stake, "Personalizing the Marriage Contract," 481–89.

100. Aubert, "Some Social Functions of Legislation."

101. See Clark, *Law of Domestic Relations* §§ 10.1–10.2, a general discussion of possibilities of tort litigation between family members.

102. See Lipton, "His-and-Hers House."

103. The canonical discussion is Hardin, "Tragedy of the Commons."

104. Seabright, "Managing Local Commons," 124–29.

105. Woolf, *Room of One's Own*, 4. But compare Spain, *Gendered Spaces*, asserting that the specialization of household spaces tends to disadvantage women.

106. Woolf, 70.

107. Compare Goffman, *Asylums*, 243–49, describing the informal privatization of common spaces within mental institutions. A space that is privatized only during limited time periods is subject to a particularly complex ownership regime sometimes referred to as a "semicommons." See Smith, "Semicommon Property Rights."

108. See Ellickson, "Property in Land," 1332–62.

109. Peter, *Hutterite Society*, 178, 202–03.

110. See chapter 5, text accompanying notes 54–63.

111. Compare *Tuckwiller v. Tuckwiller*, 413 S.W.2d 274 (Mo. 1967) (ordering an executor to honor a written contract between the decedent and a caregiver that called for the devise of the decedent's farm to the caregiver), with *Feigenspan v. Pence*, 168 S.W.2d 1074 (Mo. 1943) (declining to order specific perform-

ance of an oral contract with allegedly similar terms). On the potential complexity of interfamily relations in these contexts, particularly among the children of the person in need of care, see Engers and Stern, "Long-Term Care and Family Bargaining."

112. Compare *Marvin v. Marvin*, 557 P.2d 106 (Cal. 1976). For general discussion of disputes of this sort, see Garrison, "Is Consent Necessary?"

113. See text accompanying notes 61–73 above.

114. Stoebuck and Whitman, *Law of Property*, 175–240, provides a description of the conventional forms of co-ownership. Co-ownership interests also can be created by other means, such as the voluntary fractionalization of shares, adverse possession, wills, and intestate inheritance (see chapter 5, note 27 and accompanying text).

115. These couples typically own either as joint tenants or as tenants by the entirety, forms that confer full ownership on the surviving spouse. See chapter 2, note 25; and chapter 4, notes 49–50 and accompanying text.

116. Stoebuck and Whitman, *Law of Property*, 201–24, provides a review of the legal rules governing relations among co-owners.

117. Although most of these legal rules are defaults, some co-owner exit rights are immutable. See chapter 2, text accompanying notes 23–24.

118. Braunstein and Genn, "Home-Buying Process," 476 n.30.

119. "[T]he contractual aspects of the [co-ownership] relationship are rarely formalized by written agreement" (Lewis, "Struggling with Quicksand," 409).

120. Compare the relative brevity of *American Jurisprudence Legal Forms* 7:§ 75:1–:49 (cotenancy and joint ownership), and 14:§ 193:54–:56 (partition), with ibid., volumes 11, 11A, and 11B:§§ 161:1–:1275, nearly three full volumes on leases of real property. Similarly, compare the spareness of *Nichols Cyclopedia of Legal Forms*, 5A:§ 5.2834–.2386 (joint tenants and tenants in common) and 6D:§ 6.7535 (partition), with ibid., 5B: parts 1 and 2, two entire books on leases.

121. See Stoebuck and Whitman, *Law of Property*, 209.

122. The 100 most recent cases bearing West Keycite 373k37 ("Tenancy in Common; Mutual Rights, Duties, and Liabilities of Cotenants; Accounting") were located by searching the WestLaw database of state court decisions. Of these 100 cases, 42 were put aside because they involved either a corporate entity as a named party, a dispute involving the ownership of a mineral interest, or a title dispute (implying that the parties did not even know whether they were involved in a "game" at all).

123. In two instances, the stage in which the accounting action had been commenced was ambiguous. Thus, in only three of the fifty-eight decisions (5 percent) did the court either state or imply that the litigating co-owners intended to continue as co-owners. But compare *Swartzbaugh v. Sampson*, 54 P.2d 73 (Cal. Ct. App. 1936), a well-known decision involving a midgame action by a wife against her husband to cancel the husband's lease of his interest in real estate that the couple jointly owned and occupied.

124. *McDonald v. McDonald*, 302 P.2d 726 (N.M. 1956). The disputants were two brothers who co-owned a ranch. Because the published decision makes no mention of a ranch house, it is unlikely that this was a household dispute.

125. See, for example, Freeman, *Cotenancy and Partition*, a work published in 1886. Note 134 below cites some of the many current treatises on landlord-tenant law.

126. See chapter 4, text accompanying note 55. In England, a trust is the standard institution for the governance of co-owned property, even among intimates (Dagan and Heller, "Liberal Commons," 620 n.282).

127. See chapter 4, footnote on page 45 and accompanying text.

128. See Hogg and Abrams, *Intergroup Relations*; Tajfel, *Human Groups and Social Categories*; and Blair and Stout, "Trust, Trustworthiness," 1770–72, and sources cited therein.

129. See Hemmens and Hoch, "Shared Housing in Low Income Households," 23–25, reporting that in Chicago in the 1980s, adults residing in low-income households, especially ones lacking a conjugal unit, tended to contribute both money and services to the household economy.

130. See ibid., 23, stating that kinfolk tended to be taken in "at nominal or no rent."

131. The American Housing Survey defines a "lodger" as someone who pays rent to another household occupant (U.S. Census Bureau, *American Housing Survey*, A-17). In 1999, the heads of owner-occupied households reported the presence of 2.2 million unrelated adults, and 0.6 million lodgers (ibid., 64). See also chapter 4 above, text accompanying notes 17–18.

132. Angel and Tienda, "Cultural Pattern or Economic Need?" 1379–80.

133. In practice, a firm that specializes in the placement of au pairs is likely to be involved in any contracting between an au pair and the host family. See, for example, *Oxman v. Amoroso*, 659 N.Y.S.2d 963 (Yonkers City Ct. 1997).

134. General treatises include Friedman, *Friedman on Leases*; and Schoshinski, *American Law of Landlord and Tenant*. There also are state-specific treatises, especially in jurisdictions with a tradition of rent control. See, for example, Faber, *Handbook of Landlord-Tenant Law* (California); Karpoff, *Landlord and Tenant Law in the District of Columbia*; Warshaw, *Massachusetts Landlord-Tenant Law*; Korona, *Landlord and Tenant Law* (New Jersey); and Robert Dolan, *Rasch's Landlord & Tenant* (New York). See also, for example, Finney, Gfeller, and Sensale, *Connecticut Landlord/Tenant Relations*.

135. In the 1970s in Brown County, Wisconsin, only 10–12 percent of residential tenants had a written lease at the outset of their tenure, and only 30 percent of landlords reported that they required a security deposit (RAND, *First Annual Report*, 53, 55). On the relative informality of farm leasing practices, see Allen and Lueck, "Structure of Farmland Contracts," 367, reporting that 57 percent of a sample of cropland leases in the upper Midwest were oral.

136. For examples, see *American Jurisprudence Legal Forms* 11:§§ 161:34–:42 (offering ten lengthy form leases for residential property); *Nichols Cyclopedia of Legal Forms Annotated*, 5B:§§ 5.4318–.4319, 5.4321–.4333 (offering over a dozen). Compare Portman and Stewart, *Renters' Rights*, 2/7, urging a residential tenant to reduce basic lease terms to writing, primarily because

memories tend to be unreliable. On the increasing use of written leases, see Shepard, "Withholding Rent in Connecticut," 71 n.259, citing interviews with landlord-tenant law specialists about the nature of New Haven leases.

137. *United States Code Annotated* 42:§ 1437f(d)(1)(B)(i).

138. See Ellickson, *Order Without Law*, 275–79.

139. Since 1984, the New York State Division of Housing and Community Renewal (DHCR) has administered the rent control and rent stabilization programs in New York City (and a few other localities). These programs generate much litigation. On June 21, 2006, a search of the Westlaw database of New York cases (ny-cs), using the search terms "dhcr /10 rent & da(aft 1999)," resulted in a list of 292 reported decisions dated 2000 or thereafter.

140. New York State Unified Court System, N.Y. City Civil Court, Housing Part. On the perversities of the city's approach, see generally Salins and Mildner, *Scarcity by Design*; and Simmons-Mosley and Malpezzi, "New York City's Regulated Rental Housing Market," 40–42 (reviewing the literature).

Chapter 9: The Challenge of Unpacking the Household

1. For my own thoughts about how ambient norms of all sorts are generated, see "The Market for Social Norms."

2. On how legal formalization of a nonbiological family relationship can confer psychological benefits on those involved, see Brinig and Nock, "Does Legal Status Matter?"

3. At present, no more than eleven American states recognize common-law marriage (Dubler, "Legal History of Acting Married," 1012–13). A history of rendering care to a child does not satisfy the legal requirements for adoption, especially if the rights of absent biological parents have not been formally terminated (Romesberg, "Common Law Adoption").

4. See chapter 1, note 3.

5. Delano, *Brook Farm*.

6. On the Fourierist movement in the United States, see ibid., and also Guarneri, *Utopian Alternative*.

7. See Delano, *Brook Farm*, 254–57, for an account of the fire.

8. Ibid., 323: "Fourierism itself was not one of the major causes of Brook Farm's eventual failure." See also ibid., xiv-xv, 319–24.

9. The leaders of Brook Farm also had difficulty devising an organizational form that would attract contributions of capital. See chapter 6, notes 30–31 and accompanying text.

10. See Astrachan and Shanker, "Family Businesses' Contribution to the U.S. Economy," 217, asserting that family businesses, narrowly defined, accounted for 29 percent of U.S. GDP in 2000, and, broadly defined, accounted for 64 percent. See also Burch, *Family Control in America's Largest Corporations*.

11. Pollak, "Transaction Cost Approach," 591–93, identifies some advantages of family-governed firms. Hansmann, Kraakman, and Squire, "Rise of the Firm," 1357–60, 1365–66, provides a description of family and household enterprises in ancient Rome and medieval Italy.

12. See chapter 8, text accompanying notes 41–51, 65–73.

Appendixes A and B

1. The author can send a copy of both this database and the one prepared in conjunction with appendix B to readers desirous of more detail.

2. See chapter 4, text accompanying note 41.

3. See chapter 5, notes 44–45 and accompanying text. The estimate that a Hutterite community includes an average of 30 adults was derived from data on childbearing and family size provided in Kraybill and Bowman, *On the Backroad to Heaven*, 23; and Hostetler and Huntington, *Hutterites in North America*, 63.

4. A community's posting actually reports its number of adult "members," a term construed here to refer to its residents.

5. Pavin, "Kibbutz Movement," 57.

6. Skinner, *Walden Two*, 18, 40–44.

7. McCamant and Durrett, *Cohousing*, 208.

Works Cited

Abromowitz, David M. 1991. An Essay on Community Land Trusts: Toward Permanently Affordable Housing. *Mississippi Law Journal* 61 (Winter): 663–82.

Ackroyd, Peter. 1998. *The Life of Thomas More.* London: Chatto and Windus.

Acts 2:44. King James Version.

Adler, Matthew D., and Eric A. Posner, eds. 2001. *Cost-Benefit Analysis: Legal, Economic, and Philosophical Perspectives.* Chicago: Univ. of Chicago Press.

Adler, Matthew D., and Chris William Sanchirico. 2006. Inequality and Uncertainty: Theory and Legal Applications. *University of Pennsylvania Law Review* 155 (December): 279–377.

Akerlof, George A. 1982. Labor Contracts as Partial Gift Exchange. *Quarterly Journal of Economics* 97 (November): 543–69.

Allen, Douglas W., and Dean Lueck. 1992. The "Back Forty" on a Handshake: Specific Assets, Reputation, and the Structure of Farmland Contracts. *Journal of Law, Economics, and Organization* 8 (April): 366–76.

Alstott, Anne L. 1996. Tax Policy and Feminism: Competing Goals and Institutional Choices. *Columbia Law Review* 96 (December): 2001–82.

———. 2004. *No Exit: What Parents Owe Their Children and What Society Owes Parents.* New York: Oxford Univ. Press.

Altman, Irwin, and Joseph Ginat. 1996. *Polygamous Families in Contemporary Society.* Cambridge: Cambridge Univ. Press.

American Housing Survey for the United States: 1999. Washington, D.C.: U.S. Census Bureau.

American Jurisprudence Legal Forms, 2d. 2000. Partition. In Vol. 14 of *American Jurisprudence Legal Forms, 2d*, rev. ed., chap. 193. n.p.: West Group.

———. 2002. Husband and Wife: Nonmarital Cohabitation Agreements. In Vol. 9B of *American Jurisprudence Legal Forms, 2d*, rev. ed., chap. 139. n.p.: West Group.

———. 2006a. Leases of Real Property. In Vol. 11 of *American Jurisprudence Legal Forms, 2d*, rev. ed., chap. 161. n.p.: Thomson West.

———. 2006b. Leases of Real Property. In Vol. 11A of *American Jurisprudence Legal Forms, 2d*, rev. ed., chap. 161. n.p.: Thomson West.

———. 2006c. Leases of Real Property. In Vol. 11B of *American Jurisprudence Legal Forms, 2d*, rev. ed., chap. 161. n.p.: Thomson West.

———. 2006d. Cotenancy and Joint Ownership. In Vol. 7 of *American Jurisprudence Legal Forms, 2d*, rev. ed., chap. 75. n.p.: Thomson West.

American Law Institute. 1979. *Restatement of the Law, Second: Contracts.* Washington, D.C.: American Law Institute.

Angel, Ronald, and Marta Tienda. 1982. Determinants of Extended Household Structure: Cultural Pattern or Economic Need? *American Journal of Sociology* 87 (May): 1360–83.

Angel, Shlomo. 2000. *Housing Policy Matters: A Global Analysis.* Oxford: Oxford Univ. Press.

Apps, Patricia F., and Ray Rees. 1997. Collective Labor Supply and Household Production. *Journal of Political Economy* 105 (February): 178–90.

Aristotle. ca. 335–322 BCE/1995. *The Politics.* Translated by Ernest Barker. Revised by R. F. Stalley. Oxford: Oxford Univ. Press.

Arnott, Richard. 1988. Rent Control: The International Experience. *Journal of Real Estate Finance and Economics* 1 (January): 203–15.

Asabere, Paul K. 2004. The Pricing of the Emergent Leasehold (Possessory) Estates of Ghana. *Real Estate Economics* 32 (Winter): 673–94.

Astrachan, Joseph H., and Melissa Carey Shanker. 2003. Family Businesses' Contribution to the U.S. Economy: A Closer Look. *Family Business Review* 16 (September): 211–19.

Aubert, Vilhelm. 1967. Some Social Functions of Legislation. *Acta Sociologica* 10: 97–121.

Aviram, Amitai. 2004. A Paradox of Spontaneous Formation: The Evolution of Private Legal Systems. *Yale Law and Policy Review* 22 (Winter): 1–68.

Axelrod, Robert. 1984. *The Evolution of Cooperation.* New York: Basic Books.

Axelrod, Robert, and Douglas Dion. 1988. The Further Evolution of Cooperation. *Science* 242 (December 9): 1385–90.

Ayres, Ian, and Robert Gertner. 1989. Filling Gaps in Incomplete Contracts: An Economic Theory of Default Rules. *Yale Law Journal* 99 (October): 87–130.

Badgett, M. V. Lee. 2001. *Money, Myths, and Change: The Economic Lives of Lesbians and Gay Men.* Chicago: Univ. of Chicago Press.

Bainbridge, Stephen M. 1998. Privately Ordered Participatory Management: An Organizational Failures Analysis. *Delaware Journal of Corporate Law* 23: 979–1076.

———. 2002. Why a Board? Group Decisionmaking in Corporate Governance. *Vanderbilt Law Review* 55 (January): 1–55.

Baker, George, Robert Gibbons, and Kevin J. Murphy. 1994. Subjective Performance Measures in Optimal Incentive Contracts. *Quarterly Journal of Economics* 109 (November): 1125–56.

Baker, Matthew J., and Joyce P. Jacobsen. 2007. A Human Capital-Based Theory of Postmarital Residence Rules. *Journal of Law, Economics, and Organization* 23 (April): 208–241.

Barros, D. Benjamin. 2006. Home as a Legal Concept. *Santa Clara Law Review* 46 (January): 255–306.

Barzel, Yoram. 1997. *Economic Analysis of Property Rights.* 2nd ed. Cambridge: Cambridge Univ. Press.

Baylor University. Agreements. In *Off Campus Housing Guide*.
    http://www.baylor.edu/offcampushousing/index.php?id=681.
Bebchuk, Lucian Arye, and Mark J. Roe. 1999. A Theory of Path
    Dependence in Corporate Ownership and Governance. *Stan-
    ford Law Review* 52 (November): 127–70.
Becker, Gary S. 1974. A Theory of Social Interactions. *Journal of
    Political Economy* 82 (November–December): 1063–93.
———. 1981. Altruism in the Family and Selfishness in the
    Marketplace. *Economica* 48 (February): 1–15.
———. 1991. *A Treatise on the Family*. Enl. ed. Cambridge,
    Mass.: Harvard Univ. Press.
Becker, Gary S., and Kevin M. Murphy. 1988. The Family and
    the State. *Journal of Law and Economics* 31 (April): 1–18.
Becker, Mary. 1999. Patriarchy and Inequality: Towards a Sub-
    stantive Feminism. *University of Chicago Legal Forum* 1999:
    21–88.
Bellamy, Edward. 1887/1951. *Looking Backward 2000–1887*.
    New York: Modern Library.
Bellia, Jr., Anthony J. 2002. Promises, Trust, and Contract Law.
    American Journal of Jurisprudence 47: 25–40.
Benkler, Yochai. 2004. Sharing Nicely: On Shareable Goods and
    the Emergence of Sharing as a Modality of Economic Produc-
    tion. *Yale Law Journal* 114 (November): 273–358.
Ben-Porath, Yoram. 1980. The F-Connection: Families, Friends,
    and Firms and the Organization of Exchange. *Population and
    Development Review* 6 (March): 1–30.
Ben-Rafael, Eliezer. 1997. *Crisis and Transformation: The Kibbutz
    at Century's End*. Albany: State Univ. of New York Press.
Berger, Curtis J. 1990. Timesharing in the United States. In U.S.
    Law in an Era of Democratization. Supplement, *American
    Journal of Comparative Law* 38: 131–51.
Bergstrom, Theodore C. 1996. Economics in a Family Way. *Jour-
    nal of Economic Literature* 34 (December): 1903–34.
Berk, Sarah Fenstermaker. 1985. *The Gender Factory: The Apportion-
    ment of Work in American Households*. New York: Plenum Press.
Berle, Adolph A., and Gardiner C. Means. 1932. *The Modern
    Corporation and Private Property*. New York: Commerce Clear-
    ing House.

Bernard, Jessie. 1982. *The Future of Marriage.* 2nd ed. New Haven, Conn.: Yale Univ. Press.

Bernheim, B. Douglas, and Sergei Severinov. 2003. Bequests as Signals: An Explanation for the Equal Division Puzzle. *Journal of Political Economy* 111 (August): 733–64.

Bernheim, B. Douglas, and Oded Stark. 1988. Altruism Within the Family Reconsidered: Do Nice Guys Finish Last? *American Economic Review* 78 (December): 1034–45.

Bernstein, Lisa. 1996. Merchant Law in a Merchant Court: Rethinking the Code's Search for Immanent Business Norms. *University of Pennsylvania Law Review* 144 (May): 1765–1821.

Bianchi, Suzanne M., Melissa A. Milkie, Liana C. Sayer, and John P. Robinson. 2000. Is Anyone Doing the Housework? Trends in the Gender Division of Household Labor. *Social Forces* 79 (September): 191–228.

Black, Dan, Seth G. Sanders, and Lowell J. Taylor. 2007. The Economics of Lesbian and Gay Families. *Journal of Economic Perspectives* 21 (Spring): 53–70.

Black, Donald. 1976. *The Behavior of Law.* New York: Academic Press.

Blackstone, William. 1765–69. *Commentaries.*

Blair, Margaret M. 1995. *Ownership and Control: Rethinking Corporate Governance for the Twenty-First Century.* Washington, D.C.: Brookings Institute.

Blair, Margaret M., and Lynn A. Stout. 2001. Trust, Trustworthiness, and the Behavioral Foundations of Corporate Law. *University of Pennsylvania Law Review* 149 (June): 1735–1810.

Blau, Peter M. 1964. *Exchange and Power in Social Life.* New York: Wiley.

Block, Cheryl D. 1998. Truth and Probability—Ironies in the Evolution of Social Choice Theory. *Washington University Law Quarterly* 76: 975–1037.

Blumstein, Philip, and Pepper Schwartz. 1983. *American Couples: Money, Work, Sex.* New York: Morrow.

Boehm, Christopher. 1999. *Hierarchy in the Forest: The Evolution of Egalitarian Behavior.* Cambridge, Mass.: Harvard Univ. Press.

Booth, William James. 1993. *Households: The Moral Architecture of the Economy.* Ithaca, N.Y.: Cornell Univ. Press.

Bourassa, Steven C., and William G. Grigsby. 2000. Income Tax Concessions for Owner-Occupied Housing. *Housing Policy Debate* 11 (3): 521–46.

Bowles, Roger, and Nuno Garoupa. 2002. Household Dissolution, Child Care and Divorce Law. *International Review of Law and Economics* 22 (December): 495–510.

Bowman, Karlyn. 2000. The Good Life. *American Enterprise* 11 (June): 60–61.

Brandon, Peter David. 2001. State Intervention in Imperfect Families: The Child, the State, and Imperfect Parenting Reconsidered from a Theory of Comparative Advantage. *Rationality and Society* 13 (August): 285–303.

Braunstein, Michael, and Hazel Genn. 1991. Odd Man Out: Preliminary Findings Concerning the Diminishing Role of Lawyers in the Home-Buying Process. *Ohio State Law Journal* 52 (Spring): 469–80.

Brinig, Margaret F. 2000. *From Contract to Covenant: Beyond the Law and Economics of the Family.* Cambridge, Mass.: Harvard Univ. Press.

———. 2001. Unmarried Partners and the Legacy of *Marvin v. Marvin:* The Influence of *Marvin v. Marvin* on Housework During Marriage. *Notre Dame Law Review* 76 (October): 1311–45.

Brinig, Margaret F., and Douglas W. Allen. 2000. "These Boots Are Made for Walking": Why Most Divorce Filers Are Women. *American Law and Economics Review* 2 (Spring): 126–69.

Brinig, Margaret F., and Steven L. Nock. 2003. How Much Does Legal Status Matter? Adoptions by Kin Caregivers. *Family Law Quarterly* 36 (Fall): 449–74.

———. 2004. Marry Me, Bill: Should Cohabitation Be the (Legal) Default Option? *Louisiana Law Review* 64 (Spring): 403–42.

Brinkley, Joel. 1989. Debts Make Israelis Rethink an Ideal: The Kibbutz. *New York Times,* March 5: Late city final ed., sec. 1.

Brown, Barbara B., John R. Burton, and Anne L. Sweaney. 1998. Neighbors, Households, and Front Porches: New Urbanist Community Tool or Mere Nostalgia? *Environment and Behavior* 30 (September): 579–600.

Browning, Martin, Francois Bourguignon, Pierre-Andre Chiappori, and Valerie Lechene. 1994. Incomes and Outcomes: A Structural Model of Intrahousehold Allocation. *Journal of Political Economy* 102 (December): 1067–96.

Brozan, Nadine. 2002. For Co-op Complexes, Complex Choices. *New York Times*, February 3: Late ed.— final, sec. 11.

Bryant, W. Keith, and Cathleen D. Zick, 2006. *The Economic Organization of the Household.* 2nd ed. Cambridge.: Cambridge Univ. Press.

Buchan, Nancy R., Rachel T. A. Croson, and Robyn M. Dawes. 2002. Swift Neighbors and Persistent Strangers: A Cross-Cultural Investigation of Trust and Reciprocity in Social Exchange. *American Journal of Sociology* 108 (July): 168–206.

Buchanan, James M. 1983. Rent Seeking, Noncompensated Transfers, and Laws of Succession. *Journal of Law and Economics* 26 (April): 71–85.

Buchanan, James M., and Gordon Tullock. 1962. *The Calculus of Consent: Logical Foundations of Constitutional Democracy.* Ann Arbor: Univ. of Michigan Press.

Burch, Jr., Philip H. 1972. *The Managerial Revolution Reassessed: Family Control in America's Largest Corporations.* Lexington, Mass.: Lexington Books.

Bushee, Frederick A. 1905. Communistic Societies in the United States. *Political Science Quarterly* 20 (December): 625–64.

Buss, David M. 2004. *Evolutionary Psychology: The New Science of Mind.* 2nd ed. Boston: Allyn and Bacon / Pearson.

Calabresi, Guido, and Jon T. Hirschoff. 1972. Toward a Test for Strict Liability in Torts. *Yale Law Journal* 81 (May): 1055–85.

Calabresi, Guido, and A. Douglas Melamed. 1972. Property Rules, Liability Rules, and Inalienability: One View of the Cathedral. *Harvard Law Review* 85 (April): 1089–1128.

Caldwell, Christopher. 2006. Islam on the Outskirts of the Welfare State. *New York Times Magazine*, February 5: Late ed.— final, p. 55.

Calthorpe, Peter. 1993. *The Next American Metropolis: Ecology, Community, and the American Dream.* New York: Princeton Architectural Press.

Camerer, Colin, Samuel Issacharoff, George Loewenstein, Ted

O'Donoghue, and Matthew Rabin. 2003. Regulation for Conservatives: Behavioral Economics and the Case for "Asymmetric Paternalism." *University of Pennsylvania Law Review* 151 (January): 1211–54.

Camerer, Colin F., and Robin M. Hogarth. 1999. The Effects of Financial Incentives in Experiments: A Review and Capital-Labor-Production Framework. *Journal of Risk and Uncertainty* 19 (December): 7–42.

Caplin, Andrew, Sewin Chan, Charles Freeman, and Joseph Tracy. 1997. *Housing Partnerships: A New Approach to a Market at a Crossroads.* Cambridge, Mass.: MIT Press.

Caplow, Theodore. 1982. Christmas Gifts and Kin Networks. *American Sociological Review* 47 (June): 383–92.

Capozza, Dennis R., and Gordon A. Sick. 1991. Valuing Long Term Leases: The Option to Redevelop. *Journal of Real Estate Finance and Economics* 4 (June): 209–23.

Carden, Maren Lockwood. 1969. *Oneida: Utopian Community to Modern Corporation.* Baltimore, Md.: Johns Hopkins Univ. Press.

Casper, Lynne M., and Suzanne M. Bianchi. 2002. *Continuity and Change in the American Family.* Thousand Oaks, Calif.: Sage Publications.

Catholic University of America, ed. 2003a. Benedictines. In Vol. 2 of *New Catholic Encyclopedia*, 2nd ed., 273–74. Detroit: Gale Group.

———. 2003b. Benedictines. In Vol. 2 of *New Catholic Encyclopedia*, 2nd ed., 267–73. Detroit: Gale Group.

Census Bureau. *See* U.S. Census Bureau.

Cheal, David. 1988. *The Gift Economy.* London: Routledge.

Chiuri, Maria Concetta, and Tullio Jappelli. 2003. Financial Market Imperfections and Home Ownership: A Comparative Study. *European Economic Review* 47 (October): 857–75.

Clark, Jr., Homer H. 1988. *The Law of Domestic Relations in the United States.* Student and 2nd ed. St. Paul, Minn.: West Pub. Co.

Coase, R. H. 1937. The Nature of the Firm. *Economica* 4 (November): 386–405.

———. 1960. The Problem of Social Cost. *Journal of Law and Economics* 3 (October): 1–44.

————. 1988. *The Firm, the Market, and the Law.* Chicago: Univ. of Chicago Press.

Cohen, Lloyd. 1987. Marriage, Divorce, and Quasi Rents; Or, "I Gave Him the Best Years of My Life." *Journal of Legal Studies* 16 (June): 267–303.

Cohousing Association of the United States. http://www.cohousing .org/cmty/groups-o.html.

————. Frequently Asked Questions (FAQ). http://www.co housing.org/resources/faq.html#kitchen.

Cole, Ian, and Robert Furbey. 1994. *The Eclipse of Council Housing.* London: Routledge.

Coleman, James S. 1990. *Foundations of Social Theory.* Cambridge, Mass.: Harvard Univ. Press.

Cooper, Byron D. 1999. Continuing Problems with Michigan's Joint Tenancy "With Right of Survivorship." *Michigan Bar Journal* 78 (September): 966–69.

Costa, Dora L. 1998. *The Evolution of Retirement: An American Economic History, 1880–1990.* Chicago: Univ. of Chicago Press.

Cott, Nancy F. 1997. *The Bonds of Womanhood: "Woman's Sphere" in New England, 1780–1835.* 2nd ed. New Haven, Conn.: Yale Univ. Press.

Cowen, Tyler. 2007. *Discover Your Inner Economist: Use Incentives to Fall in Love, Survive Your Next Meeting, and Motivate the Dentist.* New York: Dutton.

Cox, Cheryl Anne. 1998. *Household Interests: Property, Marriage Strategies, and Family Dynamics in Ancient Athens.* Princeton, N.J.: Princeton Univ. Press.

Crowley, David, and Susan E. Reid, eds. 2002. *Socialist Spaces: Sites of Everyday Life in the Eastern Bloc.* Oxford: Berg. *See also* Gerasimova 2002.

Dagan, Hanoch, and Michael A. Heller. 2001. The Liberal Commons. *Yale Law Journal* 110 (January): 549–623.

Dahl, Robert A., and Charles E. Lindblom. 1953. *Politics, Economics, and Welfare.* New York: Harper.

Davis, James H. 1992. Some Compelling Intuitions About Group Consensus Decisions, Theoretical and Empirical Research, and Interpersonal Aggregation Phenomena: Selected Examples

1950–1990. *Organizational Behavior and Human Decision Processes* 52 (June): 3–38.

Dawes, Robyn M., Alphons J. C. van de Kragt, and John M. Orbell. 1990. Cooperation for the Benefit of Us—Not Me, or My Conscience. In *Beyond Self-Interest*, edited by Jane J. Mansbridge, 97–110. Chicago: Univ. of Chicago Press.

Dawkins, Richard. 1989. *The Selfish Gene*. New ed. Oxford: Oxford Univ. Press.

Deaton, Angus, and Christina Paxson. 1998. Economies of Scale, Household Size, and the Demand for Food. *Journal of Political Economy* 106 (October): 897–930.

Delano, Sterling F. 2004. *Brook Farm: The Dark Side of Utopia*. Cambridge, Mass.: Harvard Univ. Press, Belknap Press.

Dercon, Stefan, and Pramila Krishnan. 2000. In Sickness and in Health: Risk Sharing within Households in Rural Ethiopia. *Journal of Political Economy* 108 (August): 688–727.

De Ruijter, Esther, Tanja van de Lippe, and Werner Raub. 2003. Trust Problems in Household Outsourcing. *Rationality and Society* 15 (November): 473–507.

De Tocqueville. *See* Tocqueville.

Developments in the Law: Legal Responses to Domestic Violence. 1993. *Harvard Law Review* 106 (May): 1498–1620.

Developments in the Law: The Constitution and the Family. 1980. *Harvard Law Review* 93 (April): 1156–1383.

Devereux, John, and Luis Locay. 1992. Specialization, Household Production, and the Measurement of Economic Growth. In Papers and Proceedings of the Hundred and Fourth Annual Meeting of the American Economic Association, edited by Ronald L. Oaxaca and Wilma St. John. Special issue, *American Economic Review* 82 (May): 399–403.

Diakonoff, I. M. 1982. The Structure of Near Eastern Society Before the Middle of the 2nd Millennium bce. *Oikumene* 3: 7–100.

Diamond, Shari Seidman, Mary R. Rose, and Beth Murphy. 2006. Revisiting the Unanimity Requirement: The Behavior of the Non-Unanimous Civil Jury. *Northwestern University Law Review* 100: 201–30.

Dietz, Robert D., and Donald R. Haurin. 2003. The Social and

Private Micro-Level Consequences of Homeownership. *Journal of Urban Economics* 54: 401–50.

Dixit, Avinash K. 2004. *Lawlessness and Economics: Alternative Modes of Governance.* Princeton, N.J.: Princeton Univ. Press.

Dolan, Robert F. 1998. *Rasch's Landlord and Tenant: Including Summary Proceedings.* Vols. 1–3 of *New York Real Property Practice,* 4th ed. St. Paul, Minn.: West Group.

Donaldson, David, and B. Curtis Eaton. 1976. Firm-Specific Human Capital: A Shared Investment or Optimal Entrapment? *Canadian Journal of Economics* 9 (August): 462–72.

Duany, Andres, Elizabeth Plater-Zyberk, and Jeff Speck. 2000. *Suburban Nation: The Rise of Sprawl and the Decline of the American Dream.* New York: North Point Press.

Dubler, Ariela R. 2000. Wifely Behavior: A Legal History of Acting Married. *Columbia Law Review* 100 (May): 957–1021.

Edin, Kathryn, and Laura Lein. 1997. *Making Ends Meet: How Single Mothers Survive Welfare and Low-Wage Work.* New York: Russell Sage Foundation.

Eichner, Maxine. 2005. Dependency and the Liberal Polity: On Martha Fineman's *The Autonomy Myth. California Law Review* 93 (July): 1285–1321.

Eisenberg, Melvin Aron. 1997. The World of Contract and the World of Gift. *California Law Review* 85 (July): 821–66.

Ellen, Ingrid Gould, and Brendan O'Flaherty. 2002. Do Housing and Social Policies Make Households Too Small? Evidence from New York. Unpublished manuscript, on file with author.

Ellickson, Bryan, Birgit Grodal, Suzanne Scotchmer, and William R. Zame. 1999. Clubs and the Market. *Econometrica* 67 (September): 1185–1217.

Ellickson, Robert C. 1982. Cities and Homeowners Associations. *University of Pennsylvania Law Review* 130 (June): 1519–80.

———. 1991. *Order Without Law: How Neighbors Settle Disputes.* Cambridge, Mass.: Harvard Univ. Press.

———. 1993. Property in Land. *Yale Law Journal* 102 (April): 1315–1400.

———. 1996. Controlling Chronic Misconduct in City Spaces: Of Panhandlers, Skid Rows, and Public-Space Zoning. *Yale Law Journal* 105 (March): 1165–1248.

————. 2001. The Market for Social Norms. *American Law and Economics Review* 3 (Spring): 1–49.

Ellickson, Robert C., Carol M. Rose, and Bruce A. Ackerman, eds. 2002. *Perspectives on Property Law.* 3rd ed. New York: Aspen Law and Business.

Ellickson, Robert C., and Charles DiA. Thorland. 1995. Ancient Land Law: Mesopotamia, Egypt, Israel. *Chicago-Kent Law Review* 71: 321–411.

Ellin, Abby. 2003. Taming Roommate Chaos. *New York Times*, March 16: Late ed.— final, sec. 3.

Ellman, Ira Mark. 2001. "Contract Thinking" was *Marvin's* Fatal Flaw. *Notre Dame Law Review* 76 (October): 1365–80.

Engels, Friedrich. 1884/1972. *The Origin of the Family, Private Property and the State: In the Light of the Researches of Lewis H. Morgan.* Edited by Eleanor Burke Leacock. New York: International Publishers.

Engers, Maxim, and Steven Stern. 2002. Long-Term Care and Family Bargaining. *International Economic Review* 43 (February): 73–114.

Ertman, Martha M. 1998. Commercializing Marriage: A Proposal for Valuing Women's Work through Premarital Security Agreements. *Texas Law Review* 77 (November): 17–112.

Ertman, Martha M., and Joan C. Williams, eds. 2005. *Rethinking Commodification: Cases and Readings in Law and Culture.* New York: New York Univ. Press.

Faber, Stuart J. 1978. *Handbook of Landlord-Tenant Law: With Forms.* Los Angeles: Lega-Books.

Fargues, Philippe. 1996. The Arab World: The Family as Fortress. In *The Impact of Modernity*, vol. 2 of *A History of the Family*, edited by André Burguière, Christiane Klapisch-Zuber, Martine Segalen, and Françoise Zonabend; translated by Sarah Hanbury-Tenison, 339–74. Cambridge, Mass.: Harvard Univ. Press, Belknap Press.

Fehr, Ernst, Urs Fischbacher, and Michael Kosfeld. 2005. Neuroeconomic Foundations of Trust and Social Preferences: Initial Evidence. *American Economic Review* 95 (May): 346–51.

Fehr, Ernst, and Simon Gächter. 2000. Fairness and Retaliation:

The Economics of Reciprocity. *Journal of Economic Perspectives* 14 (Summer): 159–81.

Fellowship for Intentional Community. Communities Directory Online. http://directory.ic.org/iclist/.

———. Communities Directory: Hutterian Brethren. http://directory.ic.org/records/?action=view&page=view&record_id =570.

———. Communities Directory: Order of Saint Benedict. http://directory.ic.org/records/?action=view&page=view&record_id =878.

Fenster, Mark. 1999. Community by Covenant, Process, and Design: Cohousing and the Contemporary Common Interest Community. *Journal of Land Use and Environmental Law* 15 (Fall): 3–54.

Fineman, Martha Albertson. 1995. *The Neutered Mother, the Sexual Family, and Other Twentieth Century Tragedies.* New York: Routledge.

———. 2004. *The Autonomy Myth: A Theory of Dependency.* New York: New Press.

Finney, Valerie, Alena C. Gfeller, and Michele D. Sensale. 2004. *Handling Legal Issues in Connecticut Landlord/Tenant Relations.* Eau Claire, Wis.: NBI.

Fischel, William A. 2001. *The Homevoter Hypothesis: How Home Values Influence Local Government Taxation, School Finance, and Land-Use Policies.* Cambridge, Mass.: Harvard Univ. Press.

Flache, Andreas. 2001. Individual Risk Preferences and Collective Outcomes in the Evolution of Exchange Networks. *Rationality and Society* 13 (August): 304–48.

Fleishman, Sandra. 2001. The Buddy System; A New Theory of Buying Power: With Double the Income, Even Singles Can Afford Double the House. *Washington Post*, March 17: final ed., Real Estate.

Folbre, Nancy. 2001. *The Invisible Heart: Economics and Family Values.* New York: New Press.

Fox, John O. 2001. *If Americans Really Understood the Income Tax: Our Most Expensive Ignorance.* Boulder, Colo.: Westview Press.

Franks, David D., and E. Doyle McCarthy, eds. 1989. *The Sociol-*

ogy of Emotions: Original Essays and Research Papers. Greenwich, Conn.: JAI Press. *See also* Hochschild 1989.

Frantz, Carolyn J., and Hanoch Dagan. 2004. Properties of Marriage. *Columbia Law Review* 104 (January): 75–133.

Frazier, E. Franklin.1948. *The Negro Family in the United States.* Rev. and abr. ed. New York: Citadel Press.

Freeman, A. C. 1886. *Cotenancy and Partition: A Treatise on the Law of Co-ownership as It Exists Independent of Partnership Relations Between the Co-owners.* 2nd ed. San Francisco: Bancroft-Whitney.

Friedman, Lawrence M. 2004. *Private Lives: Families, Individuals, and the Law.* Cambridge, Mass.: Harvard Univ. Press.

Friedman, Milton R. 2004. *Friedman on Leases.* Edited and revised by Patrick A. Randolph, Jr. 5th ed. New York: Practising Law Institute.

Frost, Robert. 1939. The Death of the Hired Man. In *Collected Poems of Robert Frost,* 49–55. New York: Henry Holt.

Fu, Yuming. 1991. A Model of Housing Tenure Choice: Comment. *American Economic Review* 81 (March): 381–83.

Fukuyama, Francis. 1995. *Trust: The Social Virtues and the Creation of Prosperity.* New York: Free Press.

Garcia, Stephen M., Avishalom Tor, Max H. Bazerman, and Dale T. Miller. 2005. Profit Maximization versus Disadvantageous Inequality: The Impact of Self-Categorization. *Journal of Behavioral Decision Making* 18 (July): 187–98.

Garnett, Nicole Stelle. 2001. On Castles and Commerce: Zoning Law and the Home-Business Dilemma. *William and Mary Law Review* 42 (April): 1191–1244.

Garrison, Marsha. 2005. Is Consent Necessary? An Evaluation of the Emerging Law of Cohabitant Obligation. *UCLA Law Review* 52 (February): 815–97.

Gautschi, Thomas. 2000. History Effects in Social Dilemma Situations. *Rationality and Society* 12 (May): 131–62.

Geddes, Rick, and Dean Lueck. 2002. The Gains from Self-Ownership and the Expansion of Women's Rights. *American Economic Review* 92 (September): 1079–92.

Gerasimova, Katerina. 2002. Public Privacy in the Soviet Communal Apartment. In *Socialist Spaces: Sites of Everyday Life in the Eastern Bloc*, edited by David Crowley and Susan E. Reid, 207–30. Oxford: Berg.

Ginsborg, Paul. 2001. *Italy and Its Discontents: Family, Civil Society, State, 1980–2001*. London: Allen Lane.

Glaeser, Edward L., David I. Laibson, Jose A. Scheinkman, and Christine L. Soutter. 2000. Measuring Trust. *Quarterly Journal of Economics* 115 (August): 811–46.

Glaeser, Edward L. and Erzo F. P. Luttmer. 2003. The Misallocation of Housing Under Rent Control. *American Economic Review* 93 (November): 1027–46.

Glendon, Mary Ann. 1981. *The New Family and the New Property*. Toronto: Butterworths.

Glenn, Evelyn Nakano. 1983. Split Household, Small Producer and Dual Wage Earner: An Analysis of Chinese-American Family Strategies. *Journal of Marriage and the Family* 45 (February): 35–46.

Gneezy, Uri, and Aldo Rustichini. 2000. A Fine Is a Price. *Journal of Legal Studies* 29 (January): 1–17.

Godelier, Maurice. 1999. *The Enigma of the Gift*. Translated by Nora Scott. Chicago: Univ. of Chicago Press.

Goffman, Erving. 1961. *Asylums: Essays on the Social Situation of Mental Patients and Other Inmates*. Garden City, N.J.: Anchor Books.

———. 1977. The Arrangement Between the Sexes. *Theory and Society* 4 (Autumn): 301–31.

Goodman, Allen C., and John L. Goodman, Jr. 1997. The Co-op Discount. *Journal of Real Estate Finance and Economics* 14 (January-March): 223–33.

Goody, Jack. 1972. The Evolution of the Family. In *Household and Family in Past Time*, edited by Peter Laslett with the assistance of Richard Wall, 103–24. Cambridge.: Cambridge Univ. Press.

Gordon, James S. 1987. *The Golden Guru: The Strange Journey of Bhagwan Shree Rajneesh*. Lexington, Mass.: S. Greene Press.

Granovetter, Mark S. 1973. The Strength of Weak Ties. *American Journal of Sociology* 78 (May): 1360–80.

Green, Leslie. 1998. Rights of Exit. *Legal Theory* 4: 165–85.

Green, Penelope. 2005. 5 New Roommates Play "Getting To Know You." *New York Times*, July 10: Late ed.— final, section 11.

Greif, Avner. 2006. *Institutions and the Path to the Modern Econ-omy: Lessons from Medieval Trade.* Cambridge: Cambridge Univ. Press.

———. 2006. Family Structure, Institutions, and Growth: The Origins and Implications of Western Corporations. *American Economic Review* 96 (May): 308–12.

Greven, Jr. Philip J. 1970. *Four Generations: Population, Land, and Family in Colonial Andover, Massachusetts.* Ithaca, N.Y.: Cornell Univ. Press.

Gronau, Reuben. 1986. Home Production—A Survey. In Vol. 1 of *Handbook of Labor Economics,* edited by Orley Ashenfelter and Richard Layard, 273–304. Amsterdam: North-Holland.

Grossbard, Shoshana. 2007. Repack the Household: A Response to Robert Ellickson's *Unpacking the Household. Yale Law Jour-nal Pocket Part* 116: 341–47, http://thepocketpart.org/2007/04/16/grossbard.html.

Grossbard-Shechtman, Shoshana A. 1993. *On the Economics of Marriage: A Theory of Marriage, Labor, and Divorce.* Boulder, Colo.: Westview Press.

Grossberg, Michael. 1985. *Governing the Hearth: Law and the Family in Nineteenth-Century America.* Chapel Hill: Univ. of North Carolina Press.

Grossman, Sanford J., and Oliver D. Hart. 1986. The Costs and Benefits of Ownership: A Theory of Vertical and Lateral Inte-gration. *Journal of Political Economy* 94 (August): 691–719.

Guarneri, Carl J. 1991. *The Utopian Alternative: Fourierism in Nineteenth-Century America.* Ithaca, N.Y.: Cornell Univ. Press.

Gulati, G. Mitu, T. M. Thomas Isaac, and William A. Klein. 2002. When a Workers' Cooperative Works: The Case of Ke-rala Dinesh Beedi. *UCLA Law Review* 49 (June): 1417–54.

Haddock, David D., and Daniel D. Polsby. 1996. Family as a Ra-tional Classification. *Washington University Law Quarterly* 74 (Spring): 15–46.

Hadfield, Gillian K. 1993. Households at Work: Beyond Labor Market Policies to Remedy the Gender Gap. *Georgetown Law Journal* 82 (November): 89–107.

———. 1999. A Coordination Model of the Sexual Division of Labor. *Journal of Economic Behavior & Organization* 40 (Octo-ber): 125–53.

Hafen, Bruce C. 1983. The Constitutional Status of Marriage, Kinship, and Sexual Privacy—Balancing the Individual and Social Interests. *Michigan Law Review* 81 (January): 463–574.

Hajnal, J. 1983. Two Kinds of Pre-Industrial Household Formation System. In *Family Forms in Historic Europe*, edited by Richard Wall in collaboration with Jean Robin and Peter Laslett, 65–104. Cambridge: Cambridge Univ. Press.

Hanawalt, Barbara A. 1986. *The Ties that Bound: Peasant Families in Medieval England*. New York: Oxford Univ. Press.

Hansmann, Henry. 1991. Condominium and Cooperative Housing: Transactional Efficiency, Tax Subsidies, and Tenure Choice. *Journal of Legal Studies* 20 (January): 25–71.

———. 1996. *The Ownership of Enterprise*. Cambridge, Mass.: Harvard Univ. Press, Belknap Press.

Hansmann, Henry, Reinier Kraakman, and Richard Squire. 2006. Law and the Rise of the Firm. *Harvard Law Review* 119 (March): 1333–1403.

Hardin, Garrett. 1968. The Tragedy of the Commons. *Science* 162 (December): 1243–48.

Hareven, Tamara K. 1991. The Home and Family in Historical Perspective. *Social Research* 58 (Spring): 253–85.

Harvard Law Review. See Developments in the Law.

Hasday, Jill Elaine. 2005. Intimacy and Economic Exchange. *Harvard Law Review* 119 (December): 491–530.

Hawrylyshyn, Oli. 1976. The Value of Household Services: A Survey of Empirical Estimates. *Review of Income and Wealth* 22 (June): 101–31.

Heller, Michael A. 1998. The Tragedy of the Anticommons: Property in the Transition from Marx to Markets. *Harvard Law Review* 111 (January): 621–88.

Hemmens, George, and Charles Hoch. 1996. Shared Housing in Low Income Households. In *Under One Roof: Issues and Innovations in Shared Housing*, edited by George Hemmens, Charles J. Hoch, and Jana Carp, 17–32. Albany: State Univ. of New York Press.

Henderson, J. Vernon, and Yannis M. Ioannides. 1983. A Model of Housing Tenure Choice. *American Economic Review* 73 (March): 98–113.

————. 1987. Owner Occupancy: Investment vs. Consumption Demand. *Journal of Urban Economics* 21 (March): 228–41.

Hengel, Martin. 1974. *Property and Riches in the Early Church: Aspects of a Social History of Early Christianity.* Translated by John Bowden. 1st American ed. Philadelphia: Fortress Press.

Herlihy, David. 1985. *Medieval Households.* Cambridge, Mass.: Harvard Univ. Press.

Hersch, Joni. 2003. Marriage, Household Production, and Earnings. In *Marriage and the Economy: Theory and Evidence from Advanced Industrial Societies,* edited by Shoshana A. Grossbard-Shechtman, 201–21. Cambridge: Cambridge Univ. Press.

Hersch, Joni, and Leslie S. Stratton. 2000. Household Specialization and the Male Marriage Wage Premium. *Industrial and Labor Relations Review.* 54 (October): 78–94.

Hevesi, Dennis. 2000. Making Roommates of Perfect Strangers. *New York Times,* August 20: late ed.— final, sec. 11.

Hill, Claire A. 2004. Law and Economics in the Personal Sphere. *Law and Social Inquiry* 29 (Winter): 219–60.

Himmelberg, Charles, Christopher Mayer, and Todd Sinai. 2005. Assessing High House Prices: Bubbles, Fundamentals and Misperceptions. *Journal of Economic Perspectives* 19 (Fall): 67–92.

Hines, N. William. 1966. Real Property Joint Tenancies: Law, Fact, and Fancy. *Iowa Law Review* 51: 582–624.

Hirschman, Albert O. 1970. *Exit, Voice, and Loyalty: Responses to Decline in Firms, Organizations, and States.* Cambridge, Mass.: Harvard Univ. Press.

Hochschild, Arlie Russell. 1989. The Economy of Gratitude. In *The Sociology of Emotions: Original Essays and Research Papers,* ed. David D. Franks and E. Doyle McCarthy, 95–113. Greenwich, Conn.: JAI Press.

Hoffman, Elizabeth, and Matthew L. Spitzer. 1985. Experimental Law and Economics: An Introduction. *Columbia Law Review* 85 (June): 991–1036.

Hogg, Michael A., and Dominic Abrams. 1988. *Social Identifications: A Social Psychology of Intergroup Relations and Group Processes.* London: Routledge.

Homans, George Caspar. 1961. *Social Behavior: Its Elementary Forms.* Robert K. Merton, general ed. New York: Harcourt, Brace and World.

Hostetler, John A., and Gertrude Ender Huntington. 1996. *The Hutterites in North America*. 3rd ed. Case Studies in Cultural Anthropology. Fort Worth, Tex.: Harcourt Brace College Publishers.

Hsieh Jih-chang, and Chuang Ying-Chang, eds. 1985. *The Chinese Family and Its Ritual Behavior*. Nan-kang, T'iai-pei, Taiwan: Institute of Ethnology, Academia Sinica.

Hughes, James W. 1996. Economic Shifts and the Changing Homeownership Trajectory. *Housing Policy Debate* 7 (2): 293–325.

Hunter, Virginia J. 1994. *Policing Athens: Social Control in the Attic Lawsuits, 420–320 b.c.* Princeton, N.J.: Princeton Univ. Press.

Hutterian Brethren Schmiedeleut Conference. Hutterites.org. www.hutterianbrethren.org.

Ihara, Toni, Ralph Warner, and Frederick Hertz. 2004. *Living Together: A Legal Guide for Unmarried Couples*. 12th ed. Berkeley, Calif.: Nolo.

Jensen, Michael C., and William H. Meckling. 1976. Theory of the Firm: Managerial Behavior, Agency Costs, and Ownership Structure. *Journal of Financial Economics* 3 (October): 305–60.

Johnson, Richard W., and Julie DaVanzo. 1998. Economic and Cultural Influences on the Decision to Leave Home in Peninsular Malaysia. *Demography* 35 (February): 97–114.

Johnston, Jason Scott. 1996. The Statute of Frauds and Business Norms: A Testable Game-Theoretic Model. *University of Pennsylvania Law Review* 144 (May): 1859–1907.

Joint Center for Housing Studies of Harvard University. 2005. *The State of the Nation's Housing 2005*. Cambridge, Mass.: Joint Center for Housing Studies of Harvard Univ.

Jolls, Christine, Cass R. Sunstein, and Richard Thaler. 1998. A Behavioral Approach to Law and Economics. *Stanford Law Review* 50 (May): 1471–1550.

Karpoff, Julian. 1977. *Landlord and Tenant Law in the District of Columbia*. Alexandria, Va.: Potomac Law Pub.

Karst, Kenneth L. 1980. The Freedom of Intimate Association. *Yale Law Journal* 89 (March): 624–92.

Kaufman, Joanne. 2002. A House Divided: Perils of Co-Ownership. *New York Times*, August 9: Late ed.— final, sec. F.

Kennedy, Duncan. 2002. The Limited Equity Coop as a Vehicle

for Affordable Housing in a Race and Class Divided Society. *Howard Law Journal* 46 (Fall): 85–125.

Kerr, Norbert L. 1992. Group Decision Making at a Multialternative Task: Extremity, Interfaction Distance, Pluralities, and Issue Importance. *Organizational Behavior and Human Decision Processes* 52 (June): 64–95.

Kershner, Isabel. 2007. The Kibbutz Sheds Socialism and Regains Lost Popularity. *New York Times*, August 27: Late ed.—final, sec. A.

Kertzer, David I. 1991. Household History and Sociological Theory. *Annual Review of Sociology* 17: 155–79.

Keser, Claudia, and Frans van Winden. 2000. Conditional Cooperation and Voluntary Contributions to Public Goods. *Scandinavian Journal of Economics* 102 (March): 23–39.

Kimel, Dori. 2001. Neutrality, Autonomy, and Freedom of Contract. *Oxford Journal of Legal Studies* 21 (Autumn): 473–94.

Kooreman, Peter, and Sophia Wunderink. 1997. *The Economics of Household Behavior.* Basingstoke, U.K.: Macmillan Press.

Kornhauser, Marjorie E. 1993. Love, Money, and the IRS: Family, Income-Sharing, and the Joint Income Tax Return. *Hastings Law Journal* 45 (November): 63–111.

Korona, Raymond I. 2001. *Landlord and Tenant Law.* Vols. 22, 23, and 23A of *New Jersey Practice*, 5th ed. n.p.: West Group.

Kramarow, Ellen A. 1995. The Elderly Who Live Alone in the United States: Historical Perspectives on Household Change. *Demography* 32 (August): 335–52.

Kraybill, Donald B., and Carl F. Bowman. 2001. *On the Backroad to Heaven: Old Order Hutterites, Mennonites, Amish, and Brethren.* Baltimore, Md.: Johns Hopkins Univ. Press.

Kronman, Anthony T. 1985. Contract Law and the State of Nature. *Journal of Law, Economics, and Organization* 1 (Spring): 5–32.

Kumar, Krishan. 1987. *Utopia and Anti-Utopia in Modern Times.* Oxford: Blackwell.

Landa, Janet Tai. 1994. *Trust, Ethnicity, and Identity: Beyond the New Institutional Economics of Ethnic Trading Networks, Contract Law, and Gift-Exchange.* Ann Arbor: Univ. of Michigan Press.

Laslett, Peter. 1972a. Introduction: The History of the Family. In *Household and Family in Past Time*, edited by Peter Laslett with the assistance of Richard Wall, 1–89. Cambridge: Cambridge Univ. Press.

————. 1972b. Mean Household Size in England Since the Sixteenth Century. In *Household and Family in Past Time*, edited by Peter Laslett with the assistance of Richard Wall, 125–58. Cambridge: Cambridge Univ. Press.

————. 1983. Family and Household as Work Group and Kin Group: Areas of Traditional Europe Compared. In *Family Forms in Historic Europe*, edited by Richard Wall in collaboration with Jean Robin and Peter Laslett, 513–63. Cambridge: Cambridge Univ. Press.

Laslett, Peter, and Richard Wall, eds. 1972. *Household and Family in Past Time*. Cambridge: Cambridge Univ. Press. *See also* Goody 1972; Laslett 1972a; Laslett 1972b; Nakane 1972; Pryor 1972.

Lazear, Edward P., and Robert T. Michael. 1980. Family Size and Distribution of Real Per Capita Income. *American Economic Review* 70 (March): 91–107.

Lea, Michael J., and Michael L. Wasylenko. 1983. Tenure Choice and Condominium Conversion. *Journal of Urban Economics* 14 (September): 127–44.

LeDuff, Charlie. 2000. For Migrants, Hard Work in Hostile Suburbs. *New York Times*, September 24: Late ed.—final, sec. 1.

Lee, Gary R., Karen Seccombe, and Constance L. Shehan. 1991. Marital Status and Personal Happiness: An Analysis of Trend Data. *Journal of Marriage and the Family* 53 (November): 839–44.

Lefcoe, George. 2005. *Real Estate Transactions*. 5th ed. n.p.: Matthew Bender.

Leggett, Karby. 2005. Pay-As-You-Go Kibbutzim. *Wall Street Journal*, May 26.

Lehavi, Amnon (Professor, Radzyner School of Law, Herzliya, Israel). 2006. E-mail message to author, Feb. 23, 08:07:34 EST.

Lennon, Mary Clare, and Sarah Rosenfield. 1994. Relative Fairness and the Division of Housework: The Importance of Options. *American Journal of Sociology* 100 (September): 506–31.

Leslie, Melanie B. 1999. Enforcing Family Promises: Reliance, Reciprocity, and Relational Contract. *North Carolina Law Review* 77 (January): 551–636.

Levmore, Saul. 1995. Love It or Leave It: Property Rules, Liability Rules, and Exclusivity of Remedies in Partnership and Marriage. In *Partnerships*, edited by Deborah A. DeMott and J. Dennis Hynes. Special issue, *Law and Contemporary Problems* 58 (Spring): 221–49.

Lewin, Tamar. 2003. First Test for Freshmen: Picking Roommates. *New York Times*, August 7: Late ed.—final, sec. A.

Lewis, Evelyn Alicia. 1994. Struggling with Quicksand: The Ins and Outs of Cotenant Possession Value Liability and a Call for Default Rule Reform. *Wisconsin Law Review* 1994 (March / April): 331–447.

Ligos, Melinda. 2003. Wanted: Roommate, as Economic Necessity. *New York Times*, August 24: Late ed.—final, sec. 3.

Lipton, Lauren. 2003. The His-and-Hers House—With More Space, Couples Build in Separate Lairs; A "Gentlemen's Room." *Wall Street Journal*, August 15: Weekend Journal, The Home Front.

Lithwick, Dahlia, and Brandt Goldstein. 2003. *Me v. Everybody: Absurd Contracts for an Absurd World*. New York: Workman Pub.

Locay, Luis. 1990. Economic Development and the Division of Production Between Households and Markets. Part 1. *Journal of Political Economy* 98 (October): 965–82.

Löfgren, Orvar. 1984. Family and Household: Images and Realities: Cultural Change in Swedish Society. In *Households: Comparative and Historical Studies of the Domestic Group*, ed. Robert McC. Netting, Richard R. Wilk, and Eric J. Arnould, 446–69. Berkeley: Univ. of California Press.

Loh, Eng Seng. 1996. Productivity Differences and the Marriage Premium for White Males. *Journal of Human Resources* 31 (Summer): 566–89.

Lundberg, Shelly J., and Robert A. Pollak. 1993. Separate Spheres Bargaining and the Marriage Market. *Journal of Political Economy* 101 (December): 988–1010.

———. 1996. Bargaining and Distribution in Marriage. *Journal of Economic Perspectives* 10 (Autumn): 139–58.

————. 2007. The American Family and Family Economics. *Journal of Economic Perspectives* 21 (Spring): 3–26.

Lundberg, Shelly J., Robert A. Pollak, and Terence J. Wales. 1997. Do Husbands and Wives Pool Their Resources? Evidence from the United Kingdom Child Benefit. *Journal of Human Resources* 32 (Summer): 463–80.

Macaulay, Stewart. 1963. Non-Contractual Relations in Business: A Preliminary Study. *American Sociological Review* 28 (February): 55-67.

MacKinnon, Catharine A. 1989. *Toward a Feminist Theory of the State.* Cambridge, Mass.: Harvard Univ. Press.

Macy, Michael W., and John Skvoretz. 1998. The Evolution of Trust and Cooperation Between Strangers: A Computational Model. *American Sociological Review* 63 (October): 638–60.

Mahar, Heather. 2003. Why Are There So Few Prenuptial Agreements? Faculty Discussion Paper No. 436. John M. Olin Center for Law, Economics, and Business, Harvard Law School. http://www.harvard.edu/programs/olin_center/papers/pdf/436.pdf.

Maine, Henry Sumner. 1861/2002. *Ancient Law.* New Brunswick, N.J.: Transaction Publishers.

Mansbridge, Jane J. 1980. *Beyond Adversary Democracy.* New York: Basic Books.

Manuel, Frank E., and Fritzie P. Manuel. 1979. *Utopian Thought in the Western World.* Cambridge, Mass.: Belknap Press.

Maryanski, Alexandra, and Jonathan H. Turner. 1992. *The Social Cage: Human Nature and the Evolution of Society.* Stanford, Calif.: Stanford Univ. Press.

Mason, Andrew, Sang-Hyop Lee, and Gerard Russo. 2001. Population Momentum and Population Aging in Asia and Near-East Countries. East-West Center Working Papers, Population Series, No. 107. Honolulu: East-West Center.

Mause, Karsten. 2008. The Tragedy of the Commune: Learning from Worst-Case Scenarios. *Journal of Socio-Economics,* 37 (February): 308–27.

Mauss, Marcel. 1925/1990. *The Gift: The Form and Reason for Exchange in Archaic Societies.* Translated by W. D. Halls. London: W. W. Norton.

McAdams, Richard H. 1997. The Origin, Development, and Regulation of Norms. *Michigan Law Review* 96 (November): 338–433.

———. 2004. Cultural Contingency and Economic Function: Bridge-Building from the Law & Economics Side. *Law and Society Review* 38 (June): 221–28.

McCamant, Kathryn, and Charles Durrett. 1994. *Cohousing: A Contemporary Approach to Housing Ourselves.* With the assistance of Ellen Hertzman. 2nd ed. Berkeley, Calif.: Ten Speed Press.

McClain, Linda C. 1992. "Atomistic Man" Revisited: Liberalism, Connection, and Feminist Jurisprudence. *Southern California Law Review* 65 (March): 1171–1264.

———. 2001. The Domain of Civic Virtue in a Good Society: Families, Schools, and Sex Equality. *Fordham Law Review* 69 (April): 1617–66.

McKean, Margaret A. 1992. Success on the Commons: A Comparative Examination of Institutions for Common Property Resource Management. *Journal of Theoretical Politics* 4 (July): 247–81.

Medick, Hans. 1976. The Proto-Industrial Family Economy: The Structural Function of Household and Family During the Transition from Peasant Society to Industrial Capitalism. *Social History* 3 (October): 291–315.

Merrill, Thomas W. 1998. Property and the Right to Exclude. *Nebraska Law Review* 77: 730–55.

Merrill, Thomas W., and Henry E. Smith. 2001a. The Property/Contract Interface. *Columbia Law Review* 101 (May): 773–852.

———. 2001b. What Happened to Property in Law and Economics? *Yale Law Journal* 111 (November): 357–98.

Mertes, Kate. 1988. *The English Noble Household 1250 to 1600: Good Governance and Politic Rule.* Oxford: B. Blackwell.

Miceli, Thomas J., and C. F. Sirmans. 2000. Partition of Real Estate; Or, Breaking Up Is (Not) Hard To Do. *Journal of Legal Studies* 29 (June): 783–96.

Michael, Robert T., Victor R. Fuchs, and Sharon R. Scott. 1980. Changes in the Propensity to Live Alone: 1950–1976. *Demography* 17 (February): 39–56.

Milgrom, Paul, and John Roberts. 1992. *Economics, Organization, and Management.* Englewood Cliffs, N.J.: Prentice-Hall.

Minault, Gail, ed. 1981. *The Extended Family: Women and Political Participation in India and Pakistan.* Columbia, Mo.: South Asia Books.

Mitchell, Thomas W. 2001. From Reconstruction to Deconstruction: Undermining Black Landownership, Political Independence, and Community through Partition Sales of Tenancies in Common. *Northwestern University Law Review* 95 (Winter): 505–80.

Mnookin, Robert H., and Lewis Kornhauser. 1979. Bargaining in the Shadow of the Law: The Case of Divorce. *Yale Law Journal* 88 (April): 950–97.

Moench, Tom. 2005a. Colors of Empowerment. In *The Cohousing Handbook*, edited by Chris ScottHanson and Kelly ScottHanson, rev. ed., 26–27. Philadelphia: New Society.

———. 2005b. Decision-making. In *The Cohousing Handbook*, edited by Chris ScottHanson and Kelly ScottHanson, rev. ed., 30–31. Philadelphia: New Society.

Molander, Per. 1992. The Prevalence of Free Riding. *Journal of Conflict Resolution* 36 (December): 756–71.

Molm, Linda D., Gretchen Peterson, and Nobuyuki Takahashi. 2003. In the Eye of the Beholder: Procedural Justice in Social Exchange. *American Sociological Review* 68 (February): 128–52.

Morantz, Alison D. 2006. There's No Place Like Home: Homestead Exemption and Judicial Constructions of Family in Nineteenth-Century America. *Law and History Review* 24 (Summer): 245–95.

More, Thomas. 1516/1989. *Utopia.* Edited by George M. Logan and Robert M. Adams. Cambridge: Cambridge Univ. Press.

Morgan, S. Philip, and Kiyosi Hirosima. 1983. The Persistence of Extended Family Residence in Japan: Anachronism or Alternative Strategy? *American Sociological Review* 48 (April): 269–81.

Muravchik, Joshua. 2002. Socialism's Last Stand. *Commentary* 113 (March): 47–53.

Murstein, Bernard I., Mary Cerreto, and Marcia G. Mac Donald. 1977. A Theory and Investigation of the Effect of Exchange-

Orientation on Marriage and Friendship. *Journal of Marriage and the Family* 39 (August): 543–48.

Nakane, Chie. 1972. An Interpretation of the Size and Structure of the Household in Japan over Three Centuries. In *Household and Family in Past Time*, edited by Peter Laslett with the assistance of Richard Wall, 517–43. Cambridge: Cambridge Univ. Press.

National Association of Realtors. 2006. *2005 Profile of Home Buyers & Sellers*. http://www.realtor.org/prodser.nsf/pwebres?Open View&count=1000.

Nelson, Grant S., and Dale A. Whitman. 2002. *Real Estate Finance Law*. 4th ed. St. Paul, Minn.: West Group.

Nelson, Julie. 1988. Household Economies of Scale in Consumption: Theory and Evidence. *Econometrica* 56 (November): 1301–14.

Nelson, Stephen J. 2000. Timesharing 101: A TUG Introduction to Timesharing. Timeshare User's Group. November. http://www.tug2.net/advice/TimeShare-101.htm#_The_resale_market.

Nemeth, Charlan. 1977. Interactions Between Jurors as a Function of Majority vs. Unanimity Decision Rules. *Journal of Applied Social Psychology* 7 (1): 38–56.

Netting, Robert McC. 1989. Smallholders, Householders, Freeholders: Why the Family Farm Works Well Worldwide. In *The Household Economy: Reconsidering the Domestic Mode of Production*, ed. Richard R. Wilk, 221–44. Boulder, Colo.: Westview Press.

New Catholic Encyclopedia. See Catholic University of America 2003a and 2003b.

New York State Unified Court System. N.Y. City Civil Court, Housing Part. http://www.nycourts.gov/courts/nyc/housing/index.shtml.

Nichols, Clark A. 1992. Partition. In Vol. 6D of *Nichols Cyclopedia of Legal Forms Annotated*, vol. 7 revised by Dennis Jensen and Allen D. Choka, rev. ed., § 6.7510–.7535. Deerfield, Ill.: Clark Boardman Callaghan.

———. 2001. Joint Tenants and Tenants in Common. In Vol. 5A, Part One of *Nichols Cyclopedia of Legal Forms Annotated*, re-

vised by Christopher J. Miller and Edward J. Smith, rev. ed., §
5.2800–.2840. n.p.: West Group.

———. 2002. Leases (Real Property). In Vol. 5B, Parts One and
Two of *Nichols Cyclopedia of Legal Forms Annotated,* revised by
Amelia Legutki, Christopher J. Miller, Cora M. Thompson,
Lisa A. Tracey, and Kenneth Zaleski, rev. ed., § 5.4200–.5160.
n.p.: West Group.

Nock, Steven L. 1998. *Marriage in Men's Lives.* New York: Oxford Univ. Press.

———. 2000. Time and Gender in Marriage. *Virginia Law Review* 86 (November): 1971–87.

———. 2001. When Married Spouses Are Equal. *Virginia Journal of Social Policy and the Law* 9 (Fall): 48–70.

Obrinsky, Mark. 2005. NMHC 50: The More Things Change,
the More They Stay the Same. In *NMHC 50,* 10–15. Washington, D.C.: National Multi Housing Council. http://www
.nmhc.org/Content/servefile.cfm?FileID=4574.

Okin, Susan Moller. 1989. *Justice, Gender, and the Family.* New
York: Basic Books.

———. 2004. Justice and Gender: An Unfinished Debate. *Fordham Law Review* 72 (April): 1537–67.

Olsen, Frances E. 1985. The Myth of State Intervention in the
Family. *University of Michigan Journal of Law Reform* 18 (Summer): 835–64.

Order of Saint Benedict. Geographic Search Form. http://www
.osb.org/geog/searchform.asp.

Ostrom, Elinor. 1990. *Governing the Commons: The Evolution of
Institutions for Collective Action.* Cambridge: Cambridge Univ.
Press.

Pahl, Jan. 1989. *Money and Marriage.* Houndmills, U.K.: Macmillan.

Pasternak, Burton, Carol R. Ember, and Melvin Ember. 1983.
On the Conditions Favoring Extended Family Households. In
*Marriage, Family, and Kinship: Comparative Studies of Social
Organization,* ed. Melvin Ember and Carol R. Ember, 125–49.
n.p.: HRAF Press. Originally published in *Journal of Anthropo-
logical Research* 32 (1976): 109–23.

Pavin, Avraham. 1998. Members' Perceptions of Kibbutz Reforms. *Kibbutz Trends* 31–32 (Fall/Winter): 56–61.

———. 2003. The Kibbutz Movement: Facts & Figures 2003. *Kibbutz Trends* 48 (Winter): 57–59.

Peter, Karl A. 1987. *The Dynamics of Hutterite Society: An Analytical Approach.* Edmonton: Univ. of Alberta Press.

Peters, H. Elizabeth. 1986. Marriage and Divorce: Informational Constraints and Private Contracting. *American Economic Review* 76 (June): 437–54.

Plato. ca. 360 BCE. *The Republic.*

Polinsky, A. Mitchell. 1972. Probabilistic Compensation Criteria. *Quarterly Journal of Economics* 86 (August): 407–25.

Pollak, Robert A. 1985. A Transaction Cost Approach to Families and Households. *Journal of Economic Literature* 23 (June): 581–608.

———. 2007. Bargaining Around the Hearth. *Yale Law Journal Pocket Part* 116: 348–356. http://thepocketpart.org/2007/04/16/pollak.html.

Pomeroy, Sarah B. 1997. *Families in Classical and Hellenistic Greece: Representations and Realities.* Oxford: Clarendon Press.

POMS. *See Property Owners and Managers Survey.*

Porell, Frank W. 1985. One Man's Ceiling Is Another Man's Floor: Landlord/Manager Residency and Housing Condition. *Land Economics* 61 (May): 106–18.

Portman, Janet, and Marcia Stewart. 2005. *Renters' Rights: The Basics.* 4th ed. Berkeley, Calif.: Nolo.

Posner, Eric A. 1997. Altruism, Status, and Trust in the Law of Gifts and Gratuitous Promises. *Wisconsin Law Review* 1997 (2): 567–609.

Posner, Richard A. 1995a. *Aging and Old Age.* Chicago: Univ. of Chicago Press.

———. 1995b. *Overcoming Law.* Cambridge, Mass.: Harvard Univ. Press.

———. 2003. *Economic Analysis of Law.* 6th ed. New York: Aspen Publishers.

Postgate, J. N. 1992. *Early Mesopotamia: Society and Economy at the Dawn of History.* London: Routledge.

Property Owners and Managers Survey (POMS). 2004. Washington, D.C.: U.S Census Bureau. http://www.census.gov/hhes/www/housing/poms/poms.html.

Pryor, Jr., Edward T. 1972. Rhode Island Family Structure: 1875 and 1960. In *Household and Family in Past Time*, edited by Peter Laslett with the assistance of Richard Wall, 571–89. Cambridge: Cambridge Univ. Press.

Putnam, Robert D. 1993. *Making Democracy Work: Civic Traditions in Modern Italy*. With the assistance of Robert Leonardi and Raffaella Nanetti. Princeton, N.J.: Princeton Univ. Press.

———. 2000. *Bowling Alone: The Collapse and Revival of American Community*. New York: Simon and Schuster.

Quah, Euston. 1993. *Economics and Home Production: Theory and Measurement*. Brookfield, Vt.: Ashgate Pub.

Rabin, Matthew. 1993. Incorporating Fairness into Game Theory and Economics. *American Economic Review* 83 (December): 1281–1302.

Radin, Margaret Jane. 1987. Market-Inalienability. *Harvard Law Review* 100 (June): 1849–1937.

RAND. 1974. *First Annual Report of the Housing Assistance Supply Experiment*. Report no. R-1659–HUD. n.p.: RAND Corporation.

Rasmusen, Eric, and Jeffrey Evans Stake. 1998. Lifting the Veil of Ignorance: Personalizing the Marriage Contract. *Indiana Law Journal* 73 (Spring): 453–502.

Rawls, John. 1971. *A Theory of Justice*. Cambridge, Mass.: Harvard Univ. Press, Belknap Press.

Regan, Jr., Milton C. 1993. *Family Law and the Pursuit of Intimacy*. New York: New York Univ. Press.

———. 1999. *Alone Together: Law and the Meanings of Marriage*. New York: Oxford Univ. Press.

Reid, Margaret G. 1934. *Economics of Household Production*. New York: Wiley.

Rendon, Jim. 2004. Splitting the Cost of Buying a House. *New York Times*, July 11: Late ed.— final, sec. 11.

Restatement of the Law, Second: Contracts. See American Law Institute 1979.

Robinson, John P., and Geoffrey Godbey. 1997. *Time for Life: The Surprising Ways Americans Use Their Time.* University Park: Pennsylvania State Univ. Press.

Roe, Mark J. 1996. Chaos and Evolution in Law and Economics. *Harvard Law Review* 109 (January): 641–68.

Romano, Roberta, ed. 1993. *Foundations of Corporate Law.* New York: Oxford Univ. Press.

Romesberg, Lorri Ann. 1999. Note: Common Law Adoption: An Argument for Statutory Recognition of Non-Parent Caregiver Visitation. *Suffolk University Law Review* 33: 163–84.

Rose, Carol M. 1992. Giving, Trading, Thieving, and Trusting: How and Why Gifts Become Exchanges, and (More Importantly) Vice Versa. *Florida Law Review* 44 (July): 295-317.

Rosenbloom, Stephanie. 2006. For Men, a Fear of Commitment. *New York Times.* February 12: Late ed.— final, sec. 11.

Rosenfeld, Michael J., and Byung-Soo Kim. 2005. The Independence of Young Adults and the Rise of Interracial and Same-Sex Unions. *American Sociological Review* 70 (August): 541–62.

Ross, H. Laurence. 1980. *Settled Out of Court: The Social Process of Insurance Claims Adjustment.* 2nd ed. New York: Aldine Pub.

Roth, Alvin E., Vesna Prasnikar, Masahiro Okuno-Fujiwara, and Shmuel Zamir. 1991. Bargaining and Market Behavior in Jerusalem, Ljubljana, Pittsburgh, and Tokyo: An Experimental Study. *American Economic Review* 81 (December): 1068-95.

Ruggles, Steven. 1994. The Transformation of American Family Structure. *American Historical Review* 99 (February): 103–28.

Ruskola, Teemu. 2000. Conceptualizing Corporations and Kinship: Comparative Law and Development Theory in a Chinese Perspective. *Stanford Law Review* 52 (July): 1599–1729.

Russell, Raymond, Robert Hannemann, and Shlomo Getz. 2000. Processes of Deinstitutionalization and Reinstitutionalization Among Israeli Kibbutzim, 1990–1998. Paper presented at the Annual Meeting of the American Sociological Association, Washington, D.C., August 12–16, 2000. http://research.haifa .ac.il/~kibbutz/pdf/rusty2000.PDF.

Sahlins, Marshall. 1972. *Stone Age Economics.* Chicago: Aldine-Atherton.

Salins, Peter D., and Gerard C. S. Mildner. 1992. *Scarcity by Design: The Legacy of New York City's Housing Policies.* Cambridge, Mass.: Harvard Univ. Press.

Saller, Richard P. 1994. *Patriarchy, Property, and Death in the Roman Family.* Cambridge: Cambridge Univ. Press.

Sally, David. 1995. Conversation and Cooperation in Social Dilemmas: A Meta-Analysis of Experiments from 1958 to 1992. *Rationality and Society* 7 (January): 58–92.

Salsich, Jr., Peter W. 1995. Solutions to the Affordable Housing Crisis: Perspectives on Privatization. *John Marshall Law Review* 28 (Winter): 263–315.

Sandelin, Rob. 1997a. Dealing with Government Agencies. Northwest Intentional Communities Association. http://www .ic.org/nica/Construction/build1b.htm.

———. 1997b. Legal Issues for Communities: A Primer. Northwest Intentional Communities Association. http://www.ic.org/ nica/Legal/Legal1a.html.

Santi, Lawrence L. 1987. Change in the Structure and Size of American Households: 1970 to 1985. *Journal of Marriage and the Family* 49 (November): 833–37.

Sassler, Sharon. 2004. The Process of Entering Into Cohabiting Unions. *Journal of Marriage and Family* 66 (May): 491–505.

Saunders, Peter R. 1990. *A Nation of Home Owners.* London: Unwin Hyman.

Scannapieco, Maria, and Sondra Jackson. 1996. Kinship Care: The African American Response to Family Preservation. *Social Work* 41 (March): 190–96.

Schill, Michael H., Ioan Voicu, and Jonathan Miller. 2007. The Condominium versus Cooperative Puzzle: An Empirical Analysis of Housing in New York City. *Journal of Legal Studies* 36 (June): 275–324.

Schneider, Carl E., and Margaret F. Brinig. 2000. *An Invitation to Family Law: Principles, Process, and Perspectives.* 2nd ed. St. Paul, Minn.: West Group.

Schoshinski, Robert S. 1980. *American Law of Landlord and Tenant.* Rochester, N.Y.: Lawyers Co-operative Pub. Co.

Schultz, Vicki. 2000. Life's Work. *Columbia Law Review* 100 (November): 1881–1964.

Schwartz, Alan. 1979. The Case for Specific Performance. *Yale Law Journal* 89 (December): 271–306.

Schwartz, Alan, and Robert E. Scott. 2003. Contract Theory and the Limits of Contract Law. *Yale Law Journal* 113 (December): 541–619.

Schwarz, Peter M., Jennifer L. Troyer, and Jennifer Beck Walker. 2007. Animal House: Economics of Pets and the Household. *The B.E. Journal of Economic Analysis and Policy* 7: 1–27.

Scott, Elizabeth S. 2000. Social Norms and the Legal Regulation of Marriage. *Virginia Law Review* 86 (November): 1901–70.

Scott, Elizabeth S., and Robert E. Scott. 1998. Marriage as Relational Contract. *Virginia Law Review* 84 (October): 1225–1334.

Scott, Robert E. 2003. A Theory of Self-Enforcing Indefinite Agreements. *Columbia Law Review* 103 (November): 1641–99.

ScottHanson, Chris, and Kelly ScottHanson. 2005. *The Cohousing Handbook: Building a Place for Community*. Rev. ed. Philadelphia: New Society. *See also* Moench 2005a *and* Moench 2005b.

Seabright, Paul. 1993. Managing Local Commons: Theoretical Issues in Incentive Design. *Journal of Economic Perspectives* 7 (Autumn): 113–34.

Sgritta, Giovanni B. 1988. The Italian Family: Tradition and Change. *Journal of Family Issues* 9 (September): 372–96.

Shammas, Carole. 2002. *A History of Household Government in America*. Charlottesville: Univ. of Virginia Press.

Shammas, Carole, Marylynn Salmon, and Michel Dahlin. 1987. *Inheritance in America from Colonial Times to the Present*. New Brunswick, N.J.: Rutgers Univ. Press.

Shepard, Steven M. 2005. Withholding Rent in Connecticut. Unpublished manuscript on file with author.

Shiffrin, Seana Valentine. 2005. What Is Really Wrong with Compelled Association? *Northwestern University Law Review* 99 (Winter): 839–88.

Shiller, Robert J. 2005. *Irrational Exuberance*. 2nd ed. Princeton, N.J.: Princeton Univ. Press.

Shultz, Marjorie Maguire. 1982. Contractual Ordering of Marriage: A New Model for State Policy. *California Law Review* 70 (March): 204–334.

Siegel, Reva B. 1994. Home as Work: The First Woman's Rights Claims Concerning Wives' Household Labor, 1850–1880. *Yale Law Journal* 103 (March): 1073–1217.

Silbaugh, Katharine B. 1996. Turning Labor Into Love: Housework and the Law. *Northwestern University Law Review* 91 (Fall): 1–86.

———. 1998. Marriage Contracts and the Family Economy. *Northwestern University Law Review* 93 (Fall): 65–143.

Simmons-Mosley, Tammie X, and Stephen Malpezzi. 2006. Household Mobility in New York City's Regulated Rental Housing Market. *Journal of Housing Economics* 15 (March): 38–62.

Simon, William H. 1991. Social-Republican Property. *UCLA Law Review* 38 (August): 1335–1413.

Singer, Jana B. 1992. The Privatization of Family Law. *Wisconsin Law Review* 1992 (September/October): 1443–1567.

Skinner, B. F. 1948/1976. *Walden Two*. New York: Macmillan.

Smith, Henry E. 1998. Intermediate Filing in Household Taxation. *Southern California Law Review* 72 (November): 145–245.

———. 2000. Semicommon Property Rights and Scattering in the Open Fields. *Journal of Legal Studies* 29 (January): 131–69.

———. 2006. Modularity in Contracts: Boilerplate and Information Flow. *Michigan Law Review* 104 (March): 1175–1222.

Sobel, Joel. 2002. Can We Trust Social Capital? *Journal of Economic Literature* 40 (March): 139–54.

———. 2005. Interdependent Preferences and Reciprocity. *Journal of Economic Literature* 43 (June): 392–436.

Solot, Dorian, and Marshall Miller. 2002. *Unmarried to Each Other: The Essential Guide to Living Together as an Unmarried Couple*. New York: Marlowe.

Solove, Daniel J. 2002. Conceptualizing Privacy. *California Law Review* 90 (July): 1087–1155.

Sosis, Richard, and Bradley J. Ruffle. 2003. Religious Ritual and Cooperation: Testing for a Relationship on Israeli Religious and Secular Kibbutzim. *Current Anthropology* 44: 713–22.

Spain, Daphne. 1992. *Gendered Spaces*. Chapel Hill: Univ. of North Carolina Press.

Sprecher, Susan. 1998. The Effect of Exchange Orientation on

Close Relationships. *Social Psychology Quarterly* 61 (September): 220–31.

Stack, Carol B. 1975. *All Our Kin: Strategies for Survival in a Black Community.* New York: Harper & Row.

Statistical Abstract of the United States. (The volumes for various years, specifically, 1998, 1999, 2001, and 2006, are cited.) Washington, D.C.: U.S. Census Bureau.

Sternlieb, George. 1969. *The Tenement Landlord.* Paperback ed. New Brunswick, N.J.: Rutgers Univ. Press.

Sternlieb, George, and Robert W. Burchell. 1973. *Residential Abandonment: The Tenement Landlord Revisited.* New Brunswick, N.J.: Center for Urban Policy Research, Rutgers Univ.

Stoebuck, William B., and Dale A. Whitman. 2000. *The Law of Property.* 3rd ed. St. Paul, Minn.: West Group.

Stoner, Katherine E., and Shae Irving. 2004. *Prenuptial Agreements: How to Write a Fair and Lasting Contract.* Berkeley, Calif.: Nolo.

Strahilevitz, Lior Jacob. 2005. A Social Networks Theory of Privacy. *University of Chicago Law Review* 72 (Summer): 919–88.

———. 2006. Information Asymmetries and the Rights to Exclude. *Michigan Law Review* 104 (August): 1835–98.

Sutton, Robert P. 2005. *Modern American Communes: A Dictionary.* Westport, Conn.: Greenwood Press.

Swarthmore Student Housing. RA Resources. Swarthmore College. http://www.swarthmore.edu/Admin/ housing/raresource/ roommate.htm (accessed September 25, 2006; site now discontinued).

Sweet, James A., and Larry L. Bumpass. 1987. *American Families and Households.* New York: Russell Sage Foundation.

Tajfel, Henri. 1981. *Human Groups and Social Categories: Studies in Social Psychology.* Cambridge: Cambridge Univ. Press.

Taylor, J. Robert. 2005. Timeshare Ownership Equals Disaster. *Palo Alto Weekly,* Nov. 11: Online ed. http://www.paloaltoonline .com/weekly/morgue/2005/2005_11_11.taylor11.shtml.

Taylor, Michael. 1982. *Community, Anarchy, and Liberty.* Cambridge: Cambridge Univ. Press.

Teitelbaum, Lee E. 1985. Family History and Family Law. *Wisconsin Law Review* 1985 (September/October): 1135–81.

Thomas, Jonathan P., and Timothy Worrall. 2002. Gift-Giving, Quasi-Credit and Reciprocity. *Rationality and Society* 14 (August): 308–52.

Tienda, Marta, and Ronald Angel. 1982. Headship and Household Composition Among Blacks, Hispanics, and Other Whites. *Social Forces* 61 (December): 508–31.

Titmuss, Richard M. 1971. *The Gift Relationship: From Human Blood to Social Policy.* New York: Vintage Books.

Tocqueville, Alexis de. 1840/1988. *Democracy in America.* Edited by J. P. Mayer. Translated by George Lawrence. 1st Perennial library ed. New York: HarperPerennial.

Uniform Condominium Act (National Conference of Commissioners on Uniform State Laws 1980).

Uniform Partnership Act (National Conference of Commissioners on Uniform State Laws 1914).

United Nations. Human Settlements Data Bank. http://hq .unhabitat.org/programmes/guo/guo_hsdb4.asp (accessed Oct. 9, 2006; site now discontinued).

United Nations Economic Commission for Europe. *Bulletin of Housing Statistics for Europe and North America 2004.* http:// www.unece.org/env/hs/prgm/hsstat/Bulletin_04.htm.

United States Census Bureau. *See* U.S. Census Bureau.

University of Iowa Tenant Landlord Association. Roommate Issues. University of Iowa. http://www.uiowa.edu/~tla/tenant/ roommate.shtml.

University of Massachusetts Amherst Housing Technology Services. Housing and Residence Life. University of Massachusetts Amherst. http://www.housing.umass.edu/announce/state_of_ housing.html (accessed Sept. 1, 2006; site now discontinued).

U.S. Bureau of Labor Statistics. Various years, beginning in 2003. *American Time Use Surveys.* http://www.bls.gov/tus/.

U.S. Census Bureau.* *2000 Census of Population and Housing: Summary File 1; Technical Documentation.* http://www.census .gov/prod/cen2000/doc/sf1.pdf. 2005.

---

* To simplify the location of specific works issued by the U.S. Census Bureau, these works are listed in alphabetical order by title, rather than in chronological order. The year of publication is indicated at the end of the citation.

———. *America's Families and Living Arrangements: 2003.* Current Population Reports, P20–553. 2004.

———. *American Housing Survey for the United States: 1999.* Current Housing Reports, Series H150/99–RV. 2003.

———. *Historical Statistics of the United States: Colonial Times to 1970,* Part 1. Bicentennial ed. 1975.

———. *Home-Based Workers in the United States: 1997.* Current Population Reports. http://www.census.gov/prod/2002pubs/p70–78.pdf. 2001.

———. *Married-Couple and Unmarried-Partner Households: 2000.* 2003.

———. *Property Owners and Managers Survey (POMS).* http://www.census.gov/hhes/www/housing/poms/poms.html. 2004.

———. *Statistical Abstract of the United States.* (Cited for various years, specifically, 1998, 1999, 2001, and 2006).

———. Total Population in Households and Group Quarters by Sex and Selected Age Groups, for the United States: 2000, Table 1. 2001. http://www.census.gov/population/cen2000/grpqtr/grpqtr01.pdf.

———. *We the People: Asians in the United States.* Census 2000 Special Reports, CENSR-17. 2004.

Varady, David P., and Barbara J. Lipman. 1994. What Are Renters Really Like? Results from a National Survey. *Housing Policy Debate* 5 (4): 491–531.

Wall, Richard, Jean Robin, and Peter Laslett, eds. 1983. *Family Forms in Historic Europe.* Cambridge: Cambridge Univ. Press. *See also* Hajnal 1983 *and* Laslett 1983.

Walzer, Michael. 1990. The Communitarian Critique of Liberalism. *Political Theory* 18 (February): 6–23.

Warshaw, George. 1987. *Massachusetts Landlord-Tenant Law.* Rochester, N.Y.: Lawyers Co-operative Pub. Co.

Warton, Pamela M., and Jacqueline J. Goodnow. 1995. Money and Children's Household Jobs: Parents' Views of Their Interconnections. *International Journal of Behavioral Development* 18 (June): 335–50.

Wax, Amy L. 1998. Bargaining in the Shadow of the Market: Is There a Future for Egalitarian Marriage? *Virginia Law Review* 84 (May): 509–672.

Weicher, John C. 2000. Comment on Steven C. Bourassa and William G. Grigsby's "Income Tax Concessions for Owner-Occupied Housing." *Housing Policy Debate* 11 (3): 547–59.

Whittington, Leslie A., and H. Elizabeth Peters. 1996. Economic Incentives for Financial and Residential Independence. *Demography* 33 (February): 82–97.

Wikipedia. Million Programme. http://en.wikipedia.org/wiki/Million_Programme.

Williams, Joan. 2000. *Unbending Gender: Why Family and Work Conflict and What to Do About It.* Oxford: Oxford Univ. Press.

Williams, Joseph T. 1993. Agency and Ownership of Housing. *Journal of Real Estate Finance and Economics* 7 (September): 83–97.

Williamson, Oliver E. 1975. *Markets and Hierarchies, Analysis and Antitrust Implications: A Study in the Economics of Internal Organization.* New York: Free Press.

———. 1984. Corporate Governance. *Yale Law Journal* 93 (June): 1197–1230.

Wilson, William E. 1964. Utopia, Limited. *American Heritage* 15 (October): 64–72. http://www.americanheritage.com/articles/magazine/ah/1964/6/1964_6_64.shtml.

Wines, Michael. 2000. Tight Space. No Privacy. Soviet Décor. *New York Times*, February 5: Late ed.—final, sec. A.

Wolfe, Alan. 1998. *One Nation, After All: What Middle-Class Americans Really Think About God, Country, Family, Racism, Welfare, Immigration, Homosexuality, the Right, the Left, and Each Other.* New York: Viking.

Wolfers, Justin. 2006. Did Unilateral Divorce Laws Raise Divorce Rates? A Reconciliation and New Results. *American Economic Review* 96 (December) 1802–1920.

Wolfson, Mark A. 1985. Tax, Incentive, and Risk-Sharing Issues in the Allocation of Property Rights: The Generalized Lease-or-Buy Problem. *Journal of Business* 58 (April): 159–71.

Woolf, Virginia. 1929/1957. *A Room of One's Own.* New York: Harcourt, Brace and World.

Woolgar, C. M. 1999. *The Great Household in Late Medieval England.* New Haven, Conn.: Yale Univ. Press.

Xenophon. ca. 362 BC/1994. *Oeconomicus.* Translated by Sarah B. Pomeroy. Oxford: Clarendon Press.

Zablocki, Benjamin D. 1971. *The Joyful Community: An Account of the Bruderhof, a Communal Movement Now in Its Third Generation.* Baltimore, Md.: Penguin Books.

———. 1980. *Alienation and Charisma: A Study of Contemporary American Communes.* New York: Free Press.

Zablocki, Benjamin D., and Rosabeth Moss Kanter. 1976. The Differentiation of Life-Styles. *Annual Review of Sociology* 2 (August): 269–98.

Zelizer, Viviana A. 2005. *The Purchase of Intimacy.* Princeton, N.J.: Princeton Univ. Press.

Index

Bergstrom, Theodore, 25
Bernard, Jessie, 110n
Bernstein, Lisa, 92, 97
birth rates and household size, 82
black households, 7, 38, 125, 168n27
Block, Cheryl D., 185n26
boarders in family households, 38,
   124–25, 196n131
Booth, William James, 14
Brazil, 35
Brinig, Margaret, 26n, 30n, 150n21,
   167n17
Britain, 36, 39, 84, 91, 195n126
Brook Farm, MA, 54, 74, 132–33,
   171n48, 175–76nn29–30, 198n9
Bruderhof, 114, 140
Buchanan, James M., 185n26, 191n88
Bucks Co., PA, 42
"burnt toast" stratagem of access to
   household surplus, 25
business enterprise theory: applica-
   bility to households, 6, 8, 60–75,
   63*f*; intimates, consorting with,
   133; relevance to household
   organization, 4–5, 75, 133
Buss, David, 30n

Calabresi, Guido, 18
capital: conferral of ownership on
   suppliers of, 60, 69–74,
   176nn36–37; private ownership
   of, 14, 16
Caplin, Andrew, 180n40
Census. *See* U.S. Census
children: adoption of, 129–130,
   197nn2–3; adult, 17, 38, 65,
   81–83, 114–15, 124, 178n19,
   194n111; birth rates and household size, 82; care of, by grandparent, 38, 116; custody of, 5, 26,
   93, 129–130; payment for household chores, 110–11; protection
   of, 50, 108, 129–30; rent charged
   to, 124; "Rotten Kid Theorem,"
   155n42
China, 35, 115, 162n32

Christianity, 54, 170n43. *See also*
   Benedictines; Bruderhof; Hutterian Brethren
Classical Greek households, 38,
   83–84, 114–15, 179n32
Classical Roman households, 38,
   198n11
Coase, Ronald, 6, 26n, 78, 79
cohabiting couples. *See* nonmarital
   cohabitants
Co-Housing Association of the
   United States, 145–46, 146*t*
co-housing communities, 6, 56–57;
   commitment to consensual
   decision-making in, 99–100,
   146; demographic and statistical
   evidence regarding, 41, 139, 140,
   145–46, 146*t*; homeways of, 100,
   103, 146; no financial sharing
   reported in, 140; ownership
   patterns in, 73; privatization of
   space in, 56–57, 119; as secular
   communities, 41.
college dormitories, 40, 112–13,
   190n73, 190n76
colonial American households, 25
common-law marriage, 197n3
commons, household as a, xii, 12, 98,
   117–19
communes. *See* dining, communal;
   intentional communities
community and solidarity: conventional households' contributions
   to, 58–59; liberalism as possibly
   destructive of, 51–53; unpromis-
   ing history of experiments in,
   53–59
community land trusts, 181n52
community property, 181n43
condominiums, 56, 89–90, 167n19,
   175n27, 182nn57–58
Condorcet, Marquis de, 185n26
consensus, desire of household
   members to achieve, 97–100,
   141*t*, 146, 184nn18–19
consorting with intimates, 8, 27–34,

95–109, 184n9. *See also* homeways; homeways for co-occupants
Russia, household regulation and
home ownership in, 13, 44, 48,
53, 134, 165n62

Salmon, Marylynn, 42, 164n49
Samuelson, Paul, 23
Sandelin, Rob, 73n, 169n39
scholarly perspectives on households,
4–7, 128–35
Schultz, Vicki, 58, 59n, 106n, 109n
Scott, Elizabeth and Robert, 23,
186n35
ScottHanson, Chris and Kelly,
184n16, 185n28, 191n79
secular intentional communities, 41,
54, 138, 139*t*
self-determination as key principle of
liberalism, 14, 21–22, 51–52n
self-help, methods of, 25, 103,
116–17, 186n31, 186n40. *See also*
exit, freedom of
self-sufficiency of households,
78–84, 177–78n14, 180n34
Senegal, 36
servants as household members, 38,
62, 124–25
Shammas, Carole, 42, 152n19,
164n49
Shultz, Marjorie, 106n, 134n
Simon, William, 52, 58
Singer, Jana B., 186n34
single-family detached rental units,
43, 45
single occupants or owners, 1–2, 10,
36, 41, 42, 78, 82, 160–61n11,
178n19
Sitcom Household: centrality of
households to television shows,
10; extended/multigenerational
nature of, 39; homeways in,
94–95; household surplus, distribution of, 25; landlord-tenant
relationship in, 13, 44; liberal
norms of, 15, 17–21; ownership

in, 42, 61–64, 69–71, 174–75n23;
three household relationships
illustrated by, 11–13
size of household. *See* number of
participants
Skinner, B. F., 6, 47, 58, 140
slavery, 13, 16–18, 21, 38, 83,
152n15, 179n32
slum tenements in Newark, NJ,
43–44n
small-bore legal rules, 8, 134–35: on
co-ownership, 86, 121, 123; definition of, 50; distorting choices
regarding household forms,
50–51; health and housing codes,
49; of landlord-tenant law,
126–27; limited effect on co-
occupants' homeways, 108–09,
116–17, 134–35; of ownership vs.
renting, 89–91; size of household
affected by, 82; zoning regulations,
22, 50, 53, 66, 82, 134. *See also*
private-law rules, foundational
small households, prevailing preferences for, 8, 32, 35–41
Smith, Henry E., 150n1, 173n4
Sobel, Joel, 179n31, 188n49
social activity, household as site of, 4,
63*f,* 64–66
social capital, 83, 163n46, 179n31,
180n37
social control, methods of, 30,
101–02, 133
social insurance, informally provided
within household, 77, 81–82, 83,
177n4, 183n7
social norms. *See* cultural and social
norms
social scientists, advantages of household study for, 133–34
social stability, size of household
affected by, 83–84
social ties, strength of, 27–34
solidarity. *See* community and solidarity
South Korea, 39

Lightning Source UK Ltd.
Milton Keynes UK
UKOW04f0231141015

260452UK00002B/50/P